Lecture Notes in Computer Science

Commenced Publication in 1973
Founding and Former Series Editors:
Gerhard Goos, Juris Hartmanis, and Jan van Leeuwe

Bart Goethals   Arno Siebes (Eds.)

Knowledge Discovery in Inductive Databases

Third International Workshop, KDID 2004
Pisa, Italy, September 20, 2004
Revised Selected and Invited Papers

Volume Editors

Bart Goethals
University of Antwerp, Department of Mathematics and Computer Science
Middelheimlaan 1, 2020 Antwerp, Belgium
E-mail: bart.goethals@ua.ac.be

Arno Siebes
Utrecht University, Institute of Information and Computing Sciences
PO Box 80.089, 3508TB Utrecht, The Netherlands
E-mail: arno.siebes@cs.uu.nl

Library of Congress Control Number: 2005921108

CR Subject Classification (1998): H.2, I.2

ISSN 0302-9743
ISBN 3-540-25082-4 Springer Berlin Heidelberg New York

Springer is a part of Springer Science+Business Media

springeronline.com

© Springer-Verlag Berlin Heidelberg 2005
Printed in Germany

Typesetting: Camera-ready by author, data conversion by Scientific Publishing Services, Chennai, India
Printed on acid-free paper   SPIN: 11400059   06/3142   5 4 3 2 1 0

Preface

The 3rd International Workshop on Knowledge Discovery in Inductive Databases (KDID 2004) was held in Pisa, Italy, on September 20, 2004 as part of the 15th European Conference on Machine Learning and the 8th European Conference on Principles and Practice of Knowledge Discovery in Databases (ECML/PKDD 2004).

Ever since the start of the field of data mining, it has been realized that the knowledge discovery and data mining process should be integrated into database technology. This idea has been formalized in the concept of inductive databases, introduced by Imielinski and Mannila (CACM 1996, 39(11)).

In general, an inductive database is a database that supports data mining and the knowledge discovery process in a natural and elegant way. In addition to the usual data, it also contains inductive generalizations (e.g., patterns, models) extracted from the data. Within this framework, knowledge discovery is an interactive process in which users can query the inductive database to gain insight to the data and the patterns and models within that data.

Despite many recent developments, there still exists a pressing need to understand the central issues in inductive databases. This workshop aimed to bring together database and data mining researchers and practitioners who are interested in the numerous challenges that inductive databases offers.

This workshop followed the previous two workshops: KDID 2002 held in Helsinki, Finland, and KDID 2003 held in Cavtat-Dubrovnik, Croatia.

The scientific program of the workshop included 9 papers, selected out of 23 submissions, and an invited talk by Sunita Sarawagi. During the workshop, only informal proceedings were distributed. The papers in this volume were revised by the authors based on the comments from the refereeing stage and ensuing discussions during the workshop, and were subjected to a final acceptance by the Program Committee.

We wish to thank the invited speaker, all the authors who submitted their papers to the workshop, the Program Committee members for their help in the reviewing process, and the ECML/PKDD Organization Committee for their help and local organization.

December 2004

Bart Goethals
Arno Siebes

Program Chairs

Bart Goethals
Helsinki Institute for Information Technology – Basic Research Unit
Department of Computer Science
University of Helsinki
Finland
http://www.cs.helsinki.fi/bart.goethals/

Arno Siebes
Institute of Information and Computing Sciences
Utrecht University
The Netherlands
http://www.cs.uu.nl/staff/siebes.html

Program Committee

Roberto Bayardo, *IBM Almaden, USA*
Francesco Bonchi, *ISTI-CNR, Italy*
Jean-François Boulicaut, *INSA Lyon, France*
Toon Calders, *University of Antwerp, Belgium*
Luc De Raedt, *Albert-Ludwigs-Universitaet Freiburg, Germany*
Saso Dzeroski, *Jozef Stefan Institute, Slovenia*
Minos N. Garofalakis, *Bell Labs, USA*
Johannes Gehrke, *Cornell University, USA*
Mika Klemettinen, *Nokia, Finland*
Heikki Mannila, *HIIT-BRU, University of Helsinki,*
    Helsinki University of Technology, Finland
Rosa Meo, *University of Turin, Italy*
Ryszard S. Michalski, *George Mason University, USA*
Taneli Mielikäinen, *HIIT-BRU, University of Helsinki, Finland*
Mohammed Zaki, *Rensselaer Polytechnic Institute, USA*

Table of Contents

Invited Paper

Models and Indices for Integrating Unstructured Data with a Relational
Database
Sunita Sarawagi 1

Contributed Papers

Constraint Relaxations for Discovering Unknown Sequential Patterns
Cláudia Antunes, Arlindo L. Oliveira 11

Mining Formal Concepts with a Bounded Number of Exceptions from
Transactional Data
Jérémy Besson, Céline Robardet, Jean-François Boulicaut 33

Theoretical Bounds on the Size of Condensed Representations
Nele Dexters, Toon Calders 46

Mining Interesting XML-Enabled Association Rules with Templates
Ling Feng, Tharam Dillon 66

Database Transposition for Constrained (Closed) Pattern Mining
Baptiste Jeudy, François Rioult 89

An Efficient Algorithm for Mining String Databases Under Constraints
Sau Dan Lee, Luc De Raedt 108

An Automata Approach to Pattern Collections
Taneli Mielikäinen 130

Implicit Enumeration of Patterns
Taneli Mielikäinen 150

Condensed Representation of EPs and Patterns Quantified by
Frequency-Based Measures
Arnaud Soulet, Bruno Crémilleux, François Rioult 173

Author Index 191

Models and Indices for Integrating Unstructured Data with a Relational Database

Sunita Sarawagi

IIT Bombay
sunita@iitb.ac.in

Abstract. Database systems are islands of structure in a sea of un-structured data sources. Several real-world applications now need to create bridges for smooth integration of semi-structured sources with existing structured databases for seamless querying. This integration requires extracting structured column values from the unstructured source and mapping them to known database entities. Existing methods of data integration do not effectively exploit the wealth of information available in multi-relational entities.

We present statistical models for co-reference resolution and information extraction in a database setting. We then go over the performance challenges of training and applying these models efficiently over very large databases. This requires us to break open a black box statistical model and extract predicates over indexable attributes of the database. We show how to extract such predicates for several classification models, including naive Bayes classifiers and support vector machines. We extend these indexing methods for supporting similarity predicates needed during data integration.

1 Introduction

Current research in the area of database mining integration is about finding patterns in data residing within a single structured data box. Most data around us is unstructured but is largely ignored in the data analysis phase. The only effective way to exploit this abundance of unstructured data is to map it the structured schema implicit in a database system. Not surprisingly, a lot of excitement in recent learning and KDD community has been on dealing with partially structured or semi-structured data. Although, in sheer volume structured data is small, it is precious data that captures the language in which data is to be analyzed. Ideally, we would like to be able to map the huge insanity of unstructuredness in terms of this database, and perform our querying and mining the same way.

The KDID community has a lot to offer in this quest. We need to understand and build models to statistically describe and recognize the entities stored in the database. Given the huge volume of unstructured data involved, we have to rely extensively on indexed access to both the database and the unstructured world.

Here are some examples of scenarios where a database and unstructured sources meet.

B. Goethals and A. Siebes (Eds.): KDID 2004, LNCS 3377, pp. 1–10, 2005.

Consider a company selling electronics products that maintains a table of its products with their features as column names. Companies routinely monitor the web to find competing companies offering products with similar features and to find reviews of newly introduced features. Ideally, they would like to map these unstructured webpages to additional rows and columns in their existing products database.

Another interesting area where there is strong need for integrating unstructured data with a structured database is personal information management systems. These systems organize all information about an individual in a structured fixed-schema database. For example, the PIM would contain structured entries for documents along with their titles, authors and citations organized as a bibtex entry, people including colleagues and students along with their contact information, projects with topics, members and start dates. Links between the structured entities, like members pointing to people and authors pointing to people, establish relationships between the entities. Such an interlinked database opens up the possibility of a query interface significantly richer than has been possible through grep on file-based unstructured desktops.

Given the legacy of existing file-based information systems, the creation of such a database will not happen naturally. Separate data integration processes are required to map unstructured data as it gets created as files into the existing structured database. For example, as a user downloads a paper he would like the bibtex entry of the paper to get automatically extracted and added in his PIM. When a resume appears in an email, he might want to link them to relevant projects.

This is a difficult problem involving several stages of information gathering, extraction and matching. We are very far from this goal. In this article, I will go over the pieces of the puzzle that are relevant and being solved today. We explicitly limit the scope to the following concrete problem. We are given a large multi-relational database and an optional small labeled unstructured set. Our goal is to perform the following on an input unstructured string:

- Extract attributes corresponding to columns names in the database and assign relationships through foreign keys when attributes span multiple linked tables. We call this the information extraction problem.
- Map the extracted entities to existing entries in the database if they match, otherwise, create new entries. We call this the matching problem.

On each of these subproblems a lot of work has already been done. These span a number of approaches starting from manually-tuned set of scripts to plain lookup-based methods to a bewildering set of pattern learning-based methods. However, there is still a need to develop unified solutions that can exploit existing networked structured databases along with labeled unstructured data. We would like a proposed solution to have the following properties:

- Automated, domain-independent, database-driven: Our goal is to design a system that does the integration in as domain-independent and automated a manner as possible. Ideally, the database system should be the only domain-specific component of the whole system. We should exploit it in the most effective way possible.

- Unified learning-based model for all integration tasks: Instead of building one classifier/strategy for recognizing year fields and another one for author-names and a third one for geography, we want a unified model that recognizes all of these through a single global model.
- Probabilistic output for post-querying and mining: We prefer a model that can output probabilities with each extraction/matching it outputs. Integration is not a goal by itself. It is often followed by large aggregate queries and soft-results with probabilities will provide better answers to these queries.
- Exploit all possible clues for extraction/matching in a simple combined framework: Real-life extraction problems will need to exploit a rich and diverse set of clues spanning, position, font, content, context, match in dictionary, part-of-speech, etc. We want an extensible model where it is easy to add such clues in a combined framework.
- Efficient, incremental training and inferencing: Finally we would like the system and the trained models to continuously evolve with the addition of new data and user corrections.

Conditional Random Fields [6, 11], a recently proposed form of undirected graphical models, is holding great promise in taking us toward this goal. I will present an overview of CRFs and later concentrate on how they apply for extraction and matching tasks.

2 Conditional Random Fields

We are given $\mathbf{x}$ a complex object like a record or a sequence or a graph for which we need to make n interdependent predictions $\mathbf{y} = y_1 \ldots y_n$. During normal classification we predict one variable. Here the goal is to predict n variables that are not all independent. The dependency between them is expressed as a graph G where nodes denote the random variable $\mathbf{y}$ and an edge between two nodes y_i and y_j denotes that these variables are directly dependent on each other. Any other pair of nodes y_i and y_k not connected by a direct edge are independent of each other given the rest of the nodes in the graph. This graph allows the joint probability of $\mathbf{y}$ (given $\mathbf{x}$) to be factorized using simpler terms as:

$$\Pr(\mathbf{y}|\mathbf{x}) = \frac{\Phi(\mathbf{y}, \mathbf{x})}{Z(\mathbf{x})} = \frac{\prod_c \Phi_c(\mathbf{y_c}, \mathbf{x}, c)}{Z(\mathbf{x})}$$

This provides a discriminative model of $\mathbf{y}$ in terms of $\mathbf{x}$. The c terms refer to cliques in the graph. For each clique a potential function captures the dependency between variable $\mathbf{y_c}$ in the clique. The denominator $Z(\mathbf{x})$ is a normalizer and is equal to $\sum_{\mathbf{y'}} \Phi(\mathbf{y'}, \mathbf{x})$. In exponential models, the potential function takes the form:

$$\Phi_c(\mathbf{y_c}, \mathbf{x}, c) = \exp(\sum_m w_m f_m(\mathbf{y_c}, \mathbf{x}, c))$$

The terms within the exponent are a weighted sum of features that capture various properties of the variables $\mathbf{y_c}, \mathbf{x}, \mathbf{c}$. Features can take any numerical value and are not required to be independent of one other. This is one of the strengths of the exponential models because it allows a user to exploit several properties of data that might provide clues to its label without worrying about the relationship among them. The w_m terms are the parameters of the model and are learnt during training. We will use $\mathbf{W}$ to denote the vector of all w_ms.

The inference problem for a CRF is defined as follows: given $\mathbf{W}$ and $\mathbf{x}$, find the best labels, $\mathbf{y} : y_1, y_2 \ldots, y_n$

$$\mathrm{argmax}_\mathbf{y} \Pr(\mathbf{y}|\mathbf{x}) = \mathrm{argmax}_\mathbf{y} \sum_c \mathbf{W}.\mathbf{f}(y_c, \mathbf{x}, c)$$

In general it is too expensive to enumerate all possible values of each of the ys and pick the best. However, the limited dependency among variables can be exploited to significantly reduce this complexity. The message passing algorithm is a popular method of solving various kinds of inference problems on such graphs. For a graph, without cycles it can find the best $\mathbf{y}$ and/or various marginals of the distribution in at most two passes over the graph. In a graph with cycles it is used to provide an approximation. An excellent survey of these techniques and how they solve the problems of training and inferencing appear in [5].

We will now see how various forms of information extraction and matching problems can be modeled within this unifying framework of conditional random fields.

3   Information Extraction(IE)

Traditional models for information extraction take as input labeled unstructured data and train models that can then extract the labeled fields from unseen unstructured data. We will review these first. Next, we will see how these can be extended to exploit an existing large database of structured entities.

3.1   IE Using Only Labeled Unstructured Data

The state of the art methods of IE model extraction as a sequential labeling problem. Typically, IE models treat the input unstructured text as a sequence of tokens $\mathbf{x} = x_1 \ldots x_n$ which need to be assigned a corresponding sequence of labels $\mathbf{y} = y_1 \ldots y_n$ from a fixed set $\mathcal{Y}$. The label at position i depends only on its previous label, thus the corresponding dependency graph on the variables is a *chain*. For instance, $\mathbf{x}$ might be a sequence of words, and $\mathbf{y}$ might be a sequence in $\{I, O\}^{|\mathbf{x}|}$, where $y_i = I$ indicates "word x_i is inside a name" and $y_i = O$ indicates the opposite. The simpler chain structure of the graph allows for more efficient training and inferencing as discussed in [11]. The conditional form of the CRF models allows us to exploit a variety of useful features without worrying about whether these overlap or not. For example, we can add features that capture the following diverse kinds of properties of a word: word ends in

"-ski", word is capitalized, word is part of a noun phrase, word is under node X in WordNet, word is in bold font, word is indented, next two words are "and Associates", previous label is "Other".

3.2   IE Using Labeled Data and Structured Databases

We now consider the case where in addition to the labeled data, we have large databases of entity names. For example, in trying to extract journal names from citations, we can have access to an existing list of journals in a bibtex database.

The conditional model provides one easy way to exploit such databases of entities. Assume we have columns in the database corresponding to different entity types like people and journals that we wish to extract. We simply add one additional binary feature for each such column D, f_D which is true for every token that appears in that column of entity names: *i.e.*, for any token x_i, $f_D(x_i) = 1$ if x_i matches any word of the entity column D and $f_D(x_i) = 0$ otherwise. This feature is then treated like any other binary feature, and the training procedure assigns an appropriate weighting to it relative to the other features.

The above scheme ignores the fact that entity names consist of multiple words. A better method of incorporating multi-word entity names was proposed by Borthwick *et al* [1]. They propose defining a set of four features, $f_{D.unique}$, $f_{D.first}$, $f_{D.last}$, and $f_{D.continue}$. For each token x_i the four binary dictionary features denote, respectively: (1) a match with a one-word dictionary entry, (2) a match with the first word of a multi-word entry, (3) a match with the last word of a multi-word entry, or, (4) a match with any other word of an entry. For example, the token x_i="flintstone" will have feature values $f_{D.unique}(x_i) = 0$, $f_{D.first}(x_i) = 0$, $f_{D.continue}(x_i) = 0$, and $f_{D.last}(x_i) = 1$ (for the column D consisting of just two entries: "frederick flintstone" and "barney rubble".

A major limitation of both of these approaches is that the proposed exact match features cannot handle abbreviations and misspellings in unstructured source. For example, a person names column might contain an entry of the form "Jeffrey Ullman" whereas the unstructured text might have "J. Ullmann". This problem can be solved by exploiting state-of-the-art similarity metrics like edit distance and TF-IDF match [3]. The features now instead of being binary are real-valued and return the similarity measure with the closest word in a dictionary.

A second limitation is that single word classification prevents effective use of multi-word entities in dictionaries. Similarity measures on individual words is less effective than similarity of a text segment to an entire entry in the dictionary. We address this limitation by extending CRFs to do semi-markov modeling instead of the usual markov models. In a semi-markov model we classify segments (consisting of several adjacent words) instead of individual words. The features are now defined over segments and this allows us to use as features similarity measures between a segment and the closest entry in the entity column. During inference, instead of finding a fixed sequence of labels $y_1 \ldots y_n$ we find the best method of segmenting the text and assign labels for each segment. Although, computationally this appears formidable, we can design efficient dynamic programming algorithms as shown in [4] and [9].

Experimental results on five real-life extraction tasks in the presence of large database of entity names show that the semi-markov models along with the use of similarity features increase the overall F1 accuracy from 46% to 58%.

We believe that semi-markov models hold great promise in providing effective use of multi-word databases for IE. More experiments are needed to establish the usefulness of this approach in a general multi-column setting. An interesting direction of future work is how existing foreign key/primary key relationships can be exploited to get even higher accuracies.

4   Entity Matching

We now consider the problem of matching an extracted set of entities to existing entries in the database. In the general case, an input unstructured record will be segmented into multiple types of entities. For example, a citation entry can be segmented into author names, title, journal names, year and volume. The existing database will typically consist of multiple tables with columns corresponding to the extracted entities and linked through foreign and primary keys.

4.1   Pair-Wise Single-Attribute Matching

Consider first the specific problem of matching a single extracted entity to a column of entity names, if it exists and returning "none-of-the-above" if it does not. Typically, there are several non-trivial variations of an entity name in the unstructured world. So, it is hard to hand-tune scripts that will take into account the different variations and match an extracted entity to the right database entry. We therefore pursue the learning approach where we design a classifier that takes as input various similarity measures between a pair of records and returns a "0" if the records match and a "1" otherwise. This is a straight-forward binary classification problem where the features are real-valued typically denoting various kinds of similarity functions between attributes like Edit distance, Soundex, N-grams overlap, Jaccard, Jaro-Winkler and Subset match [3]. Thus, we can use any binary classifier like SVM, decision trees, logistic regression. We use a CRF with a single variable for later extensibility. Thus, given a record pair (x_1x_2), the CRF predicts a y that can take values 0 or 1 as

$$\Pr(y|x_1, x_2) = \frac{\exp(\mathbf{W}.\mathbf{F}(y, x_1, x_2))}{Z(x_1, x_2)} \qquad (1)$$

The feature vector $\mathbf{F}(y, x_1, x_2)$ corresponds to various similarity measures between the records when $y = 1$.

An important concern about this approach is efficiency. During training we cannot afford to create pairs of records when the number of records is large. Typically, we can use some easy filters like only include pairs which have at least one common n-gram to reduce cost. During prediction too we cannot afford to explicitly compute the similarity of an input record with each entry in the database. Later we will discuss how we can index the learnt similarity criteria for considering only a subset of records with which to match.

4.2 Grouped Entity Resolution

The "match" relation is transitive in the sense that if a record r_1 matches with r_2 and r_2 matches with r_3 than r_1 has to match with r_3. When the input is a group of records instead of a single record as in the previous section, the pairwise independent classification approach can output predictions that violate the transitivity property. McCallum and Wellner [7] show how the CRF framework enables us to form a correlated prediction problem over all input records pairs, so as to enforce the transitivity constraint.

Assume new the sets of records are not already in the database. Given several records x=$x_1, x_2, \ldots x_n$, we find n^2 predictions, $\mathbf{y} = y_{ij} : 1 \leq i \leq n, 1 \leq j \leq n$ so as to enforce transitivity

$$\Pr(\mathbf{y}|\mathbf{x}) = \frac{\exp(\sum_{i,j} \mathbf{W}.\mathbf{F}(y_{ij}, x_i, x_j) + \sum_{i,j,k} w'.f(y_{ij}, y_{ik}, y_{jk}))}{Z(\mathbf{x})}$$

The value of the feature $f(y_{ij}, y_{ik}, y_{jk})$ is set to 0 whenever transitivity constraint is preserved otherwise it is set to $-\infty$. This happens when exactly two of the three arguments are set to 1.

The above formulation reduces to a graph partitioning problem whose exact solution is hard. However, it is possible to get good approximate solutions as discussed in [7]. The authors show that compared to simple pair-wise classification, the combined model increases the accuracy of two noun co-referencing tasks from 91.6% to 94% and 88.9% to 91.6% respectively.

4.3 Grouped Multi-attribute Entities

In the general case, the entity groups to be matched will each consist of multiple attributes. Grouped matching of multi-attribute records presents another mechanism of increasing accuracy by exploiting correlated predictions using a graphical model like CRF as discussed in [8]. Consider the four citation records below (from [8]).

Record	Title	Author	Venue
b1	Record Linkage using CRFs	Linda Stewart	KDD-2003
b2	Record Linkage using CRFs	Linda Stewart	9th SIGKDD
b3	Learning Boolean Formulas	Bill Johnson	KDD-2003
b4	Learning of Boolean Expressions	William Johnson"	9th SIGKDD

The similarity between b1 and b2 could be easy to establish because of the high similarity of the title and author fields. This in turn forces the venues "KDD-2003", "9th SIGKDD" to be called duplicates even though intrinsic textual similarity is not too high. These same venue names are shared between b3 and b4 and now it might be easy to call b3 and b4 duplicates in spite of not such high textual similarity between the author and title fields.

Such forms of shared inferencing are easy to exploit in the CRF framework. Associate variables for predictions for each distinct attribute pair and each record pair. In the formulation below, the first set of terms express the dependency between record pair predictions and predictions of attributes that they contain. The second set of terms exploits the text of the attribute pairs to predict if they are the same entity or not.

$$\Pr(\mathbf{y}|\mathbf{x}) = \frac{\exp(\sum_{i,j}\sum_k \mathbf{W}.\mathbf{F}(y_{ij}, A_{ij}^k) + \mathbf{W}'.\mathbf{F}'(A_{ij}^k, x_i.a^k, x_j.a^k))}{Z(\mathbf{x})}$$

The main concern about such formulations is the computation overhead and [8] presents some mechanisms for addressing them using graph partitioning algorithms. The combined model is shown to increase the match accuracy of a collection of citations from 84% to 87% ([8]).

5   Indices for Efficient Inferencing

For both the extraction and matching tasks, efficient processing will require that we break open the classification function learnt by a CRF and define appropriate indices so that we can efficiently select only that data subset that will satisfy a certain prediction. All aspects of this problem are not yet solved.

We will next consider a specific matching scenario of Section 4.1 where it is possible to design indices to reduce the number of entries in the database with which a query record is compared.

After the model in Equation 1 is trained we have a weight vector $\mathbf{W}$ for each feature in the vector $\mathbf{F}(y, x_1, x_2)$. When applying this model during inferencing, we are given a string x_q and our goal is to find the x_j-s from the database with the largest value of $\mathbf{W} \cdot \mathbf{F}(1, x_q, x_j)$. We claim that for most common similarity features, this function can be factorized as

$$\mathbf{W} \cdot \mathbf{F}(1, x_q, x_j) = w_1(x_q)f_1(x_j), \ldots w_r(x_q)f_r(x_j).$$

Consider an example: The original function is:

$$\mathbf{W} \cdot \mathbf{F}(1, x_q, x_j) = 0.3 \, tf - idf(x_j, x_q) + 0.4 \, \text{common-words}(x_j, x_q)$$

This can be rewritten as:

$$\sum_{word \ e \in x_q} (0.3 \, weight(e, x_q)weight(e, x_j) + 0.4[\![e \in x_j]\!])$$

The factorized form above allows us to index the data for efficiently finding the best match for a given query record as follows. We create inverted index for each of the r features f_i. Thus, for each feature we keep the list of (record identifiers, feature-value) pair for all records that have a non-zero value of the feature. The query records assigns a weight for a subset of these features. We create a weighted merge of these lists to find the record identifiers that will have the largest value of the dot-product. A number of techniques have been proposed in the database or IR literature to efficiently perform this merge and find the top-k matching records without performing the full merge. These details can be found in [10, 2, 12].

A number of interesting problems in designing indices for pulling parts that are likely to contain entities of a given type still remain. We can expect to see lot of work in this area in the future.

6   Conclusion

In this article we motivated the research area of developing techniques for information extraction and integration by exploiting existing large databases. Recent advances in graphical models provide a unified framework for structure extraction and reference resolution. This is a call to researchers in the KDD community to investigate the problems of developing practical models for these problems and providing methods for efficient training and inferencing.

References

1. A. Borthwick, J. Sterling, E. Agichtein, and R. Grishman. Exploiting diverse knowledge sources via maximum entropy in named entity recognition. In *Sixth Workshop on Very Large Corpora New Brunswick, New Jersey. Association for Computational Linguistics.*, 1998.
2. Surajit Chaudhuri, Kris Ganjam, Venkatesh Ganti, and Rajeev Motwani. Robust and efficient fuzzy match for online data cleaning. In *SIGMOD*, 2003.
3. William W. Cohen, Pradeep Ravikumar, and Stephen E. Fienberg. A comparison of string distance metrics for name-matching tasks. In *Proceedings of the IJCAI-2003 Workshop on Information Integration on the Web (IIWeb-03)*, 2003. To appear.
4. William W. Cohen and Sunita Sarawagi. Exploiting dictionaries in named entity extraction: Combining semi-markov extraction processes and data integration methods. In *Proceedings of the Tenth ACM SIGKDD International Conference on Knowledge Discovery and Data Mining*, 2004. To appear.
5. M. I. Jordan. Graphical models. *Statistical Science (Special Issue on Bayesian Statistics)*, 19:140–155, 2004.
6. John Lafferty, Andrew McCallum, and Fernando Pereira. Conditional random fields: Probabilistic models for segmenting and labeling sequence data. In *Proceedings of the International Conference on Machine Learning (ICML-2001)*, Williams, MA, 2001.
7. Andrew McCallum and Ben Wellner. Toward conditional models of identity uncertainty with application to proper noun coreference. In *Proceedings of the IJCAI-2003 Workshop on Information Integration on the Web*, pages 79–86, Acapulco, Mexico, August 2003.
8. Parag and P. Domingos. Multi-relational record linkage. In *Proceedings of 3rd Workshop on Multi-Relational Data Mining at ACM SIGKDD*, Seattle, WA, August 2004.

9. Sunita Sarawagi and William W. Cohen. Semi-markov conditional random fields for information extraction. In *NIPs (to appear)*, 2004.
10. Sunita Sarawagi and Alok Kirpal. Efficient set joins on similarity predicates. In *Proceedings of the ACM SIGMOD International Conference on Management of Data*, 2004.
11. F. Sha and F. Pereira. Shallow parsing with conditional random fields. In *In Proceedings of HLT-NAACL*, 2003.
12. Martin Theobald, Gerhard Weikum, and Ralf Schenkel. Top-k query evaluation with probabilistic guarantees. In *VLDB*, pages 648–659, 2004.

Constraint Relaxations for Discovering Unknown Sequential Patterns

Cláudia Antunes and Arlindo L. Oliveira

Instituto Superior Técnico / INESC-ID,
Department of Information Systems and Computer Science,
Av. Rovisco Pais 1, 1049-001 Lisboa, Portugal
{claudia.antunes, arlindo.oliveira}@dei.ist.utl.pt

Abstract. The main drawbacks of sequential pattern mining have been its lack of focus on user expectations and the high number of discovered patterns. However, the solution commonly accepted – the use of constraints – approximates the mining process to a verification of what are the frequent patterns among the specified ones, instead of the discovery of unknown and unexpected patterns.

In this paper, we propose a new methodology to mine sequential patterns, keeping the focus on user expectations, without compromising the discovery of unknown patterns. Our methodology is based on the use of constraint relaxations, and it consists on using them to filter accepted patterns during the mining process. We propose a hierarchy of relaxations, applied to constraints expressed as context-free languages, classifying the existing relaxations (*legal*, *valid* and *naïve*, previously proposed), and proposing several new classes of relaxations. The new classes range from the *approx* and *non-accepted*, to the composition of different types of relaxations, like the *approx-legal* or the *non-prefix-valid* relaxations. Finally, we present a case study that shows the results achieved with the application of this methodology to the analysis of the curricular sequences of computer science students.

1 Introduction

Sequential Pattern Mining addresses the problem of discovering maximal frequent sequences in a given database. This type of problem appears when the data to be mined has some sequential nature, i.e., when each piece of data is an ordered set of elements, like events in the case of temporal information, or nucleotides and amino-acid sequences for problems in bioinformatics.

In general, we can see sequential pattern mining as an approach to perform inter-transactional analysis, being able to deal with sequences of sets of items. Sequential pattern mining was motivated by the need to perform this kind of analysis, mostly in the retailing industry, but with applications in other areas, like the medical domain. The problem was first introduced by Agrawal and Srikant, and, in the last years, several sequential pattern mining algorithms were proposed [11], [13], [9]. Despite the reasonable efficiency of those algorithms, the lack of focus and user control has hampered the generalized use of sequential pattern mining. In general, the large

B. Goethals and A. Siebes (Eds.): KDID 2004, LNCS 3377, pp. 11–32, 2005.

number of discovered patterns makes the analysis of discovered information a difficult task.

In order to solve this problem, several authors have promoted the use of constraints to represent background knowledge and to filter the patterns of interest to the final user. This approach has been widely accepted by the data mining community, since it allows the user to control the mining process and reduces the search space, which contributes significantly to achieve better performance and scalability levels. The simplest constraint over the sequence content is to impose that only some items are of interest – *item constraints*. An example of such constraint is the use of Boolean expressions over the presence or absence of items [12]. When applied to sequential pattern mining, constraints over the content can be just a constraint over the items to consider, or a constraint over the sequence of items. More recently, regular languages have been proposed [3] and used to constrain the mining process, by accepting only patterns that are accepted by a regular language. In this case, constrained algorithms use a deterministic finite automaton (DFA) to define the regular language. Generally, these automata consist of a set of states and a set of transitions from state to state that occur on symbols chosen from an alphabet. When applied to sequential pattern mining, strings (sequences of symbols) are replaced by sequences of itemsets.

Although this approach has contributed to reduce the number of discovered patterns and to match them to the user expectations, the use of regular languages transforms the pattern mining process into the verification of which of the sequences of the language are frequent, completely blocking the discovery of novel patterns. It is important to note that by specifying the language, we are explicitly specifying which are the sequences that can be considered, and the mining process is reduced to the identification of which of these are frequent. By novel information, we mean the information that is not trivially inferred from the constraint.

1.1 Motivation

Consider, for instance, the problem of identifying typical behaviors of company customers. Suppose that the company considers that a well-behaved customer is a customer who has made all its payments at the time of the analysis. This knowledge can be represented by a context-free language, but cannot be by a regular language, since it needs to count the number of invoices and payments.

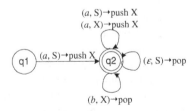

Fig. 1. Pushdown automaton for representing well-behaved customers

The pushdown automaton presented in Fig. 1 (pushdown automata are described in the next section) is able to represent that knowledge, with *a* corresponding to an invoice and *b* to a payment. In conjunction with sequential pattern mining algorithms allows for the discovery of each sequence of invoices and payments are frequent (sequences like *abab*, *aaabbb* and *aabbab*).

However, if among the recorded data there are events related to second copies of invoices, cancellations, information requests and answers to requests, for example, and there is no knowledge about their relations with the other two kinds of events, it is not possible to discover those relations with constrained sequential pattern mining. On the other hand, with an unconstrained process the existing background knowledge will be ignored. In this manner, it is clear that although constraints (formal languages in particular) can be used to represent existing domain knowledge, they are not enough to address the main data mining challenge: to discover novel information.

In this work, we propose a new mining methodology to solve the trade-off between satisfying user expectations (by using background knowledge) and mining novel information. Our methodology is based on the use of constraint relaxations, and it assumes that the user is responsible for choosing the strength of the restriction used to constrain the mining process. We propose a hierarchy of constraint relaxations (for constraints expressed as formal languages – either regular or context-free), that range from conservative to non-conservative relaxations, proposing two new types of constraints – the *approx* and the *non-accepted* relaxations, and new relaxations resulting from the composition of the different classes of relaxations.

After a concise description of the use of context-free languages to deal with sequences of itemsets (section 2), the new methodology is defined (section 3), presenting each of the relaxations (including the extension of the ones proposed in [3] – *naïve*, *legal* and *valid*). In section 4, we present a case study with the analysis of curriculum sequences, and, based on that data, we evaluate the use of constraint relaxations, by comparing the number of discovered patterns and the processing times using each relaxation. Section 5 concludes the paper with a discussion and ideas for future work.

2   Context-Free Languages for Sequences of Itemsets

Recent work [1] has shown that regular expressions can be substituted by context-free languages, without compromising the practical performance of algorithms, when dealing with strings of items. This is useful because context-free languages are more expressive than regular languages, being able to represent constraints that are more interesting. In particular, the structure of constrained sequential pattern mining algorithms does not need any change to use context-free languages as constraints. The only adaptation is the substitution of the finite automaton by a pushdown automaton (PDA), to represent the context-free language.

A *pushdown automaton* is a tuple $\mathcal{M}=(Q,\Sigma,\Gamma,\delta,q_0,Z_0,F)$, where: Q is a finite set of states; Σ is an alphabet called the input alphabet; Γ is an alphabet called the stack alphabet; δ is a mapping from $Q\times\Sigma\cup\{\varepsilon\}\times\Gamma$ to finite subsets of $Q\times\Gamma^*$; $q_0\in Q$ is the initial state; $Z_0\in\Gamma$ is a particular stack symbol called the start symbol, and $F\subseteq Q$ is the set of final states [6].

The language accepted by a pushdown automaton is the set of all inputs for which some sequence of moves causes the pushdown automaton to empty its stack and reach a final state.

When applied to the process of mining sequential patterns from sequences of itemsets instead of strings (sequences of symbols), pushdown automata have to be redefined. The problem is related with the fact that existing algorithms manipulate one item per iteration, instead of an entire itemset. In this manner, we need to perform partial transitions, corresponding to the item involved at the specific step iteration. To illustrate this situation consider the pushdown automaton defined over itemsets represented in Fig. 2 (left). This PDA generates sequences with the same number of baskets (a,b) on the left and right side of item c, which means that it generates sequences like $(a,b)c(a,b)$ or $(a,b)(a,b)c(a,b)(a,b)$. Formally, it can be defined as the tuple $M=(Q, \Sigma, \Gamma, \delta, q_1, S, \mathcal{F})$, with $Q=\{q_1, q_2\}$ the set of states, $\Sigma=\{a, b, c\}$ its alphabet, $\Gamma=\{S, X\}$ the stack alphabet, q_1 the initial state, S the initial stack symbol and $\mathcal{F}=\{q_2\}$ the set of final or accepting states. Finally, δ corresponds to the five transitions illustrated in Fig. 2-left (for example "$[(a,b),S]\rightarrow$pushX" represents the transition from state q_1 to state q_2, when the stack has the symbol S in the top and we are in the presence of (a,b)).

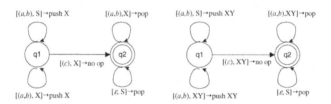

Fig. 2. Pushdown (left) and Extended Pushdown (right) automata

Consider for example that algorithm *PrefixGrowth* [10] is applied and it finds a, b and c as frequent. Then it will have to proceed to discover which items are frequent after a. At this point, there is already one problem: given that it has found a, which operation should it perform over the stack? If it pushes X, then c will be accepted after a, but if it only applies the push operation after finding b, then it will accept, as "potentially accepted", sequences like aaa, $aaaaa$ and so on, since S remains on the top of the stack.

In order to deal with itemsets, we extend the notion of PDA.

An *extended pushdown automaton* (ePDA) is a tuple $E=(Q, \Sigma, \Gamma, \delta, q_0, Z_0, \mathcal{F},)$, with Q, Σ, Γ, q_0, Z_0 and $\mathcal{F}$ defined as for pushdown automata, but δ defined as a mapping function from $Q \times P(\Sigma) \cup \{\varepsilon\} \times \Gamma^*$ to finite subsets of $Q \times \Lambda^*$, with Λ equal to Γ^* and $P(\Sigma)$ representing the powerset of Σ.

The difference to standard pushdown automata is the transition function, which manipulates itemsets and strings of stack elements instead of items and stack elements, respectively. With this extension, it is possible to explore sequences of itemsets with existing algorithms. Fig. 2-right illustrates an extension to the PDA illustrated before. Clearly, on one hand, by using extended pushdown automata, algorithms such as *SPIRIT* or *PrefixGrowth* do not need any alteration on their structure. On the other hand, their performances remain tightly connected to the number of discovered patterns and almost nothing related to the complexity of the constraint.

3 Constraint Relaxations

While the problems of representing background knowledge in sequential pattern mining and the reduction of the number of discovered patterns can be solved using formal languages, the challenge of discovering unknown information, keeping the process centered on user expectations, remains open.

At this point, it is important to clarify the meaning of some terms. By **novel information**, we mean both the information that cannot be inferred in the reference frame of the information system or of the user, and **centering the process in the user** has essentially two aspects: the management of user expectations and the use of user background knowledge in the mining process. By expectation management, we mean that the results from the process have to be in accordance with user expectations, with similarity measured by comparing them to the user's background knowledge.

In the case of sequential pattern mining using constraints expressed as context-free languages, it is clear that:

- the existing background knowledge is represented and integrated in the mining process as a context-free language;
- the process is completely centered on the user, since the process will only discover patterns that are in accordance with his background knowledge (this means that only sequences that belong to the context-free language will be of interest);
- it is not possible to discover novel information, since all the discovered patterns need necessarily be contained in the context-free language specified by the user.

Considering these limitation, we propose a new methodology to mine unknown patterns, while keeping the process centered on the user. This methodology is based on the use of constraint relaxations, instead of constraints themselves, to filter the discovered patterns during the mining process. The notion of constraint relaxation has been widely used when real-life problems are addressed, and in sequential pattern mining, they were first used to improve the performance of the algorithm [3]. The key point is that, in many cases, the user is able to specify easily a constraint that is too restrictive, but is not capable to specify a constraint that is adequate for the task at hand. For instance, the user may be able to specify a *normal behavior*, but will be hard pressed to specify an *almost normal* or *approximately normal* behavior.

A *constraint relaxation* can then be seen as an approximation to the constraint, that captures the essence of the user knowledge but that does not restrict too much the universe of possible patterns. In other words, while constraints explicitly specify which sequences can be discovered, constraint relaxations determine the way that the knowledge (expressed by the constraint) can be used to guide the mining process. In this manner, when used instead of the constraints expressed by the user, relaxations can give rise to the discovery of novel information, in the sense that the patterns discovered can no longer be directly inferred from the background knowledge, i.e. from the reference frame of the user. If these relaxations are used to mine new patterns, instead of simply used to filter the patterns that satisfy the imposed constraint, the discovery of novel information is possible. Given that the user may choose the level of relaxation allowed (the type of relaxation), it is possible to keep the focus and the interactivity of the process, while still permitting the discovery of novel and unknown information. In this manner, the goal of data mining will be achieved. Additionally, some of the unresolved challenges of pattern mining will be addressed, namely: how to use constraints to specify background knowledge and user expectations; how to reduce the number of discovered patterns by constraining the search space, and how to reduce the amount of time in processing the discovery.

In order to achieve those results, we propose four main classes of relaxations over constraints expressed as formal languages, as illustrated in Fig. 3. The differences between them result from the redefinition of the acceptability notion for the formal language that defines the constraint.

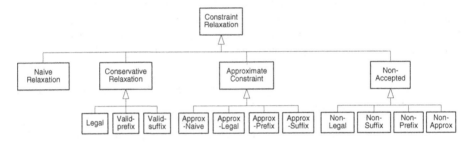

Fig. 3. Hierarchy of constraint relaxations

The first class of relaxations is the Naïve relaxation, which corresponds to a simple item constraint. However, in the context of constraints expressed as formal languages, it can be seen as a relaxation that only accepts patterns containing the items that belong to the language alphabet.

Conservative relaxations group the other already known relaxations, used by SPIRIT [3], and a third one – Valid-Prefix, similar to Valid-suffix.

It is important to note that conservative relaxations are not able to discover unknown patterns, just sub-patterns of expected ones. Approximate matching at a lexical level has been considered an extremely important tool to assist in the discovery of new facts, but ignored in most of the approaches to pattern mining. It considers two sequences similar if they are at an edit distance below a given threshold. An exception to this generalized frame is the *AproxMAP* [7], which uses this distance to count the support for each potential pattern. However, to our knowledge, edit distance has not been applied to constrain the pattern mining process.

To address the need to identify approximate matching we propose a new class of relaxations – the *Approx relaxation*, which accept the patterns that are at an acceptable edit distance from some sequence accepted by the constraint.

Another important relaxation is related with the discovery of low frequency behaviors that are still very significant to the domain. Fraud detection is the paradigm of such task. Note that the difficulties in fraud detection are related with the explosion of discovered information when the minimum support threshold decreases.

To address the problem of discovering low frequency behaviors, we propose an additional class of relaxations – the *Non-accepted relaxation*. If L is the language used to constrain the mining process, Non-accepted relaxations will only accept sequences that belong to the language that is the complement of L.

Additionally, each of these relaxations can be combined, creating compositions of relaxations, that can be used directly as filters. Examples of such compositions are *approx-legal* or *non-approx*.

Next, we will present each class of constraint relaxations. To illustrate the concepts, consider the extended pushdown automaton in Fig. 2-right.

3.1 Naïve Relaxation

As stated, the *Naïve* relaxation only prunes candidate sequences containing elements that do not belong to the alphabet of the language, For example, if we consider the specified automaton, only sequences with a's, b's and c's are accepted by the Naïve relaxation.

In this manner, a sequence is accepted by the naive criterion in exactly the same conditions than for regular languages. However, this relaxation prunes a small number of candidate sequences, which implies a limited focus on the desired patterns.

Since Naïve relaxation is anti-monotonic, no change in sequential pattern mining algorithms is needed.

3.2 Conservative Relaxations

Conservative relaxations group the *Legal* and *Valid* relaxations, used in SPIRIT, and a third one – *Valid-Prefix*, complementary to the *Valid* relaxation (called Valid-Suffix in the rest of the paper). These relaxations impose a weaker condition than the original constraint, accepting patterns that are subsequences of accepted sequences. When used in conjunction with context-free languages, those relaxations remain identical, but we have to redefine the related notions.

First of all consider the partial relation ψ, which maps from $Q \times S \times \Gamma^*$ to $Q \times \Lambda^*$ representing the achieved state $q \in Q$ and top of the stack $\lambda \in \Lambda^*$ (with Λ equal to Γ^*), when in the presence of a particular sequence $s \in S$ in a particular state $q \in Q$ and a string of stack symbols $w \in \Gamma^*$. Also, consider that $\lambda.top$ is the operation that returns the first string on λ.

$\psi(q_i, s=<s_1 \ldots s_n>, w)$ is defined as follows:
  i. (q_i, λ), if $|s|=0 \wedge \exists \lambda \in \Lambda^*$: $\lambda=w$
  ii. (q_j, λ), if $|s|=1 \wedge \exists q_j \in Q$; $\lambda \in \Lambda^*$: $\delta(q_i,s_1,w) \supset (q_j, \lambda)$
  iii. $\psi(q_j,<s_2 \ldots s_n>,\lambda.top)$, if $|s|>1 \wedge \exists q_j \in Q$; $\lambda \in \Lambda^*$: $\delta(q_i,s_1,w) \supset (q_j,\lambda)$

Additionally, consider that the elements on each itemset are ordered lexicographically (as assumed by sequential pattern mining algorithms). In this manner, it is possible to define two new predicates:

Given two itemsets $a=(a_1...a_n)$ and $b=(b_1...b_m)$, with $n<m$: a is a *prefix* of b if for all $1 \leq i \leq n$ a_i is equal to b_i and a is a *suffix* of b if for all $1 \leq i \leq n$ a_i is equal to $b_{i+(m-n)}$.

Legal. The *Legal* relaxation requires that every sequence is legal with respect to some state of the automaton, which specifies the constraint language. The extension of legal relaxation to context-free languages is non-trivial, since the presence of a stack (on the automaton) makes the identification of legal sequences more difficult. However, it is possible to extend the notion of legality of a sequence with respect to any state of an extended pushdown automaton.

A sequence $s=<s_1...s_n>$ is *legal with respect to state* q_i with the top of the stack w, iff

i. $|s|=1 \wedge \exists\, s_k \in \Sigma^*; q_j \in Q; \lambda \in \Lambda^*: \delta(q_i,s_k,w) \supset (q_j,\lambda) \wedge s_1 \subseteq s_k$

ii. $|s|=2 \wedge \exists\, s_k,s_k' \in \Sigma^*; \lambda,\lambda' \in \Lambda^*: q_j,q_j' \in Q; \delta(q_i,s_k,w) \supset (q_j',\lambda) \wedge s_1$ suffixOf s_k
     $\wedge\, \delta(q_j',s_k',\lambda.top) \supset (q_j,\lambda') \wedge s_2$ prefixOf s_k'

iii. $|s|>2 \wedge \exists\, s_k,s_k' \in \Sigma^*; \lambda,\lambda',\lambda'' \in \Lambda^*: q_j,q_j',q_j'' \in Q; \delta(q_i,s_k,w) \supset (q_j',\lambda) \wedge s_1$ suffixOf s_k
     $\wedge\, \psi(q_j',s_2...s_{n-1},\lambda.top)=(q_j'',\lambda') \wedge \delta(q_j'',s_k',\lambda'.top) \supset (q_j,\lambda'') \wedge s_n$ prefixOf s_k'

This means that any sequence with one itemset is legal with respect to an extended pushdown automaton state, if there is a transition from it, defined over a superset of the itemset (i). When the sequence is composed of two itemsets, it is legal with respect to a state, if the first itemset is a suffix of a legal transition from the current state, and the second itemset is a prefix of a legal transition from the achieved state (ii). Otherwise, the sequence is legal if the first itemset is a suffix of a legal transition from the state, $s_2...s_{n-1}$ corresponds to a valid path from the state and stack reached, and the last itemset is a prefix of a legal transition from the state and stack reached with $s_2...s_{n-1}$.

Examples of legal sequences with respect to the initial state of the specified automaton are: a, b and c (by rule i), bc and $(a,b)c$ (by rule ii) and bca and $(a,b)ca$ (by rule iii). Examples of non-legal sequences are ac (by ignoring rule ii) or acb (by ignoring rule iii).

Note that ψ is only defined for non-empty stacks. Indeed, in order to verify the legality of some sequence s, it is necessary to find a sequence of itemsets t that can be concatenated to s, creating a sequence ts accepted by the automata.

Valid-Suffix. The *Valid-Suffix* relaxation only accepts sequences that are valid suffixes with respect to any state of the automaton. Like for legal relaxation, some adaptations are needed when dealing with context-free languages.

A sequence $s=<s_1...s_n>$ is a *valid-suffix with respect to state* q_i with top of the stack w, iff

i. $|s|=1 \wedge \exists\, s_k \in \Sigma^*; \lambda \in \Lambda^*; q_j \in Q; \delta(q_i,s_k,w) \supset (q_j,\lambda) \wedge s_1$ suffixOf $s_k \wedge \lambda.top=\varepsilon$

ii. $|s|>1 \wedge \exists\, s_k',s_k'' \in \Sigma^*; \lambda',\lambda'' \in \Lambda^*; q_j,q_j',q_j'' \in Q; \delta(q_i,s_k,w) \supset (q_j',\lambda) \wedge s_1$ suffixOf s_k
     $\wedge\, \psi(q_j',s_2...s_n,\lambda.top)=(q_j,\lambda') \wedge \lambda.top=\varepsilon$

This means that a sequence is a valid-suffix with respect to a state if it is legal with respect to that state, achieves a final state and the resulting stack is empty. In particular, if the sequence only has one itemset, it has to be a suffix of a legal transition to an accepting state.

Considering the extended pushdown automaton as before, examples of such sequences are b, (a,b), $c(a,b)$ and $bc(a,b)$. Negative examples are, for instance, bca or bcb. Note that, in order to generate valid-suffix sequences with respect to any state, it is easier to begin from the final states. However, this kind of generating process is one of the more difficult when dealing with pushdown automata, since it requires a reverse simulation of their stacks.

In order to avoid this difficulty, using prefix instead of suffix validity could represent a more useful relaxation, when dealing with context-free languages. Note that valid-suffixes are not prefix-monotone, and could not be easily used by pattern-growth methods [9].

Valid-Prefix. The valid-prefix relaxation is the counterpart of valid-suffix, and requires that every sequence is legal with respect to the initial state.

A sequence $s=<s_1...s_n>$ is said to be *prefix-valid* iff:

i. $|s|=1 \wedge \exists s_k \in \Sigma^*; \lambda \in \Lambda^*: \delta(q_0,s_k,Z_0) \supset (q_j,\lambda) \wedge s_1$ prefixOf s_k

ii. $|s|>1 \wedge \exists s_k \in \Sigma^*; \lambda,\lambda' \in \Lambda^*; q_j,q_j' \in Q: \psi(q_0,s_1...s_{n-1},Z_0)=(q_j',\lambda') \wedge \delta(q_j',s_k,\lambda'.top) \supset (q_j,\lambda)$
     $\wedge s_n$ prefixOf s_k

This means that a sequence is prefix-valid if it is legal with respect to the initial state and the first itemset is a prefix of a transition from the initial state. Sequences with valid prefixes are not difficult to generate, since the simulation of the stack begins with the initial stack: the stack containing only the stack start symbol. The benefits from using the suffix-validity and prefix-validity are similar. When using the prefix-validity to generate the prefix-valid sequences with k elements, the frequent $(k-1)$-sequences are extended with the frequent 1-sequences, in accordance with the constraint. Examples of valid-prefixes are (ab) and $(ab)ca$; $(a)c$ or bc are examples of non-valid prefixes.

Note that the *legal* relaxation accepts all the patterns accepted by *valid-suffix* and *valid-prefix* relaxations. In this manner, it is a less restrictive relaxation than the other two. Although these relaxations have considerable restrictive power, which improves significantly the focus on user expectations, they do not allow for the existence of errors. This represents a strong limitation in real datasets, since little deviations may exclude many instances from the discovered patterns.

3.3 *Approx* Constraints

In order to solve this problem we propose a class of relaxations that accepts sequences that have a limited number of errors. If it is possible to correct those errors with a limited cost, then the sequence will be accepted.

A new class of relaxations, called *approx relaxations*, tries to accomplish this goal: they only accept sequences that are at a given edit distance for an accepted sequence. This edit distance is a similarity measure that reflects the cost of operations that have to be applied to a given sequence, so it would be accepted as a positive example of a given formal language. This cost of operations will be called the *generation cost*, and is similar to the edit distance between two sequences, and the operations to consider can be the *Insertion*, *Deletion* and *Replacement* [8].

Given a constraint C, expressed as a context-free language, and a real number ε which represents the maximum error allowed, a sequence *s* is said to be *approximate-accepted* by C, if its generation cost ξ(s, C) is less than or equal to ε. The *generation cost* ξ (s, C) is defined as the sum of costs of the cheapest sequence of edit operations transforming the sequence s into a sequence r accepted by the language C.

For example, considering the extended pushdown automaton defined above, $ac(a,b)$ and $(a,b)(a,b)$ are approx-accepted sequences with one error, which result from inserting a *b* on the first itemset, on the first example, and a *c* on the second position, on the second example, respectively. $c(a,b)$ and $b(a,b)$ are non-approximate accepted with one error, since two edit operations are needed to accept them.

The other four classes of approximate constraints are defined by replacing the acceptance by legality and validity notions. In this manner, an *Approx-Legal* relaxation accepts sequences that are approximately legal with respect to some state. *Approx-Suffix* and *Approx-Prefix* relaxations are defined in a similar way. Finally, *Approx-Naïve* accepts sequences that have ε items (with ε the maximum error allowed) that do not belong to the language's alphabet.

Recent work has proposed a new algorithm ε–accepts [2] to verify if a sequence was approximately generated by a given deterministic finite automata (DFA). Fortunately, the extension to deal with context-free languages is simply achieved by replacing the use of a DFA by the use of an ePDA. The results shown in this paper were achieved by using such an algorithm.

3.4 Non-accepted Relaxation

Another important issue is related with the discovery of low frequency behaviors that are still very significant to the domain.

Suppose that there is a model (expressed as a context-free language) able to describe the frequent patterns existing on a huge database (say for example that the minimum support allowed is 10%). If there are 3% of clients with a fraudulent behavior, it is possible that they are not discovered neither by using the unconstrained mining process, nor by using any of the proposed relaxations. However, the model of non-fraudulent clients may be used to discover the fraudulent ones: the fraudulent clients are known to not satisfy the model of non-fraudulent clients.

To address the problem of low frequency behaviors discovery, we propose an additional class of relaxations – the *Non-accepted relaxation*, which accept sequences that are not accepted by the constraint.

A sequence is *non-accepted* by the language if it is not generated by that language.

In fact, this is not really a relaxation, but another constraint (in particular the constraint that only accepts sequences that belong to the language that is the complement of the initial constraint). However, since they are defined based on the initial constraint, we choose to designate them as relaxations.

The benefits from using the non-accepted relaxation are mostly related to the possibility of not rediscovering already known information, which may contribute significantly to improve the performance of sequential pattern mining algorithms. Moreover, since context-free languages are not closed under complementation [6] (which means that the complement of a context-free language is not necessarily a context-free language), the use of the complement instead of the non-accepted relaxation could be prohibitive.

Note that by using this new approach, it is possible to reduce the search space, and consequently to reduce the minimum support allowed. The non-accepted relaxation will find all the patterns discovered by the rest of the introduced relaxations, representing a small improvement in the focus on user expectations. In fact, it finds all the patterns discovered by unconstrained patterns minus the ones that are accepted by the constraint. Like for approx relaxations, an interesting improvement is to associate a subset of the alphabet in conjunction with the non-accepted relaxation. This conjunction focus the mining process over a smaller part of the data, reducing the number of discovered sequences, and contributing to achieve our goal.

As before, the sub-classes of *Non-Accepted* relaxations result by combining the non-acceptance philosophy with each one of the others relaxations. While non-accepted relaxation filters only a few patterns, when the constraint is very restrictive, the non-legal relaxation filters all the patterns that are non-legal with respect to the constraint. With this relaxation is possible to discover the behaviors that completely deviate from the accepted ones, helping to discover the fraudulent behaviors.

3.5 Discussion: Novelty and Expectedness

The discussion about the concept of novel information is one of the most difficult in pattern mining. While the concept is clear in the reference frame of a knowledge acquisition system, the same is not true in the reference frame of the final user. Indeed, several interestingness measures have been proposed for the evaluation of the discovered patterns [4]. Moreover, this issue is more critical with the introduction of constraints in the mining process. In fact, in the presence of constraints the concept of novel patterns becomes unclear even in the reference frame of information systems, since they are then able to use the knowledge, represented as the constraint.

In order to bring some light into the discussion, consider that, given a model C as constraint, a pattern A is *more novel than* a pattern B, if the generation cost of A by model C is larger than the generation cost of B by model C (with the generation cost defined as above). With this concept, it is now possible to understand the reason why non-accepted patterns can be more novel than the patterns discovered by conservative relaxations. It is now clear that, despite the differences between relaxations, all of them allow for the discovery of novel information. Indeed, the conservative relaxations are able to discover failure situations, that is, situations when for, some reason, the given model is not completely satisfied (*valid-prefix* and *valid-suffix* identify failures in the beginning and ending of the model, respectively, and *legal* identifies problems in the middle of the model).

However, the great challenge of pattern mining is to discover novel information that is interesting to the user. It is clear from the definition of the novel relation, that an unexpected pattern is more novel than an expected one. In fact, the challenge resides in the balance between the discovery of novel but somehow expected patterns. The proposed relaxations cover a wide range of this balance, giving the user the option of which is the most relevant issue for the problem in hands: to discover novel information or to satisfy user expectations.

Consider the PDA and the data shown in Fig. 4: the PDA represents a more restrictive notion of well-behaved costumer – a costumer who as at most two invoices to pay. If we apply the proposed methodology to analyze that data, we will be able to discover several different patterns with the different relaxations, as shown in Table 1.

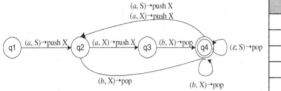

Dataset	
eababraabb	*aababbaerb*
aabbaberab	*ababaabbab*
aebraaaccd	*aebaraacbe*
abaaaccder	*abaeraacbb*
aebaraaacb	*aaacbabab*

Fig. 4. Example of a pushdown automaton and a small dataset

In order to permit an easy comparison, only maximal patterns are shown. In this manner, some patterns appear only in some columns. In the column relative to the *approx* relaxation, are shown the edit operations needed to transform each pattern to a pattern belonging to the context-free language.

Table 1. Comparison of the results achieved with and without constraints

Frequent	Accepted	Legal	Prefix	Approx.($\varepsilon=1$)	Non-Acc (w/ $\Sigma=\{a,c,d,e,r\}$)
be *baa* *era* *braa* *baba* *baer* *araa* *abab* *abaa* *raacb* *raaac* *aaacb* *aabbab* *aaaccd* *aebaraa*	*abab* *aabbab*	*baba* *abab* *abaa* *aabbab*	*abab* *abaa* *aabbab*	*abab* *aabbab* $ar \rightarrow R(r,b,2)$ $aeb \rightarrow D(e,2)$ $abaa \rightarrow R(a,b,4)$ $aacb \rightarrow R(c,b,3)$	*aer* *era* *raac* *araa* *raaac* *aaaccd*

As expected, by using the constraint itself we only discover two patterns, which satisfy the context-free language. Therefore, these results are not enough to invalidate Hipp's arguments [5] about constraints. Nevertheless, with Legal and Valid-prefixes, it is possible to discover some other intermediate patterns, which are potentially accepted by the complete constraint.

Finally, with *approx* and *non-accepted* relaxations, it is possible to discover unexpected patterns. Indeed, the approx relaxation shows the most interesting behavior, since it is possible to discover that it is usual that after sending the second invoice, customers pay their old bills (*aacb*). With non-accepted relaxation, it is also possible to discover interesting patterns. In this case, it is common that after three invoices without any payment, and the emission of two second invoices, the customer account is canceled (*aaaccd*).

4 Discovering Frequent Curricula: A Case Study

In this paper, we claim that it is possible to discover unknown information, using sequential pattern mining with constraint relaxations, without loosing the focus on user expectations. In order to validate these claims, we present the results achieved by applying this methodology to the discovery of frequent curricula instantiations from the data collected from IST student's performance in one undergraduate program on information technology and computer science. For this purpose, we will evaluate our methodology by comparing: the performance of each mining process; the number of discovered patterns and the ability to answer the relevant questions.

The curriculum has a duration of 10 semesters with 36 required subjects, a final thesis and 4 optional subjects in the last year. Four specialty areas are offered: PSI – Programming and Information Systems; SCO – Computer Systems; IAR – Artificial Intelligence and IIN – Information Systems for Factory Automation.

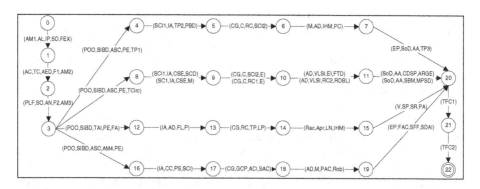

Fig. 5. DFA for specifying the model curriculum for LEIC specialty areas

There are 20 common subjects in the curriculum model, 18 on the first three semesters and the other 2 on the following two semesters. The enrollment on a specialty area was made on the fourth semester. There are 47 other subjects, distributed by each specialty area. The deterministic finite automaton on Fig. 5 shows the model curriculum for each specialty area. (The existence of two different transitions per semester for SCO students, are due to a minor reorganization of the SCO curriculum on 1995/1996.)

Data Statistics. The dataset used to analyze those questions consists on the set of sequences corresponding to the curriculum followed by students that made at least 8 enrollments. In this manner, the dataset is composed of 1440 sequences, with an average sequence length equal to 11.58 semesters. Most of the students (72%) have between 8 and 12 enrollments (they had attended classes between 8 and 12 semesters). Naturally, the number of students with an odd sequence length is reduced, since this situation corresponds to students that have registered in only one semester on that year. In terms of the number of enrollments per semester, its mean is 4.82 enrollments on subjects per semester, with most students (75%) enrolling on between 4 and 6 units.

Another interesting issue is the distribution of students per specialty area: 56% follow the PSI specialty area, 19% the SCO specialty area and the remaining 26% are equally distributed by IAR and IIN specialty areas. This distribution conditions the number of enrollments per subject. For example, subjects exclusive to Artificial Intelligence and IIN have at most 13% of support.

It is interesting to note that only 823 students (57%) have concluded the final work (TFC1 and TFC2). Since it is usual that students only take optional subjects in parallel or after finishing the final work, the support for optional subjects is at most 57%. Since the options are chosen from a large set of choices (130 subjects), their individual support is considerably lower. Indeed Management (G) is the optional subject with more students, about 40%.

4.1 Evaluation of Discovered Information

The analysis of the data referring to students' performance has essentially two main reasons: to explain the low levels of success and to identify the most common profiles of students. In this manner, we will try to answer three questions: 'what are the most common patterns on each scientific area?', 'what is the impact of some subjects on others?' and 'what are the common curricula instantiations for each specialty area, including optional subjects?'.

Finding Frequent Curricula on Scientific Areas. The discovery of the most common patterns on each scientific area is easily achieved if we look for students, who conclude the sequence of subjects in the same scientific area in at most four semesters. This constraint can be specified by the extended pushdown automaton represented on Fig. 6. In this figure, each transition represents four transitions, one per scientific area. For example, $[\sim X2, sa(X2)] \rightarrow push\ sa(X2)$ represents $[\sim AED, MTP] \rightarrow push\ MTP$, $[\sim AC, ASO] \rightarrow push\ ASO$, $[\sim AM2, AM] \rightarrow push\ AM$ and $[\sim F1, F] \rightarrow push\ F$. Consider that X_1, X_2 and X_3 are the first, second and third subjects on some of the following scientific areas: MTP, ASO, Physics and Mathematical Analysis. Also, consider that sa is a function from the set of subjects to their scientific area, for example sa(IP)=MTP.

The first thing that we are able to discover, using a constraint defined over the ePDA on Fig. 6 (with a gap equal to zero) is that the majority of students are able to conclude the sequence of MTP (61%) and ASO (57%) subjects without any failure. Additionally, 6% of students are also able to conclude all but one of those subjects in four semesters (see shadowed patterns in Table 2-left).

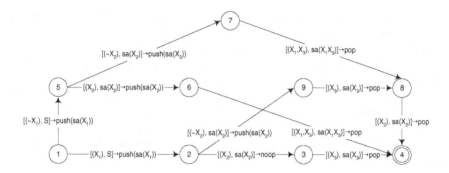

Fig. 6. ePDA for specifying the curricula on scientific areas, where students conclude three subjects in a specific scientific area at most on 4 semesters

Table 2. Discovered Patterns per Scientific Areas

Discovered Patterns			
With Constraints	Sup	With Approx Relaxation	Sup
<(IP),(AED),(PLF)>	61%	<(AM1),(~AM2),(~AM3),(AM2)>	6%
<(IP),(~AED),(PLF),(AED)>	6%	<(AM1),(~AM2),(AM2)>	6%
<(SD),(AC),(SO)>	57%	**<(AM1),(AM2),(~AM3,AM3)>**	6%
<(SD),(~AC),(SO),(AC)>	6%	<(FEX),(F1),(~F2)>	22%
<(FEX),(F1),(F2)>	35%	<(FEX),(~F1),(~F2),(F1)>	8%
<(FEX),(~F1),(F2),(F1)>	5%	<(FEX),(~F1),(F2),(F1)>	5%
<(AM1),(AM2),(AM3)>	31%	<(~F2),(F1),(F2)>	6%
		<(IP),(AED),(~PLF)>	12%
		<(IP),(~AED),(PLF),(POO)>	6%
		<(~IP),(~AED),(IP),(AED)>	5%
		<(SD),(AC),(~SO)>	13%
		<(~SD),(~AC),(SD),(AC)>	6%

It is important to note that there is no other trivial way to perform an identical analysis. Usually, the results are stored in separate records, making more difficult the sequential analysis with simple queries. Remember that those queries require several natural joins, one for each constraint on the required sequence of results. In fact, the queries must define the entire automata with those operations, which is not a simple task. No other kind of queries will be able to address this problem, because without the sequence information, we are just able to discover how many students have approved or failed in each subject.

In this manner, constrained sequential pattern mining is a natural way to perform this kind of analysis, only requiring that "experts" design the possible curricula, which is trivial, since they are publicly known.

When applying an *Approx* relaxation, we are able to discover part of the patterns followed by students that are not able to conclude all subjects in four semesters, as specified in the previous automaton. For example, one of the causes of failure on the sequence of ASO subjects is failing on the subject of Operating Systems (SO). Since this subject is the third one in the sequence and it is only offered in the *Fall* semester, students in that situation are not able to conclude the three subjects in four semesters. Similarly, students that fail on the subjects of Physics 2 (F2), Mathematical

Analysis 3 (AM3) and Functional and Logic Programming (PLF) are not able to conclude the corresponding sequences on 4 semesters, as shown in Table 2-right.

Another interesting pattern found is that 6% of students fail in the first opportunity to conclude Mathematical Analysis 3 (AM3), but seize the second opportunity, concluding that subject in the first enrollment (shadowed line in Table 2-right).

Additionally, the use of the approx relaxation also contributes to analyze the impact of some subjects on others. For example, an *approx* relaxation with one error discovers that 49% of the students that conclude MTP subjects in 3 semesters fail on AM3 and 40% on F2. Similarly, 45% of students that conclude ASO subjects in 3 semesters fail on AM3 and 39% on F2 (shadowed patterns in Table 3).

Table 3. Patterns in scientific areas with one error

Patterns	Sup	Patterns	Sup
<(IP,SD),(AED),(PLF)>	57%	<(IP,~SD),(AED),(PLF)>	8%
<(IP),(AED),(PLF,SO)>	53%	<(IP),(AED),(PLF,~SO)>	10%
<(IP),(AED,AC),(PLF)>	53%	<(IP),(AED,~AC),(PLF)>	8%
<(SD),(AC),(PLF,SO)>	51%	<(SD),(AC),(~PLF,SO)>	8%
<(IP,AM1),(AED),(PLF)>	50%	<(IP,~AM1),(AED),(PLF)>	15%
<(SD,AM1),(AC),(SO)>	47%	<(SD,~AM1),(AC),(SO)>	15%
<(IP),(AED,AM2),(PLF)>	45%	<(IP),(AED,~AM2),(PLF)>	16%
<(IP),(AED,F1),(PLF)>	45%	<(IP),(AED,~F1),(PLF)>	16%
<(SD),(AC,F1),(SO)>	41%	<(SD),(AC,~F1),(SO)>	16%
<(SD),(AC,AM2),(SO)>	41%	<(SD),(AC,~AM2),(SO)>	16%
<(IP),(AED),(PLF,F2)>	**36%**	**<(IP),(AED),(PLF,~F2)>**	**24%**
<(SD),(AC),(SO,F2)>	**34%**	**<(SD),(AC),(SO,~F2)>**	**23%**
<(FEX,AM1),(F1),(F2)>	31%	<(~AM1,FEX),(F1),(F2)>	6%
<(FEX),(F1),(SO,F2)>	31%	<(FEX),(F1),(~SO,F2)>	5%
<(IP),(AED),(PLF,AM3)>	**29%**	**<(IP),(AED),(PLF,~AM3)>**	**30%**
<(FEX),(F1,AM2),(F2)>	28%	<(FEX),(F1,~AM2),(F2)>	7%
<(SD),(AC),(SO,AM3)>	**27%**	**<(SD),(AC),(SO,~AM3)>**	**26%**
<(AM1),(AM2),(F2,AM3)>	23%	<(AM1),(AM2),(~F2,AM3)>	8%
<(FEX),(F1),(F2,AM3)>	21%	<(FEX),(F1),(F2,~AM3)>	14%

Finding Common Curricula Instantiations with Optional Subjects. The challenge on finding which students choose what optional subjects is a non-trivial task, especially because all non-common subjects can be chosen as optional by some student. A simple count of each subject support does not give the expected answer, since most of the subjects are required to some percentage of students.

The other usual approach would be to query the database to count the support of each subject, knowing that students have followed some given curriculum. However, this approach is also unable to answer the question, since a considerable number of students (more than 50%) have failed one or more subjects, following a slightly different curriculum.

In order to discover the optional subjects frequently chosen by students, we have used the methodology previously proposed – the use of constraint relaxations, defining a constraint based on the DFA shown in Fig. 7.

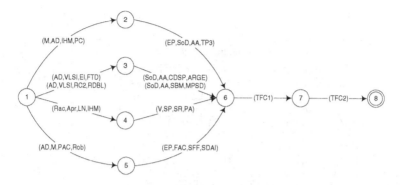

Fig. 7. DFA for finding optional subjects

This automaton accepts sequences that represent the curricula on the fourth curricular year for each specialty area (the first for PSI students, the second one for SCO, the third for IAR and the fourth for IIN). In practice, a constraint defined over this DFA filters all patterns that do not respect the model curriculum for the last two curricular years.

The use of constrained sequential pattern mining (with the specified constraint) would not contribute significantly to answer the initial question, since it would only achieve results similar to the ones obtained by the query above.

However, the use of the *Approx* relaxation described enables the discovery of several patterns. If the relaxation accepts at most two errors ($\varepsilon=2$) chosen from a restricted alphabet, composed by every non-common subject, we are able to find the frequent curricula instantiations with optional subjects. In general, students mostly attend Computer Graphics (PAC–Computed Assisted Project; IHM–Human Machine Interfaces) and Management subjects (Economy–E; Economical Theory 1–TE1; Financial Management–GF; Management–G; Management Introduction–IG), as shown in Table 4.

It is interesting to note that whenever IIN students have failed on some subject on the 4th year, they choose a specific optional subject in Economy (TE1 or IG). The same happens for PSI and IAR students (behavior identified by shadowed rules). Note that in order to discover these rules, we have to be able to admit some errors on the sequence of subjects per specialty area, which is not easily done by specifying a query to a database.

Another interesting issue is the inexistence of frequent optional subjects among IAR and SCO students. Indeed, for the last ones there is only one frequent optional subject (Management – G).

Finding Artificial Intelligence Curricula. As can be seen in previous analysis, the subjects exclusive to AI students have very low supports (about 13%). Naturally, the sequences of consecutive subjects have supports that are even lower. Indeed, the discovery of Artificial Intelligence (IAR) frequent curricula, like for IIN, is non-trivial, since the number of students in these specialty areas is reduced.

Table 4. Patterns with optional subjects attended by LEIC students

SA	Curricula Instantiations	LEIC sup	SA sup
PSI	<(M,AD,IHM,PC)(AA,SoD,EP,TP3)(TFC1,**PAC**)(TFC2,**GF**)>:22	1.5%	5%
	<(M,AD,IHM,PC)(AA,SoD,EP,TP3)(TFC1,**Econ**)(TFC2,**GF**)>:33	2.5%	8%
	<(M,AD,IHM,PC)(AA,SoD,EP,TP3)(TFC1,**Econ**)(TFC2,**IG**)>:28	2%	7%
	<(M,AD,IHM,PC)(AA,SoD,EP,TP3)(TFC1)(TFC2,**GF,IG**)>:33	2.5%	8%
	<(M,AD,IHM,PC)(AA,SoD,EP,TP3)(TFC1,**G**,**PAC**)(TFC2)>:22	1.5%	5%
	<(M,AD,IHM,PC)(AA,SoD,EP,TP3)(TFC1,**G**)(TFC2,GF)>:32	2%	8%
	<(M,AD,IHM,PC)(AA,SoD,EP,TP3)(TFC1,**G**)(TFC2,GF)>:19	1%	5%
	<(M,AD,IHM,PC)(AA,SoD,EP,TP3)(TFC1,**G**)(TFC2,GEC)>:23	1.5%	5%
	<(M,AD,IHM,PC)(AA,SoD,EP,TP3)(TFC1,**G**)(TFC2,ARGE)>:18	1%	4%
	<(M,AD,IHM,PC)(AA,SoD,EP,TP3)(TFC1,**G**,**TE1**)(TFC2)>:29	2%	7%
	<(M,AD,IHM,PC)(AA,SoD,EP,TP3)(TFC1,**TE1**,**Econ**)(TFC2)>:21	1.5%	5%
	<(M,AD,IHM,PC)(AA,SoD,EP,TP3)(TFC1,**TE1**)(TFC2,**GF**)>:44	3%	10%
	<(M,AD,IHM,PC)(AA,SoD,EP,TP3)(TFC1,**TE1**)(TFC2,**IG**)>:27	1,5%	6%
	<(M,AD,IHM,PC)(AA,SoD,EP,TP3)(**TE1**)(**GEC**)>:15	1%	4%
	<(M,AD,IHM,PC)(AA,SoD,EP)(TFC1)(TFC2,**TE2**)>:15	1%	4%
IIN	<(M,AD,PAC,Rob)(EP,SDAI,SFF)(TFC1)(TFC2,**IG**)>:15	1%	8%
	<(M,AD,PAC,Rob)(EP,FAC,SDAI,SFF)(TFC1,**IHM**)(TFC2,**GF**)>:18	1%	10%
	<(M,AD,PAC,Rob)(EP,FAC,SDAI,SFF)(TFC1,**Econ**)(TFC2,**GF**)>:18	1%	10%
	<(M,PAC,Rob)(EP,FAC,SDAI,SFF)(TFC1,**G**)(TFC2)>:17	1%	10%
	<(M,PAC,Rob)(EP,FAC,SDAI,SFF)(TFC1,**TE1**)(TFC2)>:18	1%	10%
IAR	<(IHM,Rac,LN)(SP,V,PA,SR)(TFC1,**TE1**)(TFC2)>:15	1%	10%
	<(IHM,A,Rac,LN)(SP,V,PA,SR)(TFC1)(TFC2,**GF**)>:17	1%	10%
SCO	<(C)(VLSI,RC2,RDBL,AD)(AA,CDPSD,ARGE,SoD)(TFC1,**G**)(TFC2)>:23	1.5%	8%
	<(Elect)(VLSI,RC2,RDBL,AD)(AA,CDPSD,ARGE,SoD)(TFC1,**G**)(TFC2)>:27	1.5%	10%
	<(RC1)(VLSI,RC2,RDBL,AD)(AA,CDPSD,ARGE,SoD)(TFC1,**G**)(TFC2)>:19	1%	7%

Given that the application of unconstrained sequential pattern mining algorithms found 5866 patterns in this dataset (for 20% of support, since we were not able to try lower supports due the memory requirements), and we want to find the sequence of subjects followed by IAR students, the use of constrained or unconstrained sequential pattern mining does not help in the search for an answer to the second question.

However, if we use the proposed methodology, we have two alternatives: using a DFA specifying the IAR model curriculum and an *Approx* relaxation as above, or using a DFA specifying PSI and SCO curricula models and a *Non-Accepted* relaxation with a restricted alphabet.

The patterns discovered by the second alternative (using a minimum support threshold equal to 2.5%) answer the question. (Table 5 shows the discovered patterns, excluding 8 patterns that are shared by PSI students.)

Note that we were not able to find the entire model curriculum for Artificial Intelligence, because of the reduced number of students that have concluded each subject on the first enrollment. This fact, explains the number of discovered patterns (24). However, it is smaller than the number of patterns discovered with an unconstrained approach, confirming our claim about constraint relaxations.

The Non-Accepted relaxation was defined using a constraint similar to the previous one with the DFA represented in Fig. 5 without the model curriculum for IAR and IIN. Additionally, the relaxation alphabet was composed of all the common subjects and the advanced subjects specific to the Artificial Intelligence specialty area (38 subjects).

Table 5. Artificial Intelligence frequent curricula

Patterns on Artificial Intelligence	
(AD,FL,P)(RC,TP)(IHM,A,R,LN)(SP,PA)	(FA,TAI)(AD,P)(RC,LP)(IHM,A,R,LN)(SP,V,PA,SR)
(FA,TAI)(FL,P)(RC,LP,TP)(IHM,A,R,LN)(SP,V,PA,SR)	(FA)(AD,FL,P)(RC,TP)(IHM,A,R,LN)(SP)
(FA,TAI)(AD,FL,P)(RC,LP,TP)(IHM,R,LN)(SP,V,SR)	(FA)(AD,FL,P)(RC)(IHM,A,R,LN)(SP,PA)
(FA,TAI)(AD,FL,P)(RC,LP,TP)(IHM,A,R,LN)(V,PA,SR)	(TAI)(AD,P)(RC,LP,TP)(IHM,A,R,LN)(SP,V,PA,SR)
(FA,TAI)(AD,FL,P)(RC,LP)(IHM,R,LN)(SP,V,PA,SR)	(TAI)(AD,FL,P)(RC,LP,TP)(IHM,A,R,LN)(SP,V,PA)
(FA,TAI)(AD,FL,P)(RC,LP)(IHM,A,R,LN)(SP,V,SR)	(TAI)(AD,FL,P)(RC,LP,TP)(IHM,A,R,LN)(SP,V,SR)
(FA,TAI)(AD,FL)(RC,LP,TP)(IHM,A,R,LN)(SP,V,PA,SR	(TAI)(AD,FL,P)(RC,LP)(IHM,A,R,LN)(SP,V,PA,SR)
(FA,TAI)(AD,P)(RC,LP,TP)(IHM,R,LN)(SP,V,PA,SR)	(FA,TAI)(AD,P)(RC,LP,TP)(IHM,A,R,LN)(SP,V,SR)

4.2 Efficiency Evaluation

Next, the efficiency of constrained and unconstrained sequential pattern mining are compared, we assessing the efficiency of the usage of the different constraint relaxations.

Comparison Between Constrained and Unconstrained Mining. To compare the efficiency of constrained and unconstrained sequential pattern mining, we compare the time spent by constrained and unconstrained mining, using deterministic finite automata and deterministic and non-deterministic pushdown automata that discover a similar number of patterns (they differ on one or two patterns). (The DFA used in this comparison accepts the curricula on MTP and ASO scientific areas, of students that have failed at most once per subject. The ePDA used is the one shown in Fig. 6. The nPDA used accepts sequences in each scientific area that mimic the sequence of subjects attended by students, including the possibility of failure in the first two subjects of each scientific area.)

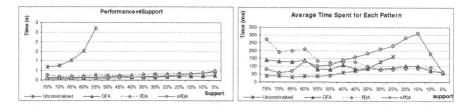

Fig. 8. Performance (on the left) and average time spent for each pattern (on the right), using different types of content constraints

It is interesting to note that the use of context-free languages implies a considerable increase on the time spent for each pattern. In fact, the time spent for each pattern may be five times slower than for unconstrained mining, and two times slower than for constrained mining with regular languages (see Fig. 8-right). The time spent for each pattern decreases with the number of discovered patterns, which is due to the decrease of the percentage of discarded sequences, the sequences that are not frequent and accepted by the constraint.

Evaluation of Constraint Relaxations. In general, mining with conservative relaxations is as efficient as mining with the entire constraint. However, the average time spent per discovered pattern is lower (Fig. 9). The results were obtained with the constraint based on the ePDA in Fig. 6.

Naturally, Non-Accepted and Approx relaxations spent much more time than the other relaxations, but this difference is mostly due to the number of patterns they discover.

It is important to note that mining with *Non-accepted* and *Approx* relaxations can be less efficient than unconstrained mining. This happens when the number of patterns discovered by these relaxations is similar to the number of discovered unconstrained patterns, as is usual for Non-accepted relaxations with a very restrictive constraint (as the ones used in this chapter).

As Fig. 9– right shows *Approx* relaxations are the most expensive per discovered pattern. In fact, even when the number of discovered patterns is considerably lower than the number of unconstrained patterns, it is possible that *Approx* relaxations spend more time than unconstrained mining.

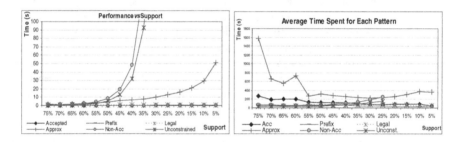

Fig. 9. Performance (on the left) and average time spent for each pattern (on the right), using different constraint relaxations

Approx **Variants.** When applied with a restricted alphabet Approx relaxations may present better performances.

Even when non-deterministic pushdown automata are used, *approx* relaxation outperforms unconstrained mining in the generality of situations, as shown in Fig. 10. These results were achieved using the constraint defined over the ePDA in Fig. 6, and restricting the items to failures.

Non-accepted Variants. The results achieved with non-accepted relaxations are similar. When combined with an item constraint, it can reduce the number of patterns that it discovers. For example, due to the memory requirements of the large number of discovered patterns, it was not possible to discover unconstrained and non-accepted patterns for supports below 25%.

Finally experiments have also shown that the ability to deal with errors is a real advantage, which makes possible the discovery of unknown patterns that are similar to accepted ones (as defined by a constraint), giving the user the ability to choose the level of similarity, by defining the number of errors accepted.

One important challenge created by this work, is to apply this methodology to the extraction of intra-transactional patterns, where there are no constraints to specify the structure of the transactions. Indeed, the definition of the corresponding relaxations would contribute to guide the traditional pattern mining processes, which may contribute to reduce the number of discovered patterns, and, consequently, to focus the process on user expectations.

References

1. Antunes, C. and Oliveira, A.L., "Inference of Sequential Association Rules Guided by Context-Free Grammars", in *Int. Conf. Grammatical Inference*, Springer (2002) 1-13
2. Antunes, C. and Oliveira, A.L., "Sequential Pattern Mining with Approximated Constraints", *Int. Conf Applied Computing*, IADIS (2004) 131-138
3. Garofalakis, M., Rastogi, R. and Shim, K., "SPIRIT: Sequential Pattern Mining with Regular Expression Constraint", in *Int. Conf. Very Large Databases*, Morgan Kaufmann (1999) 223-234,
4. Hilderman, R and Hamilton, H., "Knowledge discovery and interestingness measures: a survey", *Technical Report* CS 99-04, Dep. Computer Science, University of Regina, 1999.
5. Hipp, J. and Güntzer, U., "Is pushing constraints deeply into the mining algorithms really what we want?". *SIGKDD Explorations*, vol. 4, no. 1, ACM (2002) 50-55
6. Hopcroft, J. and Ullman, J., *Introduction to Automata Theory, Languages and Computation*. Addison Wesley. 1979.
7. Kum, H.-C., Pei, J., Wang, W. and Duncan, D., "ApproxMAP: Approximate Mining of Consensus Sequential Patterns", in *Int. Conf on Data Mining,* IEEE (2003).
8. Levenshtein, V., "Binary Codes capable of correcting spurious insertions and deletions of ones", in *Problems of Information Transmission*, 1, Kluwer (1965) 8-17
9. Pei J, Han J et al: "PrefixSpan: Mining Sequential Patterns Efficiently by Prefix-Projected Pattern Growth", in *Int. Conf Data Engineering*, IEEE (2001), 215-226
10. Pei, J., Han, J. and Wang, W., "Mining Sequential Patterns with Constraints in Large Databases", in *Conf Information and Knowledge Management*, ACM (2002) 18-25
11. Srikant R, Agrawal R.: "Mining Sequential Patterns: Generalizations and Performance Improvements", in *Int. Conf Extending Database Technology*, Springer (1996) 3-17
12. Srikant R, Agrawal R, "Mining association rules with item constraints" in *Int. Conf. Knowledge Discovery and Data Mining*, ACM (1997) 67-73
13. Zaki, M."Efficient Enumeration of Frequent Sequences", in *Int. Conf. Information and Knowledge Management*, ACM (1998) 68-75

Mining Formal Concepts with a Bounded Number of Exceptions from Transactional Data

Jérémy Besson[1,2], Céline Robardet[3], and Jean-François Boulicaut[1]

[1] INSA Lyon, LIRIS CNRS FRE 2672, F-69621 Villeurbanne cedex, France
[2] UMR INRA/INSERM 1235, F-69372 Lyon cedex 08, France
[3] INSA Lyon, PRISMA, F-69621 Villeurbanne cedex, France
{Jeremy.Besson, Celine.Robardet, Jean-Francois.Boulicaut}@insa-lyon.fr

Abstract. We are designing new data mining techniques on boolean contexts to identify a priori interesting bi-sets (i.e., sets of objects or transactions associated to sets of attributes or items). A typical important case concerns formal concept mining (i.e., maximal rectangles of true values or associated closed sets by means of the so-called Galois connection). It has been applied with some success to, e.g., gene expression data analysis where objects denote biological situations and attributes denote gene expression properties. However in such real-life application domains, it turns out that the Galois association is a too strong one when considering intrinsically noisy data. It is clear that strong associations that would however accept a bounded number of exceptions would be extremely useful. We study the new pattern domain of α/β concepts, i.e., consistent maximal bi-sets with less than α false values per row and less than β false values per column. We provide a complete algorithm that computes all the α/β concepts based on the generation of concept unions pruned thanks to anti-monotonic constraints. An experimental validation on synthetic data is given. It illustrates that more relevant associations can be discovered in noisy data. We also discuss a practical application in molecular biology that illustrates an incomplete but quite useful extraction when all the concepts that are needed beforehand can not be discovered.

1 Introduction

One of the most popular data mining techniques concerns transactional data analysis by means of set patterns. Transactional data can be represented as boolean matrices. The lines denotes transactions or objects and the columns are boolean attributes that enable to record item occurrences within transactions or properties of objects. For instance, in the toy example r_1 from Figure 1, object o_2 satisfies properties i_1 and i_2 or, alternatively, transaction o_2 contains items i_1 and i_2. Many application domains can lead to such boolean contexts. For instance, beside the classical basket analysis problem where transactions denote the items purchased by some customers, we made many experiments on boolean gene expression data sets that encode gene expression properties in

B. Goethals and A. Siebes (Eds.): KDID 2004, LNCS 3377, pp. 33–45, 2005.
© Springer-Verlag Berlin Heidelberg 2005

	Items		
	i_1	i_2	i_3
o_1	1	1	1
o_2	1	1	0
o_3	1	0	1
o_4	1	0	0
o_5	0	1	0

Fig. 1. A boolean context r_1

some biological situations (see, e.g., [4]). In this kind of application, the raw data is a collection of numerical values that quantify the activity of each gene in each studied situation. Gene expression properties, for instance over-expression, are then computed by means of discretization techniques (see, e.g., [1, 14]). For example, given r_1, we might say that all the studied genes are considered over-expressed in situation o_1.

Given eventually huge transactional data sets, hundreds of research papers have considered the efficient computation of a priori interesting association rules from the so-called frequent sets of attributes. Also, the multiple uses of (frequent) closed sets of transactions and/or attributes have been studied a lot. In this paper, we consider bi-set mining from transactional data. More precisely, we want to compute sets of objects T and sets of attributes G that are strongly associated within the data. An interesting case concerns formal concept discovery, i.e., the computation of maximal rectangles of true values [20]. For instance, in r_1, $(\{o_1, o_2\}, \{i_1, i_2\})$ is a formal concept or concept for short. In boolean gene expression data sets, concepts can be considered as putative transcription modules, i.e., maximal sets of genes that are co-regulated associated to the maximal set of situations in which they are co-regulated. Their discovery is an important step towards the understanding of gene regulation networks. It is the major application domain which motivates our research.

Collections of concepts can be used, e.g., for conceptual clustering or as condensed representations for association rules. Efficient algorithms enable to compute concepts [8, 2, 11]. When the extraction task is too hard, it is also possible to compute concepts under constraints. It can be based on (frequent) closed set computation (see, e.g., [12, 5, 13, 21, 6, 7, 16] and [10] for a recent survey). It is also possible to use an algorithm that directly mine concepts under constraints on both set components [3].

The aim of concept extraction is to identify objects and properties which are strongly associated. Within a concept, we have a maximal set of objects (i.e., a closed set) which are in relation with all the elements of a maximal set of properties and vice versa. This degree of association is often too strong in real-life data. This is typical in life sciences where we can not avoid error of measurement or when discretization methods are used and can easily lead to some wrong values. Indeed, once a discretization threshold has been computed (say 34.5) for deciding about the over-expression of a given gene, assigning false (and thus not over-expression) for a situation whose raw expression value is 34 might be or not an error. What is clear, is that concepts that would accept exceptions could be extremely useful. Assume that in a boolean context, we have a bi-set (T, G) (with, e.g., $|T| = 12$ and $|G| = 25$) such that each property from G is not shared by at most one object from T and each object from T does not have at most two properties from G. Our thesis is that it is extremely useful to extract such a bi-set for further post-processing by data owners. Indeed the presence of erroneous false values in the data set leads to the multiplication of concepts from which it might be hard to identify the relevant associations. As an illustration, in Figure 1, the bi-set $(\{o_1, o_2, o_3\}, \{i_1, i_2, i_3\})$ is not a concept but has at most 1 false value per row and at most 1 false value per column. It appears to be the union of 4 concepts which are $(\{o_1\}, \{i_1, i_2, i_3\})$, $(\{o_1, o_2, o_3\}, \{i_1\})$, $(\{o_1, o_2\}, \{i_1, i_2\})$, and $(\{o_1, o_3\}, \{i_1, i_3\})$.

Therefore, the contribution of this paper is to propose a new kind of patterns called the α/β concepts, i.e., concepts with exceptions or, more precisely, maximal consistent bi-sets of true values with a bounded number of false values per row (α threshold) and per column (β threshold). Therefore, we specify the desired patterns within a constraint-based mining framework. The constraint $\mathcal{C}_{\alpha\beta}$ is used to enforce a bounded number of exceptions. The consistency constraint denoted $\mathcal{C}_{cons}$ is important: only relevant patterns such that there is no row (resp. column) outside the bi-set which is identical to an inside one w.r.t. the bi-set columns (resp. rows) have to be mined. Finally, we also use maximality constraints (denoted $\mathcal{C}_{max}$) w.r.t. the collections specified by the other constraints and our specialization relation on bi-sets. We studied how to compute α/β concepts. This is indeed a difficult problem since we loose the Galois connection properties in this new setting. Our main theoretical result concerns the formalization of a constraint-based mining framework that can be used for computing every α/β concept. For that purpose, we start by computing every concept and then we perform unions of concepts while "pushing" the constraints $\mathcal{C}_{\alpha\beta}$, $\mathcal{C}_{cons}$, and $\mathcal{C}_{max}$ to reduce the search space. Doing so, the complete collection of α/β concepts can be computed. We provide two experimental validations. First, we consider a synthetic data set. This data set consists of some formal concepts and uniform random noise. We show that α/β concept mining enables to discover the original associations (i.e., the concepts that were existing before noise introduction) provided that the noise is not too important. Then, we discuss a practical application in molecular biology. It illustrates an incomplete but quite useful extraction when all the α/β concepts can not be discovered: instead of computing the whole collection of α/β concepts we compute a subset of them obtained from large enough concept unions. By this application we demonstrate that large α/β concepts can be computed that contain a rather small number of exceptions.

The paper is organized as follows. In Section 2, we provide the needed definitions and the formalization of the α/β concept mining task. Section 3 sketches the algorithm and discusses its properties. Section 4 concerns the experimental validation of our approach. Finally, Section 5 is a short conclusion.

2   Formalizing α/β Concept Mining

Let $\mathcal{O}$ denotes a set of objects and $\mathcal{P}$ denotes a set of properties. The transactional data or boolean context is $\mathbf{r} \subseteq \mathcal{O} \times \mathcal{P}$. $(o_i, i_j) \in \mathbf{r}$ denotes that property j holds for object i. A bi-set is an element of $\mathcal{L} = \mathcal{L}_{\mathcal{O}} \times \mathcal{L}_{\mathcal{P}}$ where $\mathcal{L}_{\mathcal{O}} = 2^{\mathcal{O}}$ and $\mathcal{L}_{\mathcal{P}} = 2^{\mathcal{P}}$.

Definition 1 (1-Rectangle). *A bi-set (T, G) is a 1-rectangle in $\mathbf{r}$ iff $\forall t \in T$ and $\forall g \in G$ then $(t, g) \in \mathbf{r}$. We say that it satisfies constraint $\mathcal{C}_{1R}(T, G)$. When a bi-set (T, G) is not a 1-rectangle, we say that it contains 0 values.*

Definition 2 (Concept). *A bi-set (T, G) is a concept in $\mathbf{r}$ iff (T, G) is a 1-rectangle and $\forall T' \subseteq \mathcal{O} \backslash T$, $(T \cup T', G)$ is not a 1-rectangle and $\forall G' \subseteq \mathcal{P} \backslash G$, $(T, G \cup G')$ is not a 1-rectangle. A concept (T, G) is thus a maximal 1-rectangle.*

Example 1. *$(\{o_1\}, \{i_1, i_3\})$ is a 1-rectangle in $\mathbf{r}_1$ but it is not a concept. An example of a concept in $\mathbf{r}_1$ is $(\{o_1, o_3\}, \{i_1, i_3\})$.*

By construction, concepts are built on two so-called closed sets that are associated by the Galois connection.

Definition 3 (Galois Connection [20]). *If $T \subseteq \mathcal{O}$ and $G \subseteq \mathcal{P}$, assume $\phi(T, \mathbf{r}) = \{i \in \mathcal{P} \mid \forall o \in T, (o, i) \in \mathbf{r}\}$ and $\psi(G, \mathbf{r}) = \{o \in \mathcal{O} \mid \forall i \in G, (o, i) \in \mathbf{r}\}$. ϕ provides the set of items that are common to a set of objects and ψ provides the set of objects that share a set of items. (ϕ, ψ) is the so-called Galois connection between $\mathcal{O}$ and $\mathcal{P}$. We use the classical notations $h = \phi \circ \psi$ and $h' = \psi \circ \phi$ to denote the Galois closure operators. A set $T \subseteq \mathcal{O}$ (resp. $G \subseteq \mathcal{P}$) is said closed iff $T = h'(T)$ (resp. $G = h(G)$).*

An important property of the Galois connection is that each closed set on one dimension is associated to a unique closed set on the other dimension. It explains why any algorithm that computes closed sets can be used for concept extraction (see, e.g., [16] for a discussion when using a frequent closed set computation algorithm in the context of gene expression data analysis).

Example 2. *$(\{o_1, o_2\}, \{i_1, i_2\})$ is a concept in $\mathbf{r}_1$. We have $h(\{i_1, i_2\}) = \{i_1, i_2\}$, $h'(\{o_1, o_2\}) = \{o_1, o_2\}$, $\phi(\{o_1, o_2\}) = \{i_1, i_2\}$, and $\psi(\{i_1, i_2\}) = \{o_1, o_2\}$.*

Many algorithms like AC-MINER[1] [6], CHARM [21] and CLOSET+ [19] extract frequent closed sets and thus very easily concepts under a minimal frequency constraint on the set of objects by an application of one of the Galois operators. This user-defined minimal frequency constraint enables to optimize the extraction tasks in dense and/or highly correlated data sets: both the search

---

[1] Even though this algorithm has been designed for the extraction of frequent δ-free sets, we often use the formal property which states that every frequent closed set is the closure of a 0-free set. In other terms, a straightforward postprocessing on AC-MINER output can provide every frequent closed set.

space and the solution space can be reduced. In practice, we can have however too large or too dense matrices (see, e.g., the case of some biological contexts in Section 4.2) such that only very high minimal frequency thresholds can lead to tractable computations. Assuming a standard boolean context, it means that only bi-sets composed of few items and many objects can be extracted whereas we would like to enforce other constraints. To overcome this problem, we have proposed in [3] the algorithm D-MINER which enables to extract formal concepts while "pushing" other meaningful constraints.

Definition 4 (Meaningful Constraints on Concepts).
Minimal size constraints: a concept (T, G) satisfies the constraint
$\mathcal{C}_{ms}(\mathbf{r}, \sigma_1, \sigma_2, (T, G))$ *iff* $|T| \geq \sigma_1$ *and* $|G| \geq \sigma_2$.
Syntactical constraints: a concept (T, G) satisfies the constraint
$\mathcal{C}_{Inclusion}(\mathbf{r}, X, Y, (T, G))$ *iff* $X \subseteq T$ *and* $Y \subseteq G$.
Minimal area constraint: a concept (T, G) satisfies the constraint
$\mathcal{C}_{area}(\mathbf{r}, \sigma, (T, G))$ *iff* $|T| \times |G| \geq \sigma$.

More precisely, D-MINER extract efficiently formal concepts which moreover satisfy some monotonic constraints w.r.t. the following specialization relation.

Definition 5 (Specialization Relation). *Our specialization relation on bi-sets from $\mathcal{L}_\mathcal{O} \times \mathcal{L}_\mathcal{P}$ is defined by $(T_1, G_1) \preceq (T_2, G_2)$ iff $T_1 \subseteq T_2$ and $G_1 \subseteq G_2$. As usual, $\prec$ is used to denote strict specialization (i.e., using $\subset$ instead of $\subseteq$).*

Definition 6 (Monotonic Constraints on Bi-sets). *Given $\mathcal{L}$ a collection of bi-sets, a constraint $\mathcal{C}$ is said monotonic w.r.t. $\subseteq$ iff $\forall \alpha, \beta \in \mathcal{L}$ such that $\alpha \subseteq \beta$, $\mathcal{C}(\alpha) \Rightarrow \mathcal{C}(\beta)$.*

Example 3. *The three previously defined constraints are examples of monotonic constraints w.r.t. our specialization relation. The concepts (T, G) satisfying $\mathcal{C}_{ms}(\mathbf{r}_1, 2, 2, (T, G))$ are $(\{o_1, o_2\}, \{i_1, i_2\})$ and $(\{o_1, o_3\}, \{i_1, i_3\})$. The concepts (T, G) satisfying $\mathcal{C}_{area}(\mathbf{r}_1, 4, (T, G))$ are $(\{o_1, o_2\}, \{i_1, i_2\})$, $(\{o_1, o_3\}, \{i_1, i_3\})$ and $(\{o_1, o_2, o_3, o_4\}, \{i_1\})$.*

A concept (T, G) is such that all its items and objects are in relation. Thus, the absence of relation between an item g and an object t leads to two concepts, one with g and without t, and another one with t and without g. D-MINER is based on this observation and it builds simultaneously the closed sets of objects and items starting from the bi-set corresponding to the whole sets of items and objects, recursively cutting it using 0 values [3].

Notice that pushing the monotonic constraint $\mathcal{C}_{area}$ within D-MINER is a solution to one of the problems addressed in [9].

The aim of concept extraction is to gather properties and objects which are strongly associated. On another hand, we already motivated the interest of relaxing the maximal 1-rectangle constraint. A simple idea is to consider all the maximal bi-sets with less than α false values per row and less than β false values per column.

Definition 7 ($\alpha\beta$-Constraint). *A bi-set (T, G) satisfies $\mathcal{C}_{\alpha\beta}$ in* **r** *iff*

$\forall o \in T, |\{i \in G \text{ such that } (o, i) \notin \mathbf{r}\}| \leq \min(\beta, |G| - 1)$ *and*
$\forall i \in G, |\{o \in T \text{ such that } (o, i) \notin \mathbf{r}\}| \leq \min(\alpha, |T| - 1)$.

Example 4. *Given* $\mathbf{r}_1$ *and* $\alpha = \beta = 1$*, the two bi-sets* $(\{o_1, o_2, o_3\}, \{i_1, i_2\})$ *and* $(\{o_1, o_2, o_4\}, \{i_1, i_2\})$ *satisfy the* $\alpha\beta$*-constraint. However,* o_3 *and* o_4 *have the same values on* i_1 *and* i_2*. It turns out that these objects can not be added simultaneously on* $(\{o_1, o_2\}, \{i_1, i_2\})$ *in order to satisfy* $\mathcal{C}_{\alpha\beta}$*.*

To ensure consistency and avoid this problem, we decided either to add all identical properties (w.r.t. the set of objects) or all identical objects (w.r.t. the set of properties) in the bi-set when $\mathcal{C}_{\alpha\beta}$ is satisfied, or to exclude all of them when it is not the case. As for concepts, α/β concepts can differ from each other either on the object component or on the property component. This is formalized by the use of the consistency constraint denoted $\mathcal{C}_{cons}$.

Definition 8 (Consistency Constraint). *A bi-set (T, G) satisfies $\mathcal{C}_{cons}$ iff*

- $\forall i \in G, \nexists j \in \mathcal{P} \setminus G \text{ such that } \psi(i) \cap T = \psi(j) \cap T$
- $\forall o \in T, \nexists w \in \mathcal{O} \setminus T \text{ such that } \phi(o) \cap G = \phi(w) \cap G$

On our way to the extraction of bi-sets with few 0 values, it is interesting to reformulate the definition of formal concepts.

Definition 9 (Maximality Constraint). *A bi-set (T, G) is maximal w.r.t. a constraint $\mathcal{C}$ and is said to satisfy $\mathcal{C}_{max|\mathcal{C}}(T, G)$ iff $\nexists(T', G')$ such that $\mathcal{C}(T', G') \wedge (T, G) \prec (T', G')$.*

Definition 10 (New Definition of Formal Concepts). *A bi-set (T, G) is a formal concept iff*

- (T, G) *satisfies* $\mathcal{C}_{1R}$
- (T, G) *is maximal w.r.t.* $\mathcal{C}_{1R}$*, i.e.,* (T, G) *satisfies* $\mathcal{C}_{max|\mathcal{C}_{1R}}$*.*

Notice that by construction, a concept satisfies the constraint $\mathcal{C}_{cons}$. Let us now define α/β concepts.

Definition 11 (α/β Concept). *A bi-set (T, G) is an α/β concept iff*

- (T, G) *satisfies* $\mathcal{C}_{\alpha\beta}$
- (T, G) *satisfies* $\mathcal{C}_{cons}$
- (T, G) *is maximal w.r.t.* $\mathcal{C}_{\alpha\beta} \wedge \mathcal{C}_{cons}$*, i.e.,* (T, G) *satisfies* $\mathcal{C}_{max|\mathcal{C}_{\alpha\beta} \wedge \mathcal{C}_{cons}}$*.*

Let us notice that, looking for an α/β concept (T, G), it makes sense that $|T| \gg \alpha$ and $|G| \gg \beta$. The $\alpha\beta$-constraint is an extension of the 1-rectangle constraint for bi-sets with 0 values. Then, α/β concepts appear to be a simple extension of concepts by changing the 1-rectangle constraint into the $\alpha\beta$-constraint in conjunction with the $\mathcal{C}_{cons}$ constraint. This is one of the important results of this work.

Example 5. $(\{o_1, o_2, o_3\}, \{i_1, i_2, i_3\})$ *is an α/β concept in* $\mathbf{r}_1$*.* $(\{o_1, o_2\}, \emptyset)$ *and* $(\{o_3, o_4, o_5\}, \{i_1, i_2\})$ *are not α/β concepts because they do not satisfy respectively* $\mathcal{C}_{max|\mathcal{C}_{cons} \wedge \mathcal{C}_{\alpha\beta}}$ *and* $\mathcal{C}_{\alpha\beta}$ *constraints.*

3   Mining α/β Concepts

The computation of every α/β concept from a given data set $\mathbf{r}$ is done in two steps. First, we compute all the concepts, i.e., a collection denoted $\mathcal{K}$. Then we search the maximal (w.r.t. a specialization relation on bi-sets) unions of concepts which satisfy the $\alpha\beta$-constraint $\mathcal{C}_{\alpha\beta}$.

Definition 12 (Union of Bi-sets). *Let $B_1 = (T_1, G_1)$ and $B_2 = (T_2, G_2)$ be two bi-sets from $\mathcal{L}_{\mathcal{O}} \times \mathcal{L}_{\mathcal{P}}$. The union of B_1 and B_2 is $B_1 \sqcup B_2 = (T_1 \cup T_2, G_1 \cup G_2)$. It can be applied on concepts that are special cases of bi-sets. By construction, unions of concepts are not concepts.*

Theorem 1. *Let $U = \{\bigsqcup_{i \in \mathcal{K}'} i \mid \mathcal{C}_{\alpha\beta}$ and $\mathcal{K}' \subseteq \mathcal{K}\}$ where $\mathcal{K}$ is the collection of concepts, the collection of α/β concepts is equal to*

$$\mathcal{K}_{\alpha\beta} = \{s \in U \mid \not\exists s\prime \in U\ s \preceq s\prime\}$$

Proof. We show that the collection of bi-sets which satisfy $\mathcal{C}_{cons}$ ($\mathcal{K}_{cons}$) is equal to the collection of the unions of concepts ($\mathcal{K}_{\sqcup}$). In other terms, the use of unions enforce the $\mathcal{C}_{cons}$ constraint.

- $\mathcal{K}_{\sqcup} \subseteq \mathcal{K}_{cons}$
  Let (X, Y) be an element of $\mathcal{K}_{\sqcup}$. Let us assume that $\neg \mathcal{C}_{cons}(X, Y)$. We consider $j \in \mathcal{P} \setminus Y$ such that $\exists i \in Y$, $\psi(i) \cap X = \psi(j) \cap X$. It exists at least one concept $(L, C) \in \mathcal{K}$ such that $(L, C) \preceq (X, Y)$ and $i \in C$ ((X, Y) is a union of concepts). However, $\forall \ell \in L$, $(\ell, i) \in \mathbf{r}$ and $L \subseteq \psi(j)$, thus $(\ell, j) \in \mathbf{r}$. Consequently, as (L, C) is a concept, $j \in C \subseteq Y$. We have a contradiction and $\mathcal{C}_{cons}$ is satisfied.
  Reciprocally, we consider $w \in \mathcal{O} \setminus X$ such that $\exists v \in X$, $\phi(v) \cap Y = \phi(w) \cap Y$. It exists at least one concept $(L, C) \in \mathcal{K}$ such that $(L, C) \preceq (X, Y)$ and $v \in L$ ((X, Y) is a union of concepts). However, $\forall c \in C$, $(v, c) \in \mathbf{r}$ and $C \subseteq \phi(w)$, thus $(w, c) \in \mathbf{r}$. Consequently, as (L, C) is a concept, $w \in L \subseteq X$. We have a contradiction and thus $\mathcal{C}_{cons}$ is satisfied.
- $\mathcal{K}_{cons} \subseteq \mathcal{K}_{\sqcup}$
  Let (X, Y) be a bi-set which satisfy $\mathcal{C}_{cons}$. $\forall i \in Y$, $\psi(i) \cap X \neq \emptyset$ and $\not\exists j \in \mathcal{P} \setminus Y$ such that $\psi(i) \cap X = \psi(j) \cap X$ consequently $\phi(\psi(i) \cap X) \subseteq Y$. As $\psi(i) \cap X \subseteq \psi(i)$ and ϕ is a decreasing operator, $\phi(\psi(i)) \subseteq \phi(\psi(i) \cap X)$ consequently $\phi(\psi(i)) \subseteq Y$.
  On the other side, $\psi(i) \cap X \neq \emptyset$. Let $v \in \psi(i) \cap X$. It does not exist $w \in \mathcal{O} \setminus \psi(i) \cap X$ such that $\phi(v) \cap Y = \phi(w) \cap Y$ consequently $\psi(\phi(v) \cap Y) \subseteq X$. As $\phi(v) \cap Y \subseteq \phi(v)$ and ψ is a decreasing operator, $\psi(\phi(v)) \subseteq \psi(\phi(v) \cap Y)$ consequently $\psi(\phi(v)) \subseteq X$.
  We can conclude that for each $(v, i) \in (X, Y)$ and $(v, i) \in \mathbf{r}$, it exists a concept $(\psi(\phi(v)), \phi(\psi(i))$ included in (X, Y). (X, Y) is the union of these concepts and thus belongs to $\mathcal{C}_{\sqcup}$.

It means that we can compute α/β concepts by generating the unions of concepts which satisfy $\mathcal{C}_{\alpha\beta}$ and $\mathcal{C}_{max|\mathcal{C}_{\alpha\beta}}$.

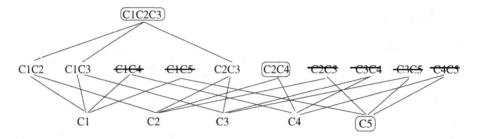

Fig. 2. Search space of α/β concepts ($\alpha = \beta = 1$) in context $\mathbf{r}_1$

Property 1. $\mathcal{C}_{\alpha\beta}$ is anti-monotonic w.r.t. our specialization relation on bi-sets.

Consequently, when considering candidate unions of concepts, we can use the anti-monotonicity of $\mathcal{C}_{\alpha\beta}$ to prune the search space. It is also possible to push $\mathcal{C}_{max|\mathcal{C}_{\alpha\beta}}$ to prune the search space. This can be done by adapting known efficient algorithms which compute maximal frequent sets (see, e.g., [10] for a recent survey), where sets are sets of concepts and the anti-monotonic minimal frequency constraint is replaced by the $\mathcal{C}_{\alpha\beta}$ constraint.

Given $\mathcal{K}$ the collection of formal concepts and two parameters α and β, we compute the following collection of sets of concepts $\{\varphi \in 2^{\mathcal{K}} \mid \mathcal{C}_{\alpha\beta}(\varphi) \wedge \mathcal{C}_{max|\mathcal{C}_{\alpha\beta}}(\varphi)$ is satisfied$\}$.

The concepts in $\mathbf{r}_1$ are:

$$c_1 = (\{o_1\}, \{i_1, i_2, i_3\}) \quad c_2 = (\{o_1, o_2\}, \{i_1, i_2\})$$
$$c_3 = (\{o_1, o_3\}, \{i_1, i_3\}) \quad c_4 = (\{o_1, o_2, o_5\}, \{i_2\})$$
$$c_5 = (\{o_1, o_2, o_3, o_4\}, \{i_1\})$$

We consider the search for α/β concepts in $\mathbf{r}_1$ when $\alpha = 1$ and $\beta = 1$.

Figure 2 illustrates how the collection of 1/1 concepts are extracted from $\mathbf{r}_1$: it provides $\{\{c_1, c_2, c_3\}, \{c_2, c_4\}, \{c_5\}\}$. The circled elements form the solution space. Stripped elements do not satisfy $\mathcal{C}_{\alpha\beta}$. Their supersets are not generated. The three α/β concepts are here $c_1 \cup c_2 \cup c_3$, $c_2 \cup c_4$, and c_5. They correspond respectively to the following bi-sets: $(\{o_1, o_2, o_3\}, \{i_1, i_2, i_3\})$, $(\{o_1, o_2, o_5\}, \{i_1, i_2\})$ and $(\{o_1, o_2, o_3, o_4\}, \{i_1\})$.

4   Experimentation

4.1   Synthetic Data

To show the relevancy of α/β concept mining in noisy data, we first designed a synthetic data set. Our goal was to show that α/β concept mining enables to discover concepts that have been introduced before the introduction of some noise. Therefore, we have built a boolean data set made of 20 non-overlapping concepts containing each 5 items and 5 objects. Secondly, we introduced a uniform random noise by modifying with the same probability (5% in Figure 3 top

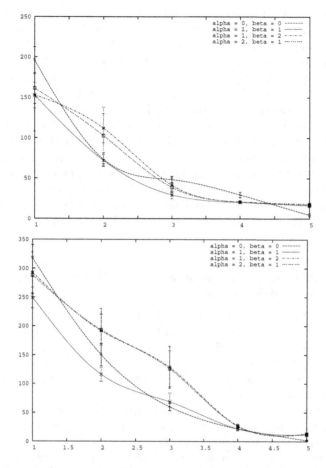

Fig. 3. Number of α/β concepts with respect to their size (both dimensions greater or equal than the X-coordinate value) with 5% (top) and 10% (bottom) of noise

and 10% in Figure 3 bottom) some of the boolean values (i.e., transforming some true values into false values and vice versa). We produced 10 data sets (with 100 lines and 100 columns) for each noise probability. When considering first concept mining phase, we extracted between 169 and 225 concepts (resp. between 289 and 373 concepts) in the 5% noise data sets (resp. in the 10% noise data sets). Figure 3 provides the average and standard deviation of the number of α/β concepts (Y-coordinate) w.r.t. their minimal number of objects and properties (X-coordinate). Each curve stands for a different value of α and β between 0 and 2. For example, on Figure 3 bottom, we have 126 α/β concepts in average with at least 3 objects and 3 items when $\alpha = 2$ and $\beta = 1$.

On the data sets with 5% noise, we have in average 196 concepts (see the curve with $\alpha = \beta = 0$) among which 48 have at least 3 properties and objects and 5 of them have at least 5 properties and objects. With 10% of noise, we got 317 concepts in average among which 60 have at least 3 properties and objects and

2 of them have at least 5 properties and objects. In this extracted collection of concepts, it is difficult to find the 20 original concepts that were occurring before noise introduction. When α and β are not null, the collection of extracted α/β concepts is roughly speaking the 20 original concepts. For example, considering $\alpha = \beta = 1$, we got 20.2 (resp. 22.1) α/β concepts of size greater than 4 in the 5% (resp. the 10%) noise data set. Even when the percentage of noise increases, the collection of α/β concepts has "captured" the embedded concepts. Nevertheless, the number of α/β concepts can increase with α or β. A lot of α/β concepts with a number of objects close to α and a number of properties close to β leads to the computation of many unions. However, when several unions have been performed, it is more and more difficult to merge concepts. α/β concepts whose the minimal number of lines and columns is large w.r.t. α and β are dense in terms of true values and considered relevant. In other terms, it is interesting not to consider small α/β concepts (w.r.t. α and β) and thus eliminate lots of meaningless α/β concepts.

4.2   Post-processing an Incomplete Collection of Concepts on Real Gene Expression Data

In many real data sets, it is not possible to extract the whole collection of concepts. In these cases, additional constraints can be pushed deeply into the concept extraction algorithms like, for instance, enforcing a minimal size for both set components when using our D-MINER algorithm [3, 4]. We could also limit the search to the so-called frequent concepts which use such a constraint on only one set component (see, e.g., [18, 15]).

Even in the case where we can not have the whole collection of concepts $\mathcal{K}$, we can still extract α/β concepts from a subset of $\mathcal{K}$. Doing so, we compute more relevant patterns as a post-processing of some concepts.

A concrete application concerns the analysis of gene expression profiles in Type 2 diabetes disease. As we already pointed out, molecular biologists are interested in discovering putative transcription modules, i.e. sets of genes that are co-regulated and the associated sets of situations where this co-regulation occurs. In the following experiment, situations corresponds to transcription factors, i.e. biological objects which are known to activate or repress the genes. We derived a boolean data set from the data in [17]. It contains 350 genes (in rows) which are in relation with some transcription factors (150 columns) known to regulate (activate or repress) them. This data set is dense since 17% of the values are true values.

We are interested in large α/β concepts that associate many genes to many transcription factors. We were not able to extract the collection of α/β concepts from the whole collection of concepts (more than 5 millions). We decided to look at the merging of large concepts containing at least 25 genes and 10 transcription factors. Using D-MINER, we extracted 1 699 concepts satisfying these size constraints. Then we computed the collections of α/β concepts with small α and β values. Table 1 provides the number of α/β concepts (for 4 values of $\alpha\beta$) per number of merged concepts.

Table 1. Number of α/β concepts produces by the union of n concepts

n	$\alpha = \beta = 1$	$\alpha = \beta = 2$	$\alpha = \beta = 3$	$\alpha = \beta = 4$
1	1450	1217	927	639
2	54	49	61	95
3	31	57	75	73
4	8	40	50	64
5	2	8	25	58
6	1	3	11	29
7	0	0	6	11
8	0	0	1	12
9	0	0	0	2
10	0	0	1	6
11	0	0	0	0
12	0	0	0	3
13	0	0	0	1
14	0	0	1	0
15	0	0	0	1
Total	1546	1374	1158	994

Table 2. α/β concept (36×12) resulting from the union of 15 concepts with $\alpha = \beta = 4$ (number of false values for each transcription factor of the α/β concept)

Number of false values
0
0
0
1
3
2
0
3
0
3
4
0

Interestingly, even though we merged only large concepts with small α and β values, large α/β concepts have appeared. For example, at most 6 concepts are merged when $\alpha = \beta = 1$ whereas 15 concepts are merged when $\alpha = \beta = 4$. In this data set, we have large bi-sets with few 0 values. Typically, the α/β concept ($\alpha = \beta = 4$) resulting from the merge of 15 concepts is made of 36 genes and 12 transcription factors and contains only 3.7% of false values (see Table 2 where each line stands for a transcription factor and the value is the number of false values in the α/β concept).

The 12 transcription factors of this α/β concept have been checked as really similar with respect to the genes which are associated. It seems useful for biologists to consider such α/β concepts with very few exceptions instead of post-processing by themselves huge collections of concepts.

5   Conclusion

We have considered the challenging problem of computing formal concepts with exceptions from transactional data sets. This is extremely important in many application domains where strongly associated sets of objets and properties can provide interesting patterns. Closed sets associated via the Galois connection are indeed strongly associated but we miss interesting associations when the data is intrinsically noisy, for instance because of measurement errors or some crispy discretization procedures. The same reasoning has lead few years ago to the computation of almost-closure [5] when looking for condensed representations of frequent itemsets. The difficulty here has been to design a complete method for computing the so-called α/β concepts. Our formalization in terms of union of concepts that satisfy $\mathcal{C}_{\alpha\beta}$ and $\mathcal{C}_{max|\mathcal{C}_{\alpha\beta}}$ is complete. We experimentally validated the added-value of the approach on both synthetic data and a real application in molecular biology. Further experiments are needed for a better understanding of the difference between collections of concepts and collections of α/β concepts.

Acknowledgement. Jérémy Besson is funded by INRA. The authors thank Sophie Rome and Christophe Rigotti for stimulating discussions and constructive feedback during the preparation of this paper.

References

1. C. Becquet, S. Blachon, B. Jeudy, J.-F. Boulicaut, and O. Gandrillon. Strong association rule mining for large gene expression data analysis: a case study on human SAGE data. *Genome Biology*, 12, 2002. See http://genomebiology.com/2002/3/12/research/0067.
2. A. Berry, J.-P. Bordat, and A. Sigayret. Concepts can not afford to stammer. In *Proceedings JIM'03*, pages 25–35, Metz, France, September 2003.
3. J. Besson, C. Robardet, and J.-F. Boulicaut. Constraint-based mining of formal concepts in transactional data. In *Proceedings PaKDD'04*, volume 3056 of *LNCS*, pages 615–624, Sydney, Australia, May 2004. Springer-Verlag.
4. J. Besson, C. Robardet, J.-F. Boulicaut, and S. Rome. Constraint-based bi-set mining for biologically relevant pattern discovery in microarray data. *Intelligent Data Analysis journal*, 9, 2004. In Press.
5. J.-F. Boulicaut and A. Bykowski. Frequent closures as a concise representation for binary data mining. In *Proceedings PaKDD'00*, volume 1805 of *LNAI*, pages 62–73, Kyoto, JP, Apr. 2000. Springer-Verlag.
6. J.-F. Boulicaut, A. Bykowski, and C. Rigotti. Free-sets: a condensed representation of boolean data for the approximation of frequency queries. *Data Mining and Knowledge Discovery journal*, 7(1):5–22, 2003.
7. A. Bykowski and C. Rigotti. DBC: a condensed representation of frequent patterns for efficient mining. *Information Systems Journal*, 28(8):949–977, 2003.
8. B. Ganter. Two basic algorithms in concept analysis. Technical report, Technisch Hochschule Darmstadt, Preprint 831, 1984.
9. F. Geerts, B. Goethals, and T. Mielikäinen. Tiling databases. In *Proceedings DS'04*, volume 3245 of *LNCS*, Padova, Italy, Oct. 2004. Springer-Verlag. To appear.

10. B. Goethals and M. J. Zaki, editors. *FIMI '03, Frequent Itemset Mining Implementations, Proceedings of the ICDM 2003 Workshop on Frequent Itemset Mining Implementations, 19 December 2003, Melbourne, Florida, USA*, volume 90 of *CEUR Workshop Proceedings*, 2003.

11. L. Nourine and O. Raynaud. A fast algortihm for building lattices. *Information Processing Letters*, 71:190–204, 1999.

12. N. Pasquier, Y. Bastide, R. Taouil, and L. Lakhal. Efficient mining of association rules using closed itemset lattices. *Information Systems*, 24(1):25–46, Jan. 1999.

13. J. Pei, J. Han, and R. Mao. CLOSET an efficient algorithm for mining frequent closed itemsets. In *Proceedings ACM SIGMOD Workshop DMKD'00*, 2000.

14. R. Pensa, C. Leschi, J. Besson, and J.-F. Boulicaut. Assessment of discretization techniques for relevant pattern discovery from gene expression data. In *Proceedings BIOKDD'04 co-located with ACM SIGKDD'04*, Seattle, USA, August 2004. In Press.

15. F. Rioult, J.-F. Boulicaut, B. Crémilleux, and J. Besson. Using transposition for pattern discovery from microarray data. In *Proceedings ACM SIGMOD Workshop DMKD'03*, pages 73–79, San Diego, USA, June 2003.

16. F. Rioult, C. Robardet, S. Blachon, B. Crémilleux, O. Gandrillon, and J.-F. Boulicaut. Mining concepts from large SAGE gene expression matrices. In *Proceedings KDID'03 co-located with ECML-PKDD'03 ISBN:953-6690-34-9*, pages 107–118, Cavtat-Dubrovnik, Croatia, September 22 2003.

17. S. Rome, K. Clément, R. Rabasa-Lhoret, E. Loizon, C. Poitou, G. S. Barsh, J.-P. Riou, M. Laville, and H. Vidal. Microarray profiling of human skeletal muscle reveals that insulin regulates 800 genes during an hyperinsulinemic clamp. *Journal of Biological Chemistry*, March 2003. In Press.

18. G. Stumme, R. Taouil, Y. Bastide, N. Pasquier, and L. Lakhal. Computing iceberg concept lattices with titanic. *Data and Knowledge Engineering*, 42:189–222, 2002.

19. J. Wang, J. Han, and J. Pei. CLOSET+: searching for the best strategies for mining frequent closed itemsets. In *Proceedings of the ninth ACM SIGKDD international conference on Knowledge discovery and data mining*, 2003.

20. R. Wille. Restructuring lattice theory: an approach based on hierarchies of concepts. In I. Rival, editor, *Ordered sets*, pages 445–470. Reidel, 1982.

21. M. J. Zaki and C.-J. Hsiao. CHARM: An efficient algorithm for closed itemset mining. In *Proceedings SIAM DM'02*, Arlington, USA, April 2002.

Theoretical Bounds on the Size of Condensed Representations

Nele Dexters and Toon Calders*

University of Antwerp, Belgium
{nele.dexters, toon.calders}@ua.ac.be

Abstract. Recent studies demonstrate the usefulness of condensed representations as a semantic compression technique for the frequent itemsets. Especially in inductive databases, condensed representations are a useful tool as an intermediate format to support exploration of the itemset space. In this paper we establish theoretical upper bounds on the maximal size of an itemset in different condensed representations. A central notion in the development of the bounds are the l-free sets, that form the basis of many well-known representations. We will bound the maximal cardinality of an l-free set based on the size of the database. More concrete, we compute a lower bound for the size of the database in terms of the size of the l-free set, and when the database size is smaller than this lower bound, we know that the set cannot be l-free. An efficient method for calculating the exact value of the bound, based on combinatorial identities of partial row sums, is presented. We also present preliminary results on a statistical approximation of the bound and we illustrate the results with some simulations.

1   Introduction

Mining frequent itemsets [1] is a core operation of many data mining algorithms. During the last decade, hundreds of algorithms have been proposed to find frequent itemsets when a database and a user-defined support threshold are given. However, when this minimal support threshold is set too low or when the data are highly correlated, the process of mining frequent itemsets can result in an immense amount of frequent sets. Even the most efficient mining algorithms cannot cope with this combinatorial blow-up. To overcome this problem, condensed representations can be used. Condensed representations were introduced in [16] in the slightly different context of arbitrary Boolean rules. Intuitively, a condensed representation can be seen as a compact view on the data that allows for answering user queries more efficiently than directly from the original data. In [16], for example, the collection of frequent sets is considered as a condensed representation that allows to speed up frequency counts of arbitrary

---

* Postdoctoral Fellow of the Fund for Scientific Research - Flanders (Belgium)(F.W.O. - Vlaanderen).

Boolean expressions over the items. In this paper we concentrate on condensed representations for the collection of frequent itemsets itself, since this collection can already be far too large to store. A condensed representation in the context of the frequent itemsets can be a sub-collection of all frequent itemsets that still contains all information to construct the frequent sets with their corresponding supports. The best-known example of a condensed representation is the *closed itemsets representation* [17]. Other examples are the *Free Sets* [4], the *Disjunction-Free Sets* [5], the *Generalized Disjunction-Free Sets* [15], and the *Non-Derivable Sets* [9].

Especially in inductive databases, condensed representations are a useful tool as an intermediate format to support exploration of the itemset space. In fact, the role of a condensed representation in an inductive database is comparable to a partly materialized view in a data warehouse: materializing all frequent itemsets off-line would speed-up the exploration enormously, but is infeasible because of the gigantic number of them. Instead, the condensed representation is materialized. This representation is much smaller, but, at the same time, contains enough information to speed up ad-hoc querying in the inductive database. When the user asks a query concerning the frequencies of itemsets, these frequencies can be computed more efficiently from the condensed representation than directly from the database. Depending on time and space constraints, the type of condensed representation can be chosen. For example, the free sets representation is less compact than the disjunction-free representation, but allows for faster computation of frequency queries.

An important question now is: how condensed is a condensed representation; do we have guarantees about the maximal size of a representation? The usefulness of a condensed representation relies critically on its size. In this paper we establish theoretical upper bounds on the maximal size of an itemset for all representations that are based on l-free sets [8]. These representations include the *Free Sets* [4], the *Disjunction-Free Sets* [5], the *Generalized Disjunction-Free Sets* [15], the *Non-Derivable Sets* [9], and all the variants of these representations, such as the disjunction-free and generalized disjunction-free generators representations [12, 14]. Hence, based on the size of the database, we present worst-case bounds on the size of the largest sets in these representations.

A central notion in the development of the bounds are thus the l-free sets. Each of the aforementioned representations can be expressed in terms of l-freeness. It was shown in [8], that these representations can be expressed as the collection of frequent l-free sets together with a part of the border, for different values of l. The border of the collection of the frequent l-free sets are the itemsets that are not frequent l-free themselves, but all their subsets are frequent l-free. For example, the free sets representation of [4], corresponds to the collection of the frequent 1-free sets plus the sets in the border that are infrequent. For more details about the connection between the l-free sets and existing condensed representations, we refer to [8].

In this paper, we will bound the maximal cardinality of an l-free set based on the size of the database. More concrete, we compute a lower bound on the size of the database in terms of the size of the l-free set, and when the database size is smaller than this lower bound, we know that the set cannot be l-free. In this paper, we thus give general results relating l-freeness of a set I with a bound on the size of the database $\mathcal{D}$ in terms of the size of I. The results for a particular l can be generalized to the case where l equals the size of I, yielding a connection between ∞-freeness and a bound on the size of $\mathcal{D}$ in terms of the size of I, and can also be extended to NDIs. Because the aforementioned representations can be expressed as the collection of frequent l-free sets plus some sets in the border, the maximal size of a set in the representations is the maximal size of a frequent l-free set plus 1, since the sets in the border can be at most 1 item larger than the largest frequent l-free set. In this way, we extend results of [9] and of [13] that relate the database size to the maximal length of respectively the non-derivable itemsets and the generalized disjunction-free sets. Hence, even though we concentrate on a bound on the l-free sets, the main goal of the paper is to establish a bound on the condensed representations that are based on the l-free sets.

An efficient method, the *sum-of-binomials triangle*, for calculating the exact value of the bound based on combinatorial identities of partial row sums is presented. From this triangle, we can conclude interesting facts concerning the size of the database.

One disadvantage of the theoretical bound is that it represents a worst-case analysis. Hence, in reality, the actual size of the largest l-free itemset will be much smaller than the exact bound. Therefore, besides the exact theoretical bound, also preliminary results on a statistical bound are provided. Based on the size of the database and the cardinality of an itemset I, the probability that I is l-free is estimated. The bound is based on some rather harsh assumptions: we assume (a) that every item has the same probability of being present in a transaction, (b) that all items are statistically independent, and (c) that the transactions are independent. Especially assumption (b) deviates from reality. As we will argue in Section 6, a result of (b) will be that the estimated probability of a set being l-free will be too high. However, as simulations and comparisons with real-life datasets show, the statistical bound allows for making more realistic estimations of the size of the largest l-free set than the theoretical bound, and it has the ability to explain many empirical observations.

The organization of the paper is as follows. In Section 2, a short review of the different used condensed representations is given. Section 3 revisits the notions of deduction rules. In Section 4 the bounds on the size of the database that are related to the l-freeness of a set are introduced. Section 5 discusses an efficient method to compute the exact bound. Section 6 gives a statistical approximation of the subject. In Section 7, our work is related to other papers. Section 8 concludes the paper and gives further research directions.

2   Condensed Representations

In the context of frequent itemsets a condensed representation is a sub-collection of all frequent sets and their corresponding supports, that still contains all information to reconstruct all the frequent sets and their supports. In this section we briefly refresh the condensed representations mentioned in the introduction. We conclude with an example covering the representations that are important for the rest of the paper.

Closed Sets [17]. The first successful condensed representation was the closed set representation introduced by Pasquier et al. [17]. In short, a *closed set* is an itemset such that its frequency does not equal the frequency of any of its supersets. The collection of the frequent closed sets together with their supports is a condensed representation. This representation will be denoted *ClosedRep*.

Generalized Disjunction-Free Sets [14, 15]. Let X, Y be two disjoint itemsets. The *disjunctive rule* $X \rightarrow \bigvee Y$ is said to *hold in the database* $\mathcal{D}$, if every transaction in $\mathcal{D}$ that contains X, also contains at least one item of Y. A set I is called *generalized disjunction-free* if there do not exist disjoint subsets X, Y of I such that $X \rightarrow \bigvee Y$ holds. The set of all generalized disjunction-free sets is denoted *GDFree*.

In [15], a representation based on the frequent generalized disjunction-free sets is introduced. It is argued that the set of frequent generalized disjunction-free sets *FGDFree* is not a representation. This problem is resolved in [15] by adding a part of the *border* of the set *FGDFree* to the representation.

Definition 1. *Let S be a set of itemsets. $\mathcal{B}(S) = \{J \mid J \notin S, \forall J' \subset J : J' \in S\}$.*

For example, the *generalized disjunction-free generators representation* (*GDFreeGenRep*) [15] does only stores the so-called *free sets* in $\mathcal{B}(S)$. Notice that hence that the maximal size of a set in the generalized disjunction-free generators representation can be the maximal size of a generalized disjunction-free set plus 1.

Free and Disjunction-Free Sets [4, 5, 12]. Free and disjunction-free sets are special cases of generalized disjunction-free sets. For free sets, the righthand side of the rules $X \rightarrow \bigvee Y$ is restricted to singletons, for disjunction-free sets to singletons and pairs. Hence, a set I is free if and only if there does not exist a rule $X \rightarrow a$ that holds with $X \cup \{a\} \subseteq I$, and I is disjunction-free if there does not exists a rule $X \rightarrow a \vee b$ that holds with $X \cup \{a, b\} \subseteq I$. The free and disjunction-free sets are denoted respectively by *Free* and *DFree*, the frequent free and frequent disjunction-free sets by *FFree* and *FDFree*.

Again, neither *FFree*, nor *FDFree* form a condensed representation. Hence, for the representations based on the free sets and the disjunction-free sets, (parts of) the border must be stored as well. See [4, 5, 12, 14, 15] for some representations consisting of *FFree* or *FDFree* together with a part of the border.

tid	Items	tid	Items
1	a,b,c,d,e	9	b,c,d
2	a,b,d,e	10	b,c,e
3	a,b,d,e	11	c,d,e
4	b,c,d,e	12	b,c
5	b,c,d,e	13	b,d
6	a,b,e	14	c,d
7	a,c,d	15	d,e
8	a,c,e	16	b

$\mathcal{D} =$

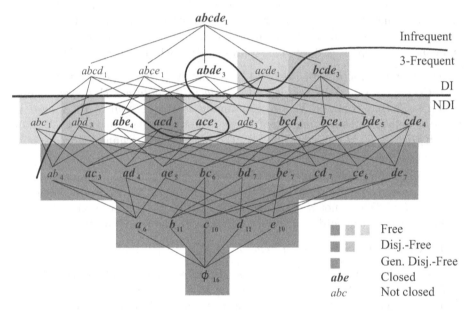

Fig. 1. Free, Disjunction-Free, Generalized Disjunction-Free, Closed, and Non-Derivable sets

Non-derivable Itemsets (NDI) [6]. The non-derivable itemsets representation is based on deduction rules to derive bounds $[l_I, u_I]$ on the support of an itemset I, based on the support of its strict subsets. These deduction rules are revisited in Section 3. We call an itemset I derivable if $l_I = u_I$. Because always $l_I \leq supp(I) \leq u_I$, in that case, we can *derive* the support of I from the supports of each strict subset J of I. Hence, in the NDI representation, only the frequent non-derivable itemsets are stored. This representation is denoted *NDIRep*.

Example 1. Consider the database $\mathcal{D}$ that is given in Figure 1. In the lattice in Figure 1, different sets of itemsets are indicated for easy reference. The free sets, disjunction-free sets, and generalized disjunction-free sets are indicated with grey boxes. The free sets are a superset of the disjunction-free sets, which are on their turn a superset of the generalized disjunction-free sets. The generalized disjunction-free sets are indicated in the darkest shade of grey. Then, the disjunction-free sets that are not generalized disjunction-free in the middle shade, and finally the free sets that are not disjunction-free in the lightest shade. The sets below the horizontal line are non-derivable, the ones above the line are derivable. The closed itemsets are in bold. The curve separates the frequent (below) from the infrequent (top) sets. The minimal support in this example is 3.

We now have the following representations:

$$ClosedRep = \{\emptyset, a, b, c, d, e, ac, ad, ae, bc, bd, be, cd, ce, de, abe, bcd, bce,$$
$$bde, cde, abde, bcde\}^{\text{supp}} \ ,$$
$$FreeRep = (FFree^{\text{supp}}, \{abc, acd, ace, acde\}) \ ,$$
$$DFreeRep = (FDFree \cup \{abc, abe, ace, ade\})^{\text{supp}} \ ,$$
$$DFreeGenRep = (FDFree^{\text{supp}}, \{ade\}^{\text{supp}}, \{abc, abe, ace\}) \ ,$$
$$GDFreeRep = (FGDFree \cup \{abc, abd, abe, ace, ade, bcd, bce, bde, cde\})^{\text{supp}} \ ,$$
$$GDFreeGenRep = (FGDFree^{\text{supp}}, \{abd, ade, bcd, bce, bde, cde\}^{\text{supp}}, \{abc, ace\}) \ ,$$
$$NDIRep = \{\emptyset, a, b, c, d, e, ac, ad, ae, bc, bd, be, cd, ce, de, abd, abe, ade,$$
$$bcd, bce, bde, cde\}^{\text{supp}} \ ,$$

The notation supp in the superscript of a set S of itemsets denotes that the itemsets in S are stored together with their supports.

3 Deduction Rules Revisited

In this section we refresh the deduction rules introduced in [6]. The deduction rules allow for deriving a lower and an upper bound on the support of an itemset, based on the support of its subsets. For example, for the itemset abc we can find the following lower bound on the support:

$$supp(abc) \geq supp(ab) + supp(ac) - supp(a).$$

We first give a complete collection of deduction rules in general. Then, the depth of a rule is defined and only rules up to a certain depth are considered. Next, the notion of an l-free set is introduced. The l-free sets are an important concept, since in [8], it was shown that many condensed representations can easily be expressed in a uniform way using the l-free sets. We will not go into detail about this uniform framework, but only give the intuition behind it. For the exact details, we refer the reader to [8].

3.1 General Concept of Deduction Rules

We start from a database $\mathcal{D}$ with $|\mathcal{D}| = m$ transactions, based on $|\mathcal{I}| = n$ items. We consider an itemset $I \subseteq \mathcal{I}$ with k elements ($|I| = k$) and we are interested in the support of I in the database $\mathcal{D}$: $supp(I, \mathcal{D})$. In [8] (in a somewhat different form), the following relation between the support of I and its subsets was shown:

Table 1. Deduction rules for the set abc. s_J denotes $supp(J)$

Upper/Lower Bounds $\delta_X(I,\mathcal{D})$	X	$\lvert I\setminus X\rvert$	$X\cup\overline{Y}$
$supp(I,\mathcal{D})\le s_{ab}+s_{ac}+s_{bc}-s_a-s_b-s_c+s_{\{\}}$	$\{\}$	3	abc
$supp(I,\mathcal{D})\ge s_{ab}+s_{ac}-s_a$	a	2	abc
$supp(I,\mathcal{D})\ge s_{ab}+s_{bc}-s_b$	b	2	$\overline{a}b\overline{c}$
$supp(I,\mathcal{D})\ge s_{ac}+s_{bc}-s_c$	c	2	$a\overline{bc}$
$supp(I,\mathcal{D})\le s_{ab}$	ab	1	$ab\overline{c}$
$supp(I,\mathcal{D})\le s_{ac}$	ac	1	$a\overline{b}c$
$supp(I,\mathcal{D})\le s_{bc}$	bc	1	$\overline{a}bc$
$supp(I,\mathcal{D})\ge 0$	abc	0	abc
		Depth l	

$X\cup\overline{Y}$	Equalities
abc	$supp(I,\mathcal{D})=s_{ab}+s_{ac}+s_{bc}-s_a-s_b-s_c+s_{\{\}}-s_{\overline{abc}}$
abc	$supp(I,\mathcal{D})=s_{ab}+s_{ac}-s_a+s_{a\overline{bc}}$
$\overline{a}b\overline{c}$	$supp(I,\mathcal{D})=s_{ab}+s_{bc}-s_b+s_{\overline{a}b\overline{c}}$
$a\overline{bc}$	$supp(I,\mathcal{D})=s_{ac}+s_{bc}-s_c+s_{\overline{ab}c}$
$ab\overline{c}$	$supp(I,\mathcal{D})=s_{ab}-s_{ab\overline{c}}$
$a\overline{b}c$	$supp(I,\mathcal{D})=s_{ac}-s_{a\overline{b}c}$
$\overline{a}bc$	$supp(I,\mathcal{D})=s_{bc}-s_{\overline{a}bc}$
abc	$supp(I,\mathcal{D})=s_{abc}$

Theorem 1. *Let $\delta_X(I,\mathcal{D})$ denote the following sum* $(X\subseteq I)$:

$$\delta_X(I,\mathcal{D})=\sum_{X\subseteq J\subset I}(-1)^{\lvert I\setminus J\rvert+1}supp(J).$$

Then, $supp(I,\mathcal{D})=\delta_X(I,\mathcal{D})+(-1)^{\lvert Y\rvert}supp(X\cup\overline{Y},\mathcal{D})$ *where* $Y=I\setminus X$, *and* $supp(X\cup\overline{Y},\mathcal{D})$ *denotes the number of transactions in $\mathcal{D}$ that contains all items in X, and none of the items in Y.*

Hence, for all $X\subseteq I$, depending on the sign of $\lvert Y\rvert$, $\delta_X(I,\mathcal{D})$ is an upper ($\lvert Y\rvert$ odd), or a lower ($\lvert Y\rvert$ even) bound on the support of I. The set $X\cup\overline{Y}$ in Theorem 1, is called a *generalized itemset based on I*. For the complete set of rules for the example where $I=\{a,b,c\}$, see Table 1. With these rules we can compute a lower and upper bound on the support of I when we assume that the supports of all its strict subsets are known. The lower bound is denoted by $LB(I,\mathcal{D})$ and the upper bound by $UB(I,\mathcal{D})$. That is:

$$LB(I,\mathcal{D})=\max\{\delta_X(I,\mathcal{D})\mid X\subseteq I, \lvert I\setminus X\rvert\ \text{even}\}$$
$$UB(I,\mathcal{D})=\min\{\delta_X(I,\mathcal{D})\mid X\subseteq I, \lvert I\setminus X\rvert\ \text{odd}\}$$

Notice that the complexity of the sum $\delta_X(I,\mathcal{D})$ depends on the cardinality of $Y=I\setminus X$. This number $\lvert Y\rvert$ is called the *depth* of the rule $\delta_X(I,\mathcal{D})$. Hence, the deeper a rule is, the more complex it is (see Table 1). Therefore, it is often interesting to only consider rules up to a fixed depth l. The lower and upper bounds calculated with rules up to depth l will be denoted $LB_l(I, \mathcal{D})$ and $UB_l(I, \mathcal{D})$. That is:

$$LB_l(I, \mathcal{D}) = \max\{\delta_X(I, \mathcal{D}) \mid X \subseteq I, |I \setminus X| \text{ even}, |I \setminus X| \leq l\}$$
$$UB_l(I, \mathcal{D}) = \min\{\delta_X(I, \mathcal{D}) \mid X \subseteq I, |I \setminus X| \text{ odd}, |I \setminus X| \leq l\}$$

When it is clear from the context we do not explicitly write down $\mathcal{D}$ in the formulas.

Example 2. Consider the following database:

TID	Items
1	a, b, c, d
2	a, b, c
3	a, b, d, e
4	c, e
5	b, d, e
6	a, b, e
7	a, c, e
8	a, d, e
9	b, c, e
10	b, d, e

In this database, the following supports hold:

$supp(\{\}) = 10 \qquad supp(a) = 6 \qquad supp(b) = 7 \qquad supp(c) = 5$
$supp(ab) = 4 \qquad supp(ac) = 3 \qquad supp(bc) = 3$

The deduction rules for abc up to level 2 are the following (see Table 1):

$supp(abc) \geq \delta_a(abc) = 1 \qquad supp(abc) \leq \delta_{ab}(abc) = 4$
$supp(abc) \geq \delta_b(abc) = 0 \qquad supp(abc) \leq \delta_{ac}(abc) = 3$
$supp(abc) \geq \delta_c(abc) = 1 \qquad supp(abc) < \delta_{bc}(abc) = 3$
$\qquad\qquad\qquad\qquad\qquad supp(abc) \geq \delta_{abc}(abc) = 0$

Hence, based on the supports of the subsets of abc, we can deduce that $LB_1(abc) = 0$, $UB_1(abc) = 3$, $LB_2(abc) = 1$ and $UB_2(abc) = 3$.

3.2 *l*-Freeness of an Itemset

A very important notion in the context of a unifying framework for the condensed representations is l-freeness:

Definition 2. *Let l be a positive integer. A set I is l-free, if $supp(I, \mathcal{D}) \neq LB_l(I, \mathcal{D})$, and $supp(I, \mathcal{D}) \neq UB_l(I, \mathcal{D})$. A set I is ∞-free, if $supp(I, \mathcal{D}) \neq LB(I, \mathcal{D})$, and $supp(I, \mathcal{D}) \neq UB(I, \mathcal{D})$.*

In [8], the following properties of l-freeness were shown: l-freeness is anti-monotone; that is, every subset of an l-free itemset is also l-free, and every superset of an itemset that is not l-free is also not l-free. l-freeness is interesting in the context of condensed representations, because the support of any non-l-free set can be derived as follows: if $supp(I, \mathcal{D}) = LB_l(I, \mathcal{D})$, then for all $I \subseteq J$, $supp(J, \mathcal{D}) = LB_l(J, \mathcal{D})$. Hence, if we observe the fact $supp(I, \mathcal{D}) = LB_l(I, \mathcal{D})$, there is no need to store any of the supersets of I in a condensed representation. The representations that rely on l-freeness hence store the frequent l-free sets, and some sets that are "on the border." For a detailed description we refer to Section 2 and [8].

From Theorem 1, the following lemma easily follows:

Lemma 1. *Let l be a positive integer, I an itemset, $X \subseteq I$. I is l-free if and only if $supp(X \cup \overline{Y}) \neq 0$ for all generalized itemsets $X \cup \overline{Y}$ that are based on I, with $|Y| \leq l$.*

Example 3. Consider the following database $\mathcal{D}$:

In this database, the following supports hold:

TID	Items
1	a, d
2	b, d, e
3	c, d, e
4	a, b, e
5	a, c, d
6	b, c, d, e
7	a, b, c, d

$$supp(\{\}) = 7 \qquad supp(a) = 4 \qquad supp(b) = 4 \qquad supp(c) = 4$$
$$supp(ab) = 2 \qquad supp(ac) = 2 \qquad supp(bc) = 2$$

The deduction rules for abc up to level 2 are the following (see Table 1):

$$supp(abc) \geq \delta_\emptyset(abc) = 1 \qquad supp(abc) \leq \delta_{ab}(abc) = 2$$
$$supp(abc) \geq \delta_a(abc) = 0 \qquad supp(abc) \leq \delta_{ac}(abc) = 2$$
$$supp(abc) \geq \delta_b(abc) = 0 \qquad supp(abc) \leq \delta_{bc}(abc) = 2$$
$$supp(abc) \geq \delta_c(abc) = 0 \qquad supp(abc) \geq \delta_{abc}(abc) = 0$$

We can deduce that $LB_2(abc) = 0$, $UB_2(abc) = 2$. Hence, $supp(abc, \mathcal{D})$ must be in the interval $[0, 2]$. Since the actual support of abc in $\mathcal{D}$ is 1, $supp(abc, \mathcal{D}) \neq LB_2(abc)$ and $supp(abc, \mathcal{D}) \neq UB_2(abc)$. Thus, abc is a 2-free set. Notice that indeed, as stated by Lemma 1, the generalized itemsets based on abc with at most 2 negations have a non-zero support. These generalized itemsets (see Table 1) are the sets abc, $\overline{a}bc$, $a\overline{b}c$, $ab\overline{c}$, $\overline{ab}c$, $\overline{a}b\overline{c}$, and $a\overline{bc}$. Each of them occurs exactly once in the database. To illustrate the other direction of Lemma 1, notice that $supp(\overline{abc}, \mathcal{D}) = 0$. $\overline{abc}$ has three negations and thus corresponds to a deduction rule of depth 3. This deduction rule ($\delta_\emptyset(abc)$) gives an upper bound of 1 for abc, and thus we see that $supp(abc, \mathcal{D}) = UB_3(abc)$, illustrating that abc is not 3-free.

3.3   Link Between *l*-Freeness and Condensed Representations

The following proposition from [8], links the *free sets* [4], the *disjunction-free sets* [5, 12], and the *generalized disjunction-free sets* [15, 14] with *l*-freeness, for different values of *l*.

Proposition 1. *Link between l-freeness with other condensed representations.*

- *I* is free $\Leftrightarrow$ *I* is $1 - $ free
- *I* is disjunction$- $ free $\Leftrightarrow$ *I* is $2 - $ free
- *I* is generalized disjunction$- $ free $\Leftrightarrow$ *I* is $\infty - $ free
- *I* is NDI $\Rightarrow$ every strict subset of *I* is $\infty - $ free

From the unified framework introduced in [8] the following proposition making the connection between the size of an *l*-free set and the different condensed representations is immediate (recall from Section 2 that the different representations can be expressed as *l*-free sets *plus the border*. Hence, the representations can contain sets that are 1 item larger than the largest *l*-free set):

Proposition 2. *Let $max(l, \mathcal{D})$ be the length of the largest frequent l-free set in $\mathcal{D}$.*

- *Every set in the free sets representation [4] has length at most $max(1, \mathcal{D}) + 1$.*
- *Every set in the disjunction-free sets representation [5, 12] has length at most $max(2, \mathcal{D}) + 1$.*

- *Every set in the generalized disjunction-free sets representation [15, 14] has length at most $max(\infty, \mathcal{D}) + 1$.*
- *Every set in the non-derivable itemsets representation [9] has length at most $max(\infty, \mathcal{D}) + 1$.*

Hence, because of Proposition 2, a theoretical bound on the size of the l-free sets immediately leads to a bound on many condensed representations.

4 Bounds on the Size of the Database

In this section we present the theoretical lower bound $d_l(k)$ on the size of the database in terms of the size k of the largest l-free set. Hence, if $\mathcal{D}$ contains an l-free set of size k, then the cardinality of $\mathcal{D}$ must be at least $d_l(k)$. This result then allows for deriving the maximal cardinality of an l-free set based on the size of a database. Indeed; the maximal size k of an l-free set is the largest integer k such that $|\mathcal{D}| \geq d_l(k)$.

4.1 Bounds for l-Free Sets

We illustrate the principle of the bound with an example. Let $I = abcd$ be a 2-free set. We will show how the lower bound $d_2(4)$ on the size of $\mathcal{D}$ can be derived. Because I is 2-free, by definition, $supp(I, \mathcal{D}) \neq LB_2(I, \mathcal{D})$ and $supp(I, \mathcal{D}) \neq UB_2(I, \mathcal{D})$. Because of Lemma 1, for all generalized itemsets $X \cup \overline{Y}$ based on I, with $|Y| \leq 2$, $supp(X \cup \overline{Y}, \mathcal{D}) \neq 0$. In the case of $abcd$, this means that

$$
\begin{aligned}
&supp(\overline{abc}d) > 0, \; supp(\overline{ab}c\overline{d}) > 0, \; supp(\overline{a}bc\overline{d}) > 0, \\
&supp(a\overline{bc}d) > 0, \; supp(a\overline{b}c\overline{d}) > 0, \; supp(ab\overline{c}\overline{d}) > 0, \\
&supp(\overline{a}bcd) > 0, \; supp(a\overline{b}cd) > 0, \; supp(ab\overline{c}d) > 0, \\
&supp(abc\overline{d}) > 0, \; supp(abcd) > 0 \; .
\end{aligned}
$$

Every transaction can make only one of these conditions true. Indeed; suppose that a transaction T supports *both* $\overline{abc}d$ and $\overline{abc}d$. Then, T must at the same time not contain b ($\overline{abc}d$) and contain b ($\overline{abc}d$), and that is clearly impossible. Hence, a database $\mathcal{D}$ in which $abcd$ is 2-free, must contain at least one transaction for each generalized itemset $X \cup \overline{Y}$ based on $abcd$ with $|Y| \leq 2$. Hence, to get the lower bound on the size of the database, we we have to count the number of generalized itemsets consisting of 4 items with at most two negated items. There are $\binom{4}{2} = 6$ generalized itemsets consisting of 4 elements with exactly two elements negated and $\binom{4}{1} = 4$ generalized itemsets of size 4 with exactly 1 item negated. There exists only 1 generalized itemset of size 4 with no items negated. Hence, every database in which $abcd$ is 2-free needs to have at least $d_2(4) = 6 + 4 + 1 = 11$ transactions.

In general, let I be l-free with $|I| = k$. Then, for every generalized itemset $X \cup \overline{Y}$ based on I with $|Y| \leq l$, there needs to be at least one supporting transaction. For each generalized itemset we thus have k items and at most l of them can be negated. We now count all the possibilities with no item of the k items negated, with 1 item negated, ..., up to when l items out of k are negated. Hence, in general, we have:

$$d_l(k) = \binom{k}{0} + \binom{k}{1} + \ldots + \binom{k}{l} = \sum_{i=0}^{l} \binom{k}{i}$$

This reasoning leads directly to the following theorem:

Theorem 2.

$$I \text{ is } 1-\text{free} \Rightarrow |\mathcal{D}| \geq \sum_{i=0}^{l} \binom{k}{i} \tag{1}$$

$$|\mathcal{D}| < \sum_{i=0}^{l} \binom{k}{i} \Rightarrow I \text{ is not } l-\text{free} \tag{2}$$

Example 4. We now show that the above bound eq. (2) is tight. This means that if we take a database with $|\mathcal{D}| = \sum_{i=0}^{l} \binom{k}{i}$, that this gives that I is l-free. We consider the case where $l = 2$, and $I = abc$ thus $k = 3$. The size of the database is $\mathcal{D} = \sum_{i=0}^{2} \binom{3}{i} = 7$.

Consider:

In this database, the following supports hold:

TID	Items
1	a, d
2	b, d, e
3	c, d, e
4	a, b, e
5	a, c, d
6	b, c, d, e
7	a, b, c, d

$supp(\{\}) = 7 \qquad supp(a) = 4 \qquad supp(b) = 4 \qquad supp(c) = 4$
$supp(ab) = 2 \qquad supp(ac) = 2 \qquad supp(bc) = 2$

The deduction rules for abc up to level 2 are the following (see Table 1):

$supp(abc) \geq \delta_a(abc) = 0 \qquad supp(abc) \leq \delta_{ab}(abc) = 2$
$supp(abc) \geq \delta_b(abc) = 0 \qquad supp(abc) \leq \delta_{ac}(abc) = 2$
$supp(abc) \geq \delta_c(abc) = 0 \qquad supp(abc) \leq \delta_{bc}(abc) = 2$
$\qquad\qquad\qquad\qquad\qquad\quad supp(abc) \geq \delta_{abc}(abc) = 0$

We can deduce that $LB_2(abc) = 0$, $UB_2(abc) = 2$. We thus have that $supp(abc, \mathcal{D}) \in [0, 2]$. If we compute $supp(abc, \mathcal{D})$ exactly by counting in the database, we find that $supp(abc, \mathcal{D}) = 1$, illustrating that $supp(abc, \mathcal{D}) \neq LB_2(abc)$ and $supp(abc, \mathcal{D}) \neq UB_2(abc)$, thus abc is a 2-free set.

4.2   Bounds for ∞-Free Sets

If we take l equal to k, the size of I, we use *all* the deduction rules to derive the support of I. Based on (1) and (2) we now have the following results:

$$I \text{ is } \infty-\text{free} \Rightarrow |\mathcal{D}| \geq \sum_{i=0}^{k} \binom{k}{i} = 2^k \tag{3}$$

$$|\mathcal{D}| < 2^k \Rightarrow I \text{ is not } \infty\text{-free} \qquad (4)$$

From eqs. (3) and (4), it follows that

Theorem 3. I is ∞-free $\Rightarrow |I| \leq \log_2(|\mathcal{D}|)$
Hence, $|I| > \log_2(|\mathcal{D}|) \Rightarrow I$ is not ∞-free

5   Exact Computation of the Bound

In Section 4.1 we derived Theorem 2. A crucial part in the equations (1) and (2) is the incomplete binomial sum that is completely determined by l and k:

$$d_l(k) =_{\text{def}} \sum_{i=0}^{l} \binom{k}{i}$$

This is the exact amount of generalized itemsets that is needed to to make a set I of size k, l-free. We can now find a recursion relation between the different $d_l(k)$'s. We illustrate the relation with an example. Suppose we want to know the value of $d_2(4)$. $d_2(4)$ corresponds to the number of generalized disjunction-free sets of size 4 with at most 2 negations. Let $abcd$ be the base of the generalized disjunction-free sets. The disjunction-free sets based on $abcd$ can be divided into two groups: the ones with d, and the ones with $\overline{d}$. Let $X \cup Y$ be a generalized itemset of the first type. Then, $X \setminus \{d\} \cup \overline{Y}$ is a generalized itemset based on abc with at most 2 negations. Similarly, if we take $\overline{d}$ out of a generalized itemset based on $abcd$ of the second type, we get a generalized itemset based on abc with at most 1 negation. Hence, there are $d_2(3)$ generalized itemsets of the first kind, and $d_1(3)$ of the second type. Hence, $d_2(4) = d_2(3) + d_1(3)$. An illustration of this example can be found in Table 2.

For general l and k, we get the following recursive relation:

$$d_l(k) = d_l(k - 1) + d_{l-1}(k - 1) \qquad (5)$$

When we rewrite this relation with the partial binomial sums, we get:

$$\sum_{i=0}^{l} \binom{k}{i} = \sum_{i=0}^{l} \binom{k-1}{i} + \sum_{i=0}^{l-1} \binom{k-1}{i}$$

This relation is also known as *Pascal's 6th Identity of Partial Row Sum Rules*.

Because $l \leq k$, we only need to know the diagonal elements $d_k(k)$ and the base-elements $d_1(k)$ to use the above recurrence relation (5). With this knowledge, we can construct a triangle with the incomplete binomial sums $d_l(k)$.

This *sum-of-binomials* triangle has several interesting properties (see Fig. 2):

- The diagonal defined by $l = k$ is easy to compute because $\sum_{i=0}^{k} \binom{k}{i} = 2^k$.
- The bottom line for $l = 0$ is always 1.

Table 2. Total amount of generalized itemsets for a set of size $k = 4$, consisting of the items a, b, c and d, for level 2 based on a subset of size $k = 3$

				$d_2(4)$		$d_2(3)$		$d_1(3)$	
	$d_2(3)$			$\sum_{i=0}^{2}\binom{4}{i} = 11$		$\sum_{i=0}^{2}\binom{3}{i} = 7$		$\sum_{i=0}^{1}\binom{3}{i} = 4$	
	$\sum_{i=0}^{2}\binom{3}{i} = 7$			$abcd$				$abcd$	
				$a\bar{b}cd$				$a\bar{b}c\bar{d}$	
$\overline{abc}$				$ab\bar{c}d$		$ab\bar{c}d$			
$\bar{a}b\bar{c}$	$\binom{3}{2} = 3$			$\bar{a}b\bar{c}d$	$\binom{4}{2} = 6$			$\bar{a}bc\bar{d}$	
$\bar{a}bc$		$\rightarrow$		$\bar{a}b\bar{c}d$		$\bar{a}b\bar{c}d$			
$ab\bar{c}$				$a\bar{b}cd$		$a\bar{b}cd$			
$a\bar{b}c$	$\binom{3}{1} = 3$			$abcd$				$abc\bar{d}$	
				$ab\bar{c}d$		$ab\bar{c}d$			
$\bar{a}bc$				$a\bar{b}cd$	$\binom{4}{1} = 4$	$a\bar{b}cd$			
abc	$\binom{3}{0} = 1$			$\bar{a}bcd$		$\bar{a}bcd$			
				$abcd$	$\binom{4}{0} = 1$	$abcd$			

- The base line for $l = 1$ is always $k + 1$. For a set of size k to be 1-free, $\binom{k}{0} + \binom{k}{1} = 1 + k$ generalized itemsets are needed.
- The line under the diagonal defined by $l = k - 1$ is always $2^k - 1$. $d_k(k) = \sum_{i=0}^{k}\binom{k}{i} = 2^k$ and $d_{k-1}(k) = \sum_{i=0}^{k-1}\binom{k}{i} = 2^k - \binom{k}{k} = 2^k - 1$.
- Parallellogramrule: the entry $d_{l'}(k')$ for a certain couple (k', l') can be calculated using (5) and therefore needs all the other entries in the parallelogram that can be constructed starting in that couple (k', l') and drawing lines parallel with the diagonal and the horizontal axes. The parallellogram is then bounded by the diagonal defined by $l = k$, the horizonthal base line defined by $l = 1$ and the lines parallel with these basic axes defined by $l = l'$ and $l = k - (k' - l')$. For an example, take $k' = 6$ and $l' = 4$.
- Sumrule: the entry $d_{l'}(k')$ for a certain couple (k', l') can also be computed by taking $\left(\sum_{i=0}^{k'-1} d_{l'-1}(i)\right) + 1$. This is taking the sum of all the entries on the lower line, one step shifted to the left, plus 1. For example, if we take $k' = 6$ and $l' = 4$ we see that $57 = (1 + 2 + 4 + 8 + 15 + 26) + 1$.

To give an idea of the complete(d) diagram, see Figure 2. When $l = 2$ we find $d_2(k) = \dfrac{k^2}{2} + o(k)$. When $l = 3$ we find $d_3(k) = \dfrac{k^3}{2 \cdot 3} + o(k^2)$. In general, $d_l(k) = \dfrac{k^l}{l!} + o(k^{l-1})$.

l	0	1	2	3	4	5	6	7	8	.	.	k	.	Limit.
l	1	2	4	8	16	32	64	128	256	.	.	2^k	.	.
.	.	.	.	.	.	.	.	.	.	.	↗	2^k-1	.	
.	.	.	.	.	.	.	.	.	.	↗	↗	.	.	.
8	1	2	4	8	16	32	64	128	**256**	↗	.	.	.	.
7	1	2	4	8	16	32	64	**128**	255	.	.	.	.	.
6	1	2	4	8	16	32	**64**	127	297	.	.	.	.	.
5	1	2	4	8	16	**32**	63	120	219	.	.	.	.	.
4	1	2	4	8	**16**	31	**57**	99	163	.	.	.	.	.
3	*1*	*2*	*4*	**8**	*15*	*26*	*42*	*64*	*93*	.	.	.	⟶	$\frac{n^3}{3!}$
2	1	2	4	7	11	16	22	29	37	.	.	.	⟶	$\frac{n^2}{2!}$
1	1	**2**	3	4	5	6	7	8	9	→	→	**k+1**	⟶	n
0	**1**	1	1	1	1	1	1	1	1	→	→	**1**	⟶	1

Fig. 2. Sum-of-binomials triangle

With the use of Proposition 2 and these bounds, we also find bounds for the various condensed representations.

6 Statistical Approximation

The theoretical bound derived in the previous sections represents a worst-case analysis. Based on the size of the database, the theoretical bound is valid for *all* databases of that size. Therefore, in reality, the theoretical bound is in general far too pessimistic. In this section we present preliminary results on a statistical bound. Based on the size of the database and the cardinality of an itemset I, the probability of I being l-free is given. This probability gives a more realistic estimate of the largest l-free set. The study is preliminary in the sense that there are a lot of assumptions. First, these assumptions are discussed. Then we develop a general theory in case of these assumptions. Finally, the results are illustrated with a couple of simulations.

6.1 Assumptions

We consider a transaction database $\mathcal{D}$ over items from $\mathcal{I}$. Let m be the number of transactions, and n the number of items. In the development of a statistical bound, we will assume the following conditions:

(a) The transactions are statistically independent. That is, the presence or absence of certain transactions does not influence other transactions. Thus, the process generating the transactions has no memory. In the market-basket model this condition corresponds to the situation in which the shoppers do not influence each other. There are many practical situations in which this assumption fails. For example, in a transaction database containing information about alarm events, it is conceivable that the existence of a transaction with a certain type of alarm increases the probability of other alarms in other transactions. Even though, the independence condition is often (implicitly) assumed in other papers as well. See for example many papers about privacy preserving data mining, such as [2] where it is assumed that the transactions are the realization of m independent identical distributed (iid) random variables and [10] where there is an implicit assumption.

(b) We assume that each item has the same probability, p, of being in a transaction. Hence, in fact, we assume that the supports of the items are more or less the same. This is often not the case in the real-life datasets. However, due to the minimal support constraint, after the first database scan, the items with the lowest supports are removed. It is also common practice to remove items with support that is too high. For example, the well-known pumsb* dataset from the *UCI KDD Repository* [11] is formed by removing all items with relative support higher than 80% from the pumsb dataset. In this way, the supports of the items are within a limited range. Even though, this restriction is a small deviation from reality and needs to be taken into account when evaluating the results.

(c) The most severe assumption is that all items are statistically independent. Hence, the probability of having items $i_1 \ldots i_k$ in a transaction T is p^k. Thus, we assume that the database is formed by a process that randomly picks items from $\mathcal{I}$ with probability p. In reality (hopefully) the database does contain correlated items. However, correlated items decrease the probability of having large l-free sets. Indeed, suppose i_1 and i_2 are correlated and $p = 0.5$. Then the existence of $i_1 i_2$ and $\overline{i_1} i_2$ is favored over the existence of $i_1 \overline{i_2}$. Therefore, the statistical bound will provide bounds that are good for random data, but that are too large for highly correlated data. Even though, the bounds found by the statistical approximation will be much better than the theoretical, worst-case bound.

For an itemset I consisting of k items, we now define a stochast X_l^k being true when all generalized itemsets $X \cup \overline{Y}$ based on I with $|I| = k$ and $|Y| \leq l$ have support different from 0. In the case that $l = k$ we write X^k. If the probability of this stochast X_l^k (X^k) almost equals 1, we know that the probability is very high that all generalized itemsets up to level l (k) have a support value that differs from 0. This means that we are almost certain that an itemset I of size k is an l-free (∞-free) set (see Lemma 1, Section 3). We try to find a general expression in terms of the probability of items, p, for the probability of this stochast X_l^k (X^k) and therefore for l-freeness (∞-freeness). With the probabilities X_l^k we can also estimate the amount of l-free (∞-free) sets as follows:

$$E[l-\text{free sets}] = \sum_{i=1}^{n} \binom{n}{i} P(X_l^k = 1)$$

$$E[\infty-\text{free sets}] = \sum_{i=1}^{n} \binom{n}{i} P(X^k = 1)$$

6.2 General Expression

We now derive a general expression for the probability of X_l^k being true.

We focus on a set I consisting of k items and a depth $l \leq k$. We now consider a generalized itemset $X \cup \overline{Y}$ with $|Y| = l_1$ ($l_1 \leq l$) and $|X \cup \overline{Y}| = k$. The probability that $X \cup \overline{Y}$ occurs in a transaction T is:

$$P(X \cup \overline{Y} \text{ in } T) = p^{k-l_1}(1-p)^{l_1} \ ,$$

and the probability that the generalized itemset does not occur in that transaction is

$$P(X \cup \overline{Y} \text{ not in } T) = 1 - p^{k-l_1}(1-p)^{l_1}.$$

The probability that $X \cup \overline{Y}$ does not occur in the database is the probability that the generalized itemset does not occur in any of the transactions in the database. Because of the assumption of independence of the transactions we find

$$P(X \cup \overline{Y} \text{ not in } \mathcal{D}) = \left[1 - p^{k-l_1}(1-p)^{l_1}\right]^m .$$

Based on this expression, the probability that the generalized itemset occurs in the database, so occurs in one or more transactions of $\mathcal{D}$, can be computed as

$$P(X \cup \overline{Y} \text{ in } \mathcal{D}) = 1 - \left[1 - p^{k-l_1}(1-p)^{l_1}\right]^m .$$

Example 5. In Table 1 (Section 3), all deduction rules and corresponding generalized itemsets for abc can be found. For $l \leq 3$, the stochast X_l^3 is defined as "all generalized itemsets $X \cup \overline{Y}$ based on abc with $|Y| \leq l$ have support $\neq 0$" and the stochast X^3 means "all generalized itemsets $X \cup \overline{Y}$ based on abc have support $\neq 0$". We can compute $P(X^3)$ ($l = k = 3$) as $P(X^3) = P($ all gen. itemsets $X \cup \overline{Y}$ based on abc have $supp \neq 0) = P(\overline{abc}$ occurs in $\mathcal{D}$, $a\overline{bc}$ occurs in $\mathcal{D}$, $\overline{a}b\overline{c}$ occurs in $\mathcal{D}$, $\overline{abc}$ occurs in $\mathcal{D}$, $ab\overline{c}$ occurs in $\mathcal{D}$, $a\overline{bc}$ occurs in $\mathcal{D}$, $\overline{a}bc$ occurs in $\mathcal{D}$, abc occurs in $\mathcal{D}$). Analogously, we can compute $P(X_1^3)$ ($l = 1$) as $P($all gen. itemsets $X \cup \overline{Y}$ based on abc with $|Y| \leq 1$ have $supp \neq 0) = P(ab\overline{c}$ occurs in $\mathcal{D}$, $a\overline{b}c$ occurs in $\mathcal{D}$, $\overline{a}bc$ occurs in $\mathcal{D}$, abc occurs in $\mathcal{D}$).

The probability that a set I of size k is l-free is now the probability that for all generalized itemsets $X \cup \overline{Y}$ with $|Y| \leq l$, $X \cup \overline{Y}$ occurs in at least one transaction. Hence,

$$P(X_l^k) = P\{X \cup \overline{Y} \text{ in } \mathcal{D} \mid X \cup Y = I, |Y| \leq l\}.$$

A major problem for finding a closed expression for this probability $P(X_l^k)$ is that the conditions in $\{X \cup \overline{Y} \text{ in } \mathcal{D} \mid X \cup Y = I, |Y| \leq l\}$ are not independent. Indeed, suppose that $m = 7$. Then $P(X_3^3)$ denotes the probability that a set of size 3 is a 3-free set. From the theoretical bound in Theorem 2, we know that a database of size 7 cannot have a 3-free set of size 3. Therefore, $P(X_3^3) = 0$, if $m = 7$. However, in the case that the size of the database is much larger than the number of generalized itemsets that need to have support larger than 1, we can assume that the conditions are independent. For m going to infinity, in the limit, independence does hold. It is important though to keep in mind that using the independence does increase the estimation of the probability we make. We will use the following approximation of $P(X_l^k)$:

$$P(X_l^k) \approx \prod_{l_1=0}^{l} \left[1 - (1 - p^{k-l_1}(1-p)^{l_1})^m\right]^{\binom{k}{l_1}}.$$

6.3   Illustration

We illustrate the approximation and the resulting formulas in the case $p = 0.5$. In the case $p = 0.5$, we can further simplify the formulas.

$$P(X_l^k) \approx \prod_{l_1=0}^{l} \left[1 - (1 - (0.5)^{k-l_1}(1-(0.5))^{l_1})^m\right]^{\binom{k}{l_1}}$$

$$= \prod_{l_1=0}^{l} \left[1 - (1 - (0.5)^k)^m\right]^{\binom{k}{l_1}}$$

$$= \left[1 - (1 - (0.5)^k)^m\right]^{\sum_{l_1=0}^{l}\binom{k}{l_1}}$$

$$= \left[1 - (1 - (0.5)^k)^m\right]^{d_l(k)}.$$

Hence, for ∞-freeness this yields the following bound:

$$P(X^k) = \left[1 - (1 - (0.5)^k)^m\right]^{2^k}.$$

6.4   Simulations

To empirically evaluate the proposed statistical bound, we performed some tests on the *Mushroom* dataset. This dataset contains characteristics from different species of mushrooms and can be found in the UCI Machine Learning Repository [3]. We use the Mushroom dataset because this dataset is small enough to find all 1-free and 2-free sets without having to impose support constraints. In this way, we can focus on l-freeness in isolation of the frequency constraint.

Bound on Length. In Table 3, the results of some simulations are given. The largest l-free set, the theoretical bound, and the statistical bound are given. The reported statistical bound is the largest value of k such that

$$\binom{n}{k} \times P(X_l^k) \geq 1.$$

Table 3. Largest ∞-free set, theoretical bound and statistical bound for some benchmark datasets

	Largest l-free			Theoretical Bound			Statistical Bound		
	$l=1$	$l=2$	$l=\infty$	$l=1$	$l=2$	$l=\infty$	$l=1$	$l=2$	$l=\infty$
mushroom	10	9	9	8123	126	12	16	12	10

That is, the largest k such that the expected number of l-free sets of length k is at least 1. We initialized p to 0.5, as we assume no prior knowledge on the supports of the items.

As can be seen in Table 3, in this situation, the statistical bound is better than the theoretical bound. Especially when l is small, the theoretical bound is far from realistic.

7   Related Work

In [7], the $\log_2(|\mathcal{D}|) + 1$-bound on the NDI-representation was already proven. In [13], it is showed, using a very similar technique, the upper bound $\log_2(|\mathcal{D}|)+1$ on the cardinality of generalized disjunction-free set. Notice that this claim is less strong than our claim that the largest ∞-free set is at most $\log_2(|\mathcal{D}|)$, and that ∞-free and generalized disjunction-free is the same. This discrepancy comes partially from a slight difference in definition between generalized disjunction-free sets in [15], and in [8]. The results in [13] are based on the definitions in [15], while the results in this paper are based on the definitions in [8]. We next explain the difference and motivate our choice to follow the definition of [8].

The original definition of generalized disjunction-free sets in [15] relies on the notion of disjunctive rules $I \setminus Y \to \bigvee Y$. A rule $I \setminus Y \to \bigvee Y$ holds in a transaction database if and only if every transaction that contains all items in $I \setminus Y$ also contains at least one item in Y. A set I is said to be generalized disjunction-free if for all *non-empty* $Y \subset I$, the rule $I \setminus Y \to \bigvee Y$ does not hold. Notice that the rule $I \setminus Y \to \bigvee Y$ holds if and only if $supp((I \setminus Y) \cup \overline{Y}) = 0$ [8]. Since $Y = \emptyset$ is not considered, a set is generalized disjunction-free according to [15] if and only if $supp((I \setminus Y) \cup \overline{Y}) \neq 0$ for all non-empty subsets Y of I. In [8], however, also the rule $I \to \emptyset$ is considered. The rule $I \to \emptyset$ only holds for sets with support equal to 0, since the right-hand side is the empty disjunction, which is always false. Therefore, the only sets for which there is a difference, are sets with support equal to 0. There are situations in which a set with support equal to 0 is generalized disjunction-free in the definition of [15], while it is not generalized disjunction-free in the definition of [8]. In our opinion, it is reasonable to say that an itemset with support 0 is not generalized disjunction-free, since the support of all its supersets can trivially be derived to be equal to 0. Therefore, in this paper, we used the definitions from [8]. This difference explains the difference between the bound of [13] and ours, as for a set I of size k to be generalized disjunction-free, there must not be 2^k transactions, but $2^k - 1$; $supp(I)$ itself can be 0. Therefore, I can only be generalized disjunction-free according to [15] if $|\mathcal{D}| \geq 2^k - 1$. This gives the bound $\log_2(|\mathcal{D}| + 1)$, which still improves the bound $\log_2(|\mathcal{D}|) + 1$ given in [13].

Notice incidentally that our bound on the l-free sets can easily be extended to a bound on frequent l-free sets, using a similar technique as in [13]. Let σ be the frequency threshold. A set I is frequent if at least σ transactions in the database contain all items of I. Therefore, for a set I of cardinality k to be frequent l-free, there need to be at least σ transactions containing all items of I, and 1 transaction for every other generalized itemset $X \cup \overline{Y}$ based on I. Hence,

$$I \text{ is } \sigma - \text{frequent } 1 - \text{free} \Rightarrow |\mathcal{D}| \geq \sum_{i=0}^{l} \binom{k}{i} + (\sigma - 1)$$

Another interesting link exists with [18]. In [18], the following question in the context of mining frequent itemsets with a standard levelwise approach is studied: given the current level and the current frequent itemsets, what is the maximal number of candidate itemsets that can be generated on the next level? The method described in [18] can be used at run-time to get ever better estimates on the size of the largest possible frequent itemset. Furthermore, the method also works for any collection of itemsets that is subset-closed. Hence, the results in [18] can also be used to get a run-time bound on the number and maximal cardinality of the l-free sets.

8   Conclusion and Future Work

In this paper an upper bound on the size of the database $\mathcal{D}$, in terms of the size of the set I is found, indicating that whenever that bound is not exceeded, the set I is no l-free set. For the case that $l = k$ the bound simplifies yielding a simple expression in terms of $|I|$ and $|\mathcal{D}|$ from which we can conclude that I is derivable or not.

The aim of this work was trying to find a simple expression only based on the size of the set I and the amounts of tuples in the database, to tell us if that set I is derivable or not. We have tried to find a reasonable approximation for the combinatorial bound that is easy to compute and useful for making conclusions. Because of the link between l-freeness and the other representations (freeness, disjunction-freeness and generalized disjunction-freeness) we can extend our results based on Proposition 1 and also make conclusions for these cases.

$$|\mathcal{D}| < k + 1 \Rightarrow I \text{ is not free}$$

$$|\mathcal{D}| < \frac{k^2 + k + 2}{2} \Rightarrow I \text{ is not disjunction} - \text{free}$$

$$|\mathcal{D}| < 2^k \Rightarrow I \text{ is not generalized disjunction} - \text{free}$$

An interesting topic for future research is to find better statistical bounds that include dependence between items.

References

1. R. Agrawal, T. Imilienski, and A. Swami. Mining association rules between sets of items in large databases. In *Proc. ACM SIGMOD Int. Conf. Management of Data*, pages 207–216, Washington, D.C., 1993.
2. R. Agrawal and R. Srikant. Privacy-preserving data mining. In *Proc. ACM SIGMOD Int. Conf. Management of Data*, pages 439–450, 2000.
3. C.L. Blake and C.J. Merz. *The UCI Repository of machine learning databases [http://www.ics.uci.edu/~mlearn/MLRepository.html]*. Irvine, CA: University of California, Department of Information and Computer Science, 1998.
4. J.-F. Boulicaut, A. Bykowski, and C. Rigotti. Approximation of frequency queries by means of free-sets. In *Proc. PKDD Int. Conf. Principles of Data Mining and Knowledge Discovery*, pages 75–85, 2000.
5. A. Bykowski and C. Rigotti. A condensed representation to find frequent patterns. In *Proc. PODS Int. Conf. Principles of Database Systems*, 2001.
6. T. Calders. Deducing bounds on the frequency of itemsets. In *EDBT Workshop DTDM Database Techniques in Data Mining*, 2002.
7. T. Calders. *Axiomatization and Deduction Rules for the Frequency of Itemsets*. PhD thesis, University of Antwerp, Belgium, 2003. http://win-www.ruca.ua.ac.be/u/calders/download/thesis.pdf.
8. T. Calders and B. Goethals. Minimal k-free representations of frequent sets. In *Proc. PKDD Int. Conf. Principles of Data Mining and Knowledge Discovery*, pages 71–82, 2002.
9. T. Calders and B. Goethals. Mining all non-derivable frequent itemsets. In *Proc. PKDD Int. Conf. Principles of Data Mining and Knowledge Discovery*, pages 74–85. Springer, 2002.
10. A. Evfimievski, R. Srikant, R. Agrawal, and J. Gehrke. Privacy preserving mining of association rules. In *Proc. KDD Int. Conf. Knowledge Discovery in Databases*, 2002.
11. S. Hettich and S. D. Bay. *The UCI KDD Archive. [http://kdd.ics.uci.edu]*. Irvine, CA: University of California, Department of Information and Computer Science, 1999.
12. M. Kryszkiewicz. Concise representation of frequent patterns based on disjunction-free generators. In *Proc. IEEE Int. Conf. on Data Mining*, pages 305–312, 2001.
13. M. Kryszkiewicz. Upper bound on the length of generalized disjunction free patterns. In *SSDBM*, 2004.
14. M. Kryszkiewicz and M. Gajek. Concise representation of frequent patterns based on generalized disjunction-free generators. In *Proc. PaKDD Pacific-Asia Conf. on Knowledge Discovery and Data Mining*, pages 159–171, 2002.
15. M. Kryszkiewicz and M. Gajek. Why to apply generalized disjunction-free generators representation of frequent patterns? In *Proc. International Syposium on Methodologies for Intelligent Systems*, pages 382–392, 2002.
16. H. Mannila and H. Toivonen. Multiple uses of frequent sets and condensed representations. In *Proc. KDD Int. Conf. Knowledge Discovery in Databases*, 1996.
17. N. Pasquier, Y. Bastide, R. Taouil, and L. Lakhal. Discovering frequent closed itemsets for association rules. In *Proc. ICDT Int. Conf. Database Theory*, pages 398–416, 1999.
18. J. Van den Bussche F. Geerts, B. Goethals. A tight upper bound on the number of candidate patterns. In *Proc. ICDM*, pages 155–162, 2001.

Mining Interesting XML-Enabled Association Rules with Templates

Ling Feng[1] and Tharam Dillon[2]

[1] Dept. of Computer Science, University of Twente, PO Box 217,
7500 AE Enschede, The Netherlands
ling@cs.utwente.nl
[2] Faculty of Information Technology, University of Technology, Sydney, Australia
tharam3@it.uts.edu.au

Abstract. XML-enabled association rule framework [FDWC03] extends the notion of associated items to XML fragments to present associations among trees rather than simple-structured items of atomic values. They are more flexible and powerful in representing both simple and complex structured association relationships inherent in XML data. Compared with traditional association mining in the well-structured world, mining from XML data, however, is confronted with more challenges due to the inherent flexibilities of XML in both structure and semantics. The primary challenges include 1) a more complicated hierarchical data structure; 2) an ordered data context; and 3) a much bigger data size. In order to make XML-enabled association rule mining truly practical and computationally tractable, in this study, we present a template model to help users specify the interesting XML-enabled associations to be mined. Techniques for template-guided mining of association rules from large XML data are also described in the paper. We demonstrate the effectiveness of these techniques through a set of experiments on both synthetic and real-life data.

1   Introduction

EXtensible Markup Language (XML) has emerged as the dominant standard for describing data and exchanging data on the Web. Its nested, self-describing structure provides a simple yet flexible means for applications to exchange data. Currently, XML is penetrating virtually all areas of Internet application programming, and bringing about a huge amount of data encoded in XML [SWK+01]. With the continuous growth in XML data sources, the ability to extract knowledge from them for decision support becomes increasingly important and desirable. Data mining, emerging during the late 1980s, has made great strides during the 1990s in transforming vast amounts of data into useful knowledge, and is expected to continue to flourish into the new millennium [HK01]. However, compared to the fruitful achievements in mining well-structured data such as relational databases and object-oriented databases, mining in the semi-structured XML world has received less exploration so far. The aim of this paper is to integrate the newly emerging XML technology into data mining technology, using association rule mining as a case in point.

B. Goethals and A. Siebes (Eds.): KDID 2004, LNCS 3377, pp. 66–88, 2005.

1.1   Challenges for Traditional Association Rule Mining

The problem of mining association rules was first introduced in [AIS93]. The most often cited application of association rules is market basket analysis using transaction databases from supermarkets. These databases contain sales transaction records, each of which details items bought by a customer in the transaction. Mining association rules is the process of discovering knowledge such as *80% of customers who bought diapers also bought beer.* which can be expressed as *diapers* $\Rightarrow$ *beer* (20%, 80%), where 80% is the *confidence level* of the rule, and 20% is the support level of the rule indicating how frequently the customers bought both diapers and beer. In general, an association rule takes the form $X \Rightarrow Y$ (s, c); where X and Y are sets of items, and s and c are support and confidence respectively.

In the XML Era, mining association rules is confronted with more challenges than in the traditional well-structured world due to the inherent flexibilities of XML in both structure and semantics. First, XML data has a more complex hierarchical structure than a database record. Second, elements in XML data have contextual positions, which thus carry the order notion. Third, XML data appears to be much bigger than traditional data. To address these challenges, the classic association rule mining framework originating with transactional databases needs to be re-examined.

1.2   Our Work

Under the traditional association rule framework, the basic unit of data to look at is database *record*, and the construct unit of a discovered association rule is *item* which has an *atomic value*. These lead us to the following two questions: 1) *what is the counterpart of record* and 2) *what is the counterpart of item* in mining association relationships from XML data?

In this study, we focus on rule detection from a collection of XML documents, which describe the same type of information (e.g., customer order, etc.). Hence, each of XML documents corresponds to a database record, and possesses a tree-like structure [Con01, Con00]. Accordingly, we extend the notion of associated item to an XML fragment (i.e., tree), and build up associations among trees rather than simple-structured items of atomic values. For consistency, we call each such kind of trees a **tree-structured item** to distinguish it from the traditional counterpart item. With the above extended notions, we propose an **XML-enabled association rule framework** in the paper. From both structural and semantic aspects, XML-enabled association rules are more powerful and flexible than the traditional ones.

While achieving considerable strengths in association description, XML-enabled association rule mining has meanwhile to resolve another serious problem. That is, XML data to be mined are usually much bigger than traditional transactional data. In order to make XML-enabled association mining truly practical and computationally tractable, we propose a template model to help such rule discovery. Previous work on traditional association rules demonstrated the effectiveness of constraint/query-based association mining [LNHP99, NLHP98, SVA97, TUA+98, MPC96, BP97, DT99]. It is applicable to XML-enabled association mining as well, since users may also have certain interesting XML portions in mind, from which to do the mining. For example, a shop owner may want to know *"which kind of people after purchasing some books tends to order a CD of the same title?"* With the presented template model, users can declare what kinds of associations are of interest so that the mining process can be more focused.

We believe that the synergy of the two areas has great potential in delivering more desirable and self-describing knowledge in manifold application areas over the Internet.

The remainder of the paper is organized as follows. We review some closely related work in Section 2. A formal definition of XML-enabled association rules and related measurements is given in Section 3. Section 4 introduces a template model for XML-enabled association rules. A performance study is presented Section 5. We conclude the paper and outline future work in Section 6.

2   Related Work

Since the problem of mining association rules was first introduced in [AIS93], a large amount of work has been done in various directions, including efficient, Apriori-like mining methods [AS94, KMR+94, SON95, PCY95a, PCY95b, PCY96, Toi96, ZPOL97, FSGM+98], mining generalized, multi-level, or quantitative association rules [SA95, SA96, HF95a, FMMT96b, FMMT96a, MY97, LSW97, KHC97, RS98], association rule mining query languages [MPC96, TUA+98], constraint-based rule mining [LNHP99, NLHP98, SVA97, TUA+98, BP97, HF95b, DT99], incremental maintenance of discovered association rules [CHNW96], parallel and distributed mining [AS96a, HKK97, CNFF96], mining correlations and causal structures [BMS97, SBMU98, SBMU00], cyclic, interesting and surprising association rule mining [ORS98, RMS98, CDF+00, CSD98], mining frequent itemsets with multiple supports [LHM99, WHH00], and so on.

In the following subsections, we review the work that is directly relevant to our study, particularly the languages for mining association rules from relational databases, constraint-based association rules, and mining associations from semi-structured data.

2.1   Mining Association Rules from Relational Databases

There were some proposals in the literature to tightly couple association rule mining with relational database systems [AS96b, HS95, TS98, and STA98]. [HS95] investigated the possibility to carry out association rule mining from relational tables using SQL query language. Following a set-oriented methodology, a simple mining algorithm, whose basic steps are sorting and merge scan join, was implemented in a relational database system. [TS98] developed SQL formulations based on SQL-92 and SQL-OR (SQL enhanced with object relational extensions) for mining generalized association rules. This work highlights that it is possible to express mining computations that are significantly more complicated than simple boolean associations in SQL using essentially the same framework [TS98].

Several languages extensions have also been proposed to extend SQL with mining operators. [MPC96] presented an SQL-like operator, named *MINE RULE*, for mining association rules. It unified the descriptions of all association-related mining problems. The procedural semantics of this operator were provided by means of an extended relational algebra. In the same year, [HFK+96] presented a data mining query language called *DMQL*, for relational databases. DMQL adopts an SQL-like syntax to facilitate high-level data mining and natural integration with relational query language SQL. [TUA+98] generalized the problem of association rule mining to query flocks, i.e., parameterized queries with a filter condition to eliminate values of the parameters that are uninteresting. By expressing the query flock in Datalog, the set of options for adapting a-priori, an optimization technique for association rule mining, can then be easily presented.

2.2 Constraint-Based Association Rule Mining

A frequently encountered phenomenon in data mining is that although a mining system may discover quite a large number of rules, many of them could be poorly focused or lack interest to users. To solve this kind of problem, *[FPSSU95]* proposed to specify a desired logical form of rules, called *metaquery*, to be discovered. In their study, a metaquery served as an important interface between human discoverers and the discovery system. A meta-rule-guided approach was further proposed in [HF95b], which applied meta-rules to discover multiple-level association rules. A meta-rule is in the form of $P_1 \wedge .... \wedge P_m \rightarrow Q_1 \wedge .... \wedge Q_m$, in which some of the predicates (and/or their variables) in the antecedent and/or consequent of the rule could be instantiated. Such kinds of meta-rules can be used to describe what forms of rules are expected and thus constrain the mining process.

In addition, some other kinds of constraints have been considered and integrated into association rule mining. [SVA97] utilized boolean expressions to constrain the presence or absence of associated items. [NLHP98, LNHP99] introduced a set of 1-variable and 2-variable constraint constructs, including domain, class and SQL-style aggregate constraints, to enable users to specify what kinds of mined rules are to be computed. Several pruning optimization techniques were also developed for mining constraint-based association rules [SVA97, NLHP98, LNHP99].

2.3 Discovery of Association Rules from Semi-structured Data

As the amount of semi-structured data available on the Web increases rapidly, extracting knowledge from semi-structured data appears to be an interesting topic. Unlike traditional well-structured data whose schema is known in advance, semi-structured data does not have a fixed schema, and the structure of data may be incomplete or irregular. One interesting work in the literature [WL97, WL98, WL00] was thus to discover similar structures among a collection of semi-structured objects, which describe the same type of information. A detailed algorithm for find structural associations inherent in semi-structured objects was given in [WL97, WHH00].

Finding structure-oriented association relationships, [SSC97] was proposed to mine association rules that relate structural data values to concepts extracted from unstructured and/or semi-structured data. An extended concept hierarchy (ECH) was applied to maintain parent, child, and sibling relationships between concepts, so that the generated rules can relate a given concept in the ECH and a given structured attribute value to the neighbours of the given concept in the ECH. The architecture and algorithm for mining such kinds of association rules were described in [SCH+98, SCHS99]. Based on the work of [WL97, SCH+98], [MU00] also proposed to first detect typical common structure of semi-structured data to filter out useless data portions, and then use the idea of concept hierarchy to generate extra rules in addition to the originally generated rules.

3   An XML-Enabled Association Rule Framework: Formulation

In this section, we define the XML-enabled association rule framework, starting with the tree structure of its associated items. The relationship among tree-structured items, as well as the containing relationship between a tree-structured item and an XML instance document, is then defined. They form the base for the definitions of XML-enabled association rules and related measurements.

3.1   Trees (Tree-Structured Items)

The basic construct in XML-enabled association rule framework is the structured item, which can be described using a rooted, ordered tree. In the paper, we also refer to tree-structured item as tree, which is made up of a series of nodes that are connected to each other through directed labeled edges. In addition, constraints can be defined over the nodes and edges. At an abstract level, a tree consists of the following five components:

- a set of nodes, N_{ode}, representing XML elements or attributes;
- a set of directed edges, E_{dge}, representing *ancestor-descendant* or *element-attribute* relationships between the nodes;
- a set of labels, L_{abel}, denoting different types of relationships between the nodes;
- a set of constraints, $C_{onstraint}$, defined over the nodes and edges;
- a unique root node $n_{root} \in N_{ode}$ of the tree.

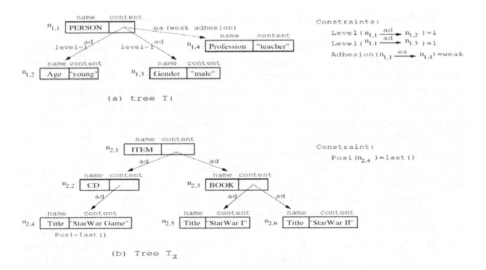

Fig. 1. Two Tree examples

3.1.1   Nodes

We categorize nodes into *basic nodes* and *complex nodes*. Basic nodes have no edges emanating from them. They are the leaf nodes in the tree diagram. Complex nodes are the internal nodes in the diagram. Each complex node has one or more labeled directed edges emanating from it, each associated with a label, and each going to another node. Figure 1 gives two tree examples. The example tree T_1 contains one complex node $n_{1,1}$, and three basic nodes $n_{1,2}$, $n_{1,3}$ and $n_{1,4}$. The example tree T_2 has three complex node $n_{2,1}$, $n_{2,2}$, $n_{2,3}$, and three basic nodes $n_{2,4}$, $n_{2,5}$ and $n_{2,6}$.

Each basic node has a *simple content*, taking values from the domains of basic data types like string, integer and float. A wildcard value $*$ is allowed to denote any content including an empty one.

On the contrary, the content of a complex node called *complex content* refers to some other nodes through directed labeled edges. Each edge connects two nodes, with a label stating the relationship between the two nodes. Before giving the formal definition of complex content, let's first define the concepts of connection, connection cluster and *connection cluster set* using the *cableset* approach presented in [Mor86, Sha91].

Definition 1. *A **connection** of a node $n \in N_{ode}$ is a pair (l, n'), where l is a label in L_{label} and is a node in N_{ode}, representing that node n is connected to node n' via relation l.*

Definition 2. *A **connection clusters** of a node $n \in N_{ode}$ is a pair (l, ns), where l is a label in L_{label} and ns are a sequence of nodes in N_{ode}, representing that node n is connected to each node in ns via relation l.*

Definition 3. *A **connection cluster set** of a node $n \in N_{ode}$ is a set of connection clusters, $\{(l_1, ns_1), ..., (l_k, ns_k)\}$, where $\forall i \forall j (1 \le i, j \le k)(i \ne j \Leftrightarrow l_i \ne l_j)$.*

Definition 4. *A **complex content** of a complex node is a connection cluster set.*

Definition 5. *A **node** $n \in N_{ode}$ is a tuple $(n_{name}, n_{content})$, consisting of a node name n_{name} and a node $n_{content}$.*

Example 1. *In Figure 1 (a), the basic nodes $n_{1,2}$, $n_{1,3}$ and $n_{1,4}$ have simple contents of string data type, which are "young", "male" and "teacher". The complex node $n_{1,1}$ links to a sequence of nodes $\langle n_{1,2}, n_{1,3} \rangle$ via relationship "ad" (denoting ancestor-descendant), and to basic node $n_{1,4}$ via relationship "ea" (denoting element-attribute). It thus has complex content $\{(ad, \langle n_{1,2}, n_{1,3} \rangle), (ea, \langle n_{1,4} \rangle)\}$.*

3.1.2   Labeled Edges

Each edge in a tree links two nodes, with a label specifying their relationship. We consider two kinds of links, namely, *ancestor-descendant* and *element-attribute* relationships, abbreviated as "ad" and "ea", respectively. Thus, $L_{label} = \{ad, ea\}$.

- An *antecedent-descendant* represents a structural relationship between an XML element and its nested subelement. It takes *parent-child* relationship as its special case.
- An *element-attribute* represents a relationship between an XML element and its attribute.

Definition 6. An **edge** $e \in E_{dge}$ is a triple $(l, n_{source}, n_{target})$, consisting of a label $l \in L_{abel}$ stating the link type, the source node of the edge $n_{source} \in N_{ode}$ and the target node of the edge $n_{target} \in N_{ode}$. An edge e can also be pictorially denoted as $"n_{source} \xrightarrow{\quad l \quad} n_{target}"$.

Example 2. In Figure 1 (a), the edge $"n_{1,1} \xrightarrow{ea} n_{1,4}"$ links PERSON element to its Profession attribute, and the edge $"n_{1,1} \xrightarrow{ad} n_{1,2}"$ links Person element to its child element Age.

3.1.3   Constraints
The following three kinds of constraints can be imposed upon nodes and edges to enhance the expressiveness of tree structured items.

1) **Level Constraint Over An *ad*-Labeled Edge** Level (e)

For an ancestor-descendant relationship $e = n_{source} \xrightarrow{ad} n_{target}$, the level constraint Level (e) = m (where m is an integer) indicates that n_{target} is the *m*-th descendant generation of n_{source}. When $m = 1$, it implies that n_{target} is a child of n_{source}. A wildcard level constraint value, denoted using *, (i.e., Level (e) = *) means any nested level among the ancestor and descendant nodes. In Figure1 (a), the constraints $Level(n_{1,1} \xrightarrow{ad} n_{1,2}) = 1$ and $Level(n_{1,1} \xrightarrow{ad} n_{1,3}) = 1$ require that both *Age* and *Gender* are direct children of PERSON element. We simplify the constraint expression by attaching the level value directly with the edge in the figure.

Unless explicitly specified, the default level constraint value over any ad relationship is *.

2) **Adhesion Constraint Over An *ea*-Labeled Edge** Adhesion(e)

Assume we have an edge $e = n_{source} \xrightarrow{ea} n_{target}$ pointing from an element node n_{source} to its attribute node n_{target}. The adhesion constraint Adhesion(e)=strong declares that n_{target} is a compulsory attribute node of element node n_{source}. An optional attribute node n_{target} of n_{source} can be specified using Adhesion(e)= weak. In Figure 1 (a), the weak adhesion constraint $Adhesion(n_{1,1} \xrightarrow{ea} n_{1,4}) = weak$ implies that *Profession* is an optional attribute of PERSON element.

The default adhesion constraint over an element-attribute relationship is strong.

3) **Position Constraint Over A Node** Posi(n)
The position constraint over a node n states its contextual position among all the nodes sharing the same ancestor and meanwhile having the same node name as *n*. A position constraint has the form of $Posi(n) = last() - v \mid first() + v \mid v$ (where *v* is a non-negative integer). Taking T_2 tree in Figure 1 (b) for example, $Posi(n_{2,4}) = last()$

implies the *Title* of the last ordered CD. A constraint like $Posi(n_{2,4}) = last() - 1$ means the title of the last to second ordered CD.

By default, a node n is assumed to have the first occurrence position, i.e., $Posi(n) = first()$. Its next sibling node n' with the same node name as n is thus constrained by $Posi(n) = first() + 1$ in turn.

Definition 7. A **well-formed tree** T is a tree that satisfies the following three conditions:

1) *T has only one unique tree node.*

2) *For any edge in T, it links two correctly-typed nodes. That is, if the link type is ea (element- attribute), the source is a complex node and the target is a basic node; and if the link type is ad (ancestor-descendant), the source is a complex node.*

3) *For any constraint in T, it is applied to a correctly-typed edged. That is, a level constraint only constrains an ad-labeled edge, and an adhesion constraint only constrains ea-labeled edge.*

In the paper, all the trees under discussion are assumed to be well-formed.

3.2   The Sub-tree (Sub-item) Relationship

We define the *sub-tree* (sub-item) *relationship* between two trees (tree-structured items) on the basis of *partial relationship* of tree nodes, which is defined as follows.

Definition 8. *Let $n = (n_{name}, n_{content})$ and $n' = (n'_{name}, n'_{content})$ be two nodes where $(n_{name} = n'_{name})$. n is a **part** of n', denoted as $(n \leq_{node} n')$, if and only if n and n' have the same position constraint $(Posi(n) = Posi(n'))$, and meanwhile satisfy one of the following requirements:*

[Case 1] *n is a basic node with a wildcard content * (i.e., $n_{content} = *$).*
[Case 2] *n and n' are basic nodes with the same simple content (i.e., $n_{content} = n'_{content}$).*
[Case 3] *n and n' are complex nodes, each with a connection cluster set as the content.*

For $\forall (l, \langle n_1 .... n_k \rangle) \in n_{content}$ there exits $(l, \langle n'_1,....n'_k \rangle) \in n'_{content}$ and a subsequence $\langle n'_{m_1},.....n'_{m_k} \rangle$ of $\langle n'_1,.....n'_k \rangle$, such that

$\forall i (1 \leq i \leq k) ((n_i \leq_{node} n'_{m_i}) \wedge (c(n \xrightarrow{l} n_i) = c(n \xrightarrow{l} n'_{m_i})))$. *Here, c denotes the level constraint if $l = ad$; and adhesion constraint if $l = ea$.*

Definition 9. *Given two trees (tree-structured items) whose root nodes are r and r', respectively. T is called a **sub-tree** (**sub-item**) of T', denoted as $(T \leq_{tree} T')$, if and only if there exists a node n' in T', such that $(r \leq_{node} n')$.*

Example 3. *Let's look at the trees in 1 and 2. T_3 is a sub-tree of T_1 ($T_3 \leq_{tree} T_1$) since root node $n_{3\,1}$ in T_3 is a part of node $n_{1,1}$ in T_1. Also, ($T_4 \leq_{tree} T_2$) and ($T_5 \leq_{tree} T_2$), since ($n_{4,1} \leq_{node} n_{2,3}$) and ($n_{5,1} \leq_{node} n_{2,1}$).*

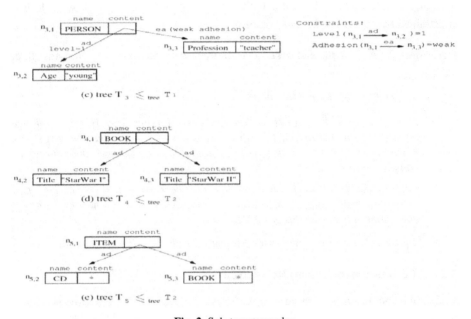

Fig. 2. Sub-tree examples

According to Definition 8 and 9, we can derive the following properties:

Property 1. *The sub-tree (sub-item) relationship has the following properties:*

1) *reflective: ($T \leq_{tree} T$)*
2) *transitive: ($T \leq_{tree} T'$) $\wedge$ ($T' \leq_{tree} T''$) $\wedge$ ($T \leq_{tree} T''$)*

Definition 10. *Two trees T and T' are **equal**, denoted as ($T =_{tree} T'$), if and only if ($T \leq_{tree} T'$) $\wedge$ ($T' \leq_{tree} T'$).*

3.3   The Containing Relationship Between an XML Document and a Tree (Tree-Structured Item)

Since an XML document possesses a hierarchical document structure, where an XML element may contain further embedded elements, and can be attached with a number of attributes, it is therefore frequently modeled using a labeled ordered tree in the literature [Con01, Con00]. Here, we first define when the content of an element/attribute in an XML document contains a tree, including a single node tree. Based on this, the *containing relationship* between an XML instance document and a tree (tree-structured item) can then be deduced.

Definition 11. *The **embedding** between an XML element/attribute and a tree (tree-structured item) T, rooted at node r = (r_{name}, $r_{content}$), can be recursively defined as follows:*

[Case 1] *r is a basic node * (i.e., tree T has only one node) with a simple content.*
*If a simple XML element/attribute 1) has a tag/attribute name r_{name} , 2) has a simple element/attribute value equal to $r_{content}$, and 3) satisfies the position constraint Posi(r), i.e., the Posi(r)-th occurrence in the host XML document, then this element/attribute **embeds** T .*
[Case 2] *r is a basic node (i.e., tree T contains only one node) with a wildcard content *.*
*If a simple XML element/attribute 1) has a tag/attribute name r_{name} , and 2) satisfies the position constraint Posi(r), then this element/attribute **embeds** T.*
[Case 3] *r is a complex node with a connection cluster set as its content.*
*If an XML element 1) has a tag name r_{name} , 2) for any connection cluster (l, n_1,...,n_k) ∈ $r_{content}$ where l = ea, the element has a set of attributes which embed the trees rooted at n_1 ,...,n_k respectively; and 3) for any connection cluster (l, n_1 ,...,n_k) ∈ $r_{content}$ where l = ad, the element has a sequence of ordered subelements which embed the trees rooted at n_1 ,...,n_k respectively, then this element **embeds** T . Note that the appearance of these attributes or subelements in the XML document must conform to the constraints Adhesion (r $\xrightarrow{ea}$ n_i) and Level (r $\xrightarrow{ad}$ n_i)($1 \leq i \leq k$) defined in T .*

Definition 12. *An XML document doc **contains** a tree (tree-structured item) T rooted at node r, denoted as (T $\in_{tree}$ doc), if and only if it has an XML element or attribute which embeds tree T .*

Example 4. *An XML instance document shown in Figure 3 contains all the example trees in Figure 1 and 2. Note that the order of CD and BOOK elements, as well as the order of Title subelements of BOOK conform to the orders declared in T_2,T_5 and T_4 .*
The position constraint over node $n_{2,4}$ posi($n_{2,4}$)=last() in T_2 is also satisfied by the given XML document.

Property 2. *If an XML document contains a tree (tree-structured item) T , then it contains any of its sub-tree (sub-item).*
The tenability of the property can be easily proven according to Definition 12 and 11.

3.4 A Formal Definition of XML-Enabled Association Rules

With the above notation, we are now in a position to formally define XML-enabled association rules and related measurements.

Definition 13. *Let $\mathcal{T}$ denote a set of trees (tree-structured items). An **XML-enabled association rule** is an implication of the form X ⇒ Y, which satisfies the following two conditions:*

1) X ⊂ $\mathcal{T}$, Y ⊂ $\mathcal{T}$, and X ∩ Y = φ ;
2) for ∀ T, T' ∈ (X ∪ Y), there exists no tree T'' such that (T'' $\leq_{tree}$ T) ∧ (T'' $\leq_{tree}$ T').

```
<ORDER>
   <PERSON  Profession="teacher"   Address="NL">
      <Name> Martin Louis </Name>
      <Age> young </Age>
      <Gender> male </Gender>
   </PERSON>
   <ITEM>
      <CD>
         <Title> Pop Music </Title>
         <Title> StarWar Game </Title>
      </CD>
      <BOOK>
         <Title> StarWar I </Title>
         <Title> StarWar II </Title>
         <Title> Lost Space </Title>
      </BOOK>
   </ITEM>
</ORDER>
```

Fig. 3. An XML document example

Different from classical association rules where associated items are usually denoted using simple structured data from the domains of basic data types, the items in XML-enabled association rules can have a hierarchical tree structure, as indicated by the first clause of the definition. Here, it is worth pointing out that when each of the tree-structured items contains only one basic root node, the XML-enabled association rules will degrade to the traditional association rules. The second clause of the definition requires that in an XML-enabled association rule, no common sub-trees exist within any two item trees in order to avoid redundant expression.

Figure 4 illustrates some XML-enabled association rule examples. Thanks to XML, XML-enabled association rules are more powerful than traditional association rules in capturing and describing association relationships. Such enhanced capabilities can be reflected from both a structural as well as a semantic point of view.

- Association items have hierarchical tree structures, which are more natural, informative and understandable (e.g., Rule 1 & 2 in Figure 4).
- Associated items inherently carry the *order* notion, enabling a uniform description of association and sequence patterns within one mining framework (e.g., Rule 1 states the sequence of books to be ordered, i.e., *"Star War I"* proceeding *"Star War II"* on a customer's order).
- Associated items can further be constrained by their context positions, hierarchical levels, and weak/strong adhesion in the corresponding XML data to be mined. (e.g., Rule 1 indicates the contextual appearances of BOOKs on the order).
- Association relationships among structures and structured-values can also be captured and described (e.g., Rule 2 states that a student orders some flowers from a shop, and leaves detailed content of FLOWER element such as the kind of flowers and quantity, etc. aside).

- Auxiliary information which states the occurrence context of association relationships can be uniformly self-described in the mining framework (e.g., Rule 1 indicates that only male people have such as order pattern).

Similar to traditional association rules, we use support and confidence as two major measurements for XML-enabled association rules.

Rule 1: If a "male" person orders a CD entitled "StarWar Game", he will immediately
        order two books in the order of "StarWar I" and "StarWar II".

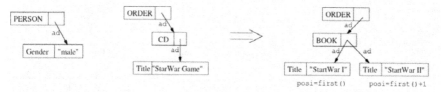

Rule 2: If a "student" living in "Tilburg" wants to order some flowers,
        s/he tends to go to a "small"-scaled shop located in "Tilburg South".

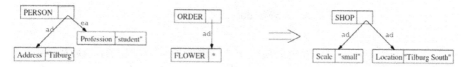

Fig. 4. XML-enabled association rule examples

Definition 14. *Let $\mathcal{D}$ be a set of XML documents. The support and confidence of an XML-enabled association rule $X \Rightarrow Y$ are defined:* $support(X \Rightarrow Y) = \dfrac{|D_{xy}|}{|\mathcal{D}|}$,

confidence $(X \Rightarrow Y) = \dfrac{|D_{xy}|}{|D_x|}$ *where* $D_{xy} = \{doc | \forall T \in (X \cup Y)(T \in_{tree} doc)\}$, *and* $D_x = \{doc | \forall T \in X (T \in_{tree} doc)\}$.

4   Template-Guided Mining of XML-Enabled Association Rules

In this section, we describe the techniques used to mine template-guided XML-enabled association rules. Our mining process proceeds in three steps.

Phase-1: Transforming Tree-Structured Data into Sequences

Different from traditional association mining where both transactions to be mined and associated items are of simple structure, XML-enabled association mining must deal with complex tree-structured data and their inherent association relationships. To prepare for efficient mining, our first step is to transform each tree in the XML database and each tree variable in the template expression into a sequence while preserving their hierarchical structures. We employ the encoding technique, recently developed by Wang et al. for efficient indexing and querying XML data [WPF03], to do such transformation. That is, a tree T is transformed into a sequence *Transform(T)* = $\langle(a_1 , p_1), (a_2 , p_2), \ldots, (a_n\ p_n)\rangle$, where a_i represents a node in the tree T , p_i is the path from the root node to node a_i, and $a_1 , a_2 , \ldots,$ an is the preorder traversal of the tree [WPF03]. For example, Doc_1 (Figure 5) can be encoded into a sequence like:

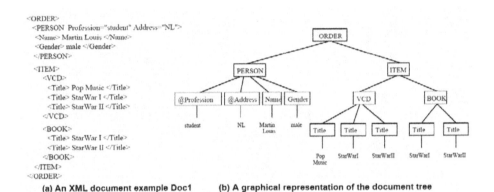

(a) An XML document example Doc1   (b) A graphical representation of the document tree

Fig. 5. An XML document example Doc_1

Transform(Doc1) = $\langle$(ORDER, $\in$), (PERSON, ORDER), (@Profession, ORDER/PERSON), ("student", ORDER/PERSON/@Profession), (@Address, ORDER/PERSON), ("NL", ORDER/ PERSON/@Address), (Name, ORDER/PERSON), ("Martin Louis", ORDER/ PER- SON/Name), (Gender, ORDER/PERSON), ("male", ORDER/PERSON/Gender), (ITEM, ORDER), (VCD, ORDER/ITEM), (Title, ORDER/ITEM/VCD), ("Pop Music", ORDER/ITEM/VCD/Title), (Title, ORDER/ITEM/VCD), ("StarWar I", ORDER/ITEM/VCD/Title), (Title, ORDER/ITEM/VCD), ("StarWar II", ORDER/ ITEM/VCD/Title), (BOOK, ORDER/ITEM), (Title, ORDER/ITEM/BOOK), ("StarWar I", ORDER/ITEM/BOOK/Title), (Title, ORDER/ITEM/BOOK),("StarWar II", ORDER/ITEM/BOOK/Title)$\rangle$

Similarly, we can convert the three tree variables in Template 1 (Figure 6) to the following three sequences: *Transform(∇T_1) = $\langle$ (ORDER, $\in$), (VCD, ORDER), (Title, ORDER/VCD), (?, ORDER/VCD/Title)$\rangle$; Transform(∇T_2)= $\langle$(ORDER, $\in$), (BOOK, ORDER), (Title, ORDER/BOOK), (?, ORDER/BOOK/Title)$\rangle$; Transform(∇T_3) = $\langle$(PERSON, $\in$), (@Profession, PERSON), (?, PERSON/ @Profession)$\rangle$.*

Phase-2: Discovering Structurally Containing Relationships by Sub-sequence Matching

With the structure-encoded sequences, checking the embedding relationship (i.e., whether an XML document contains a template tree variable) degrades to non-contiguous subsequence matching. Let *Doc* and ∇T be an XML document and a

Template 1: Of what profession do people like to order a book and meanwhile the same titled VCD?

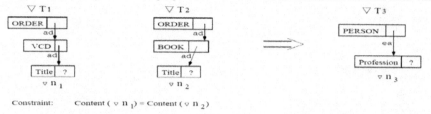

Constraint: Content (∨ n₁) = Content (∨ n₂)

Template 2: Which kind of people order some books after ordering a VCD entitled "StarWar I"?

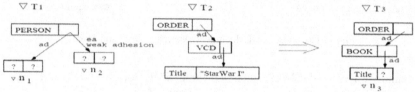

Fig. 6. Template examples

template   tree   variable,   respectively.   Assume   that
$Transform(\nabla T) = \langle (a_1, p_1), (a_2, p_2), \dots (a_n, p_n) \rangle$ and $Transform(\nabla T)$ =
$\langle (a'_1, p'_1), (a'_2, p'_2), \dots, (a'_m, p'_m) \rangle$. *Doc* structurally contains ∇T if and only if
$a'_1, \dots, a'_m$ is a non-contiguous subsequence of $a_1, \dots, a_n$ and p'_i is a non-contiguous subsequence of p_j where ($a'_i = a_j$). Here, symbol ? in a template tree variable is treated as a wildcard which can match any node label in a document. In the example, $Transform(\nabla T_1)$ is an non-contiguous subsequence of $Transform(Doc_1)$, thus, Doc_1 structurally contains ∇T_1. Also, the same for ∇T_2 and ∇T_3. Given a mining template, the output of this phase is a subset of XML documents in the database that structurally contain all its tree variables.

Phase-3: Correlating Concrete Contents with Structures

For each document obtained after Phase-2, our last step is to instantiate every symbol ? in the template expression with a concrete content extracted from the document, which also observes content constraint(s) as indicated by the template. For instance, conforming to Template 1 (Figure 6) which requires Content(∇n_1) = Content(∇n_2), two possible content instantiation combinations can be done based on Doc_1, i.e.,

Instantiation Combination 1: Content(∇n_1) = "*Star War I*",
       Content(∇n_2) = "*Star War I*", Content(∇n_3) = "*student*".
Instantiation Combination 2: Content(∇n_1) = "*Star War II*",
       Content(∇n_2) = "*Star War II*", Content(∇n_3) = "*student*".

```
<ORDER>
  <PERSON Profession="student" Address="NL">
    <Name> Alice Brown </Name>
    <Gender> female </Gender>
  </PERSON>
  <ITEM>
    <VCD>
      <Title> StarWar I </Title>
    </VCD>

    <BOOK>
      <Title> StarWar I </Title>
    </BOOK>
  </ITEM>
</ORDER>
```

(a) XML document Doc2

```
<ORDER>
  <PERSON Profession="artist" Address="NL">
    <Name> Joe Smith </Name>
    <Gender> male </Gender>
  </PERSON>
  <ITEM>
    <VCD>
      <Title> StarWar I </Title>
    </VCD>

    <BOOK>
      <Title> StarWar I </Title>
      <Title> Lord of the Ring </Title>
    </BOOK>
  </ITEM>
</ORDER>
```

(b) XML document Doc3

Fig. 7. Two more XML document examples: Doc_2 and Doc_3

Assume we have a database containing three XML documents Doc_1 (Figure 5), Doc_2 , and Doc_3 (Figure 7). To count the support of each such kind of con- tent instantiations, and thus the association rules, we employ the hash technique to hash all the content instantiation combinations extracted from all the XML documents obtained after Step 2 into a hash table, as illustrated in Figure 8 Suppose *HashFunc("Star War I", "Star War I", "student") = 1, HashFunc("Sta rWar I", "StarWar I", "artist") = 1*, and *HashFunc("Star War II", "Star War II", "student") = 4*.

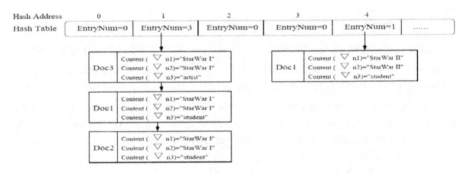

Fig. 8. Hash table for all possible content instantiation combinations extracted from Doc_1, Doc_2 and Doc_3

Note that the entry list underlying each bucket of the hash table is always maintained in a sorted order while we hash each content instantiation combination into the hash table. In this way, the same content instantiation combinations can adjacently stay together, making the support counting easy and efficient. For example, according to the hashing result in Figure 8, *Count("Star War I", "Star War I", "artist") = 1, Count("Star War I", "Star War I", "student") = 2*, and *Count("Star War I", "Star War II", "student") = 1*. Figure 9 outlines the support and confidence of the obtained association rules which conform to Template 1.

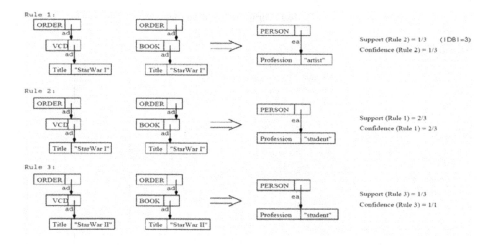

Fig. 9. Discovered XML-enabled association rules that conforms to Template 1

5   Performance Study

To assess the performance of the mining method, we have conducted a set of experiments on both synthetic and real-life data. The method used to generate synthetic XML data and templates is described in Subsection 5.1, and Subsection 5.2 presents some experimental results from this. Results obtained from real-life XML data are reported in Subsection 5.3.

5.1   Generation of Synthetic XML Data and Templates

Synthetic Data Generation. We first build a complete k-ary master tree, from which a number of subtrees are then generated to construct our database. The master tree has totally *total_label* different node labels. We allow multiple nodes in a tree to have the same label. Parameter *fanout* and *depth* specify the fanout and depth of the master tree, respectively. From the master tree, we generate *total_tree_in_db* number of subtrees. Each subtree has db tree node num nodes, which are randomly picked up from the master tree. The root of the master tree is always selected to ensure node connectivity within each subtree. This also accords with the basic assumption of our study, aiming at rule detection from a collection of XML documents, which describe the same type of information (e.g., customer order, etc.).

Template Generation. Each template consists of a set of tree variables, the number of which is indicated by the parameter *template_length*. To generate each tree variable, we first determine its size (i.e., the total number of tree nodes) via a poisson distribution function, whose maximal value should not exceed *db_tree_node_num* ∗ *template_tree_size_percent*. The nodes of the tree variable are picked up from the master tree in the same way as those of the database subtrees. The probability to assign symbol ? instead of a concrete label to a node, representing an unknown element/attribute name or an unknown content, is *template_unknown_percent*.

Table 1 summarizes all the parameters used and their settings.

Table 1. Parameters and Setting

Parameter	Meaning	Setting	Default
Master Tree Parameters			
fanout	fanout of the master tree	3	3
depth	depth of the master tree	4	4
total_label	number of different node labels in the master tree	40	40
Database Parameters			
total_tree_in_db	number of trees in the database	10K-100K	10K
db_tree_node_num	size of each tree in the database	18-22	20
Template Parameters			
template_length	number of tree variables in a template	2-4	3
template_tree_size_percent	maximum size of a tree variable in a template with respect to *db_tree_node_num*	50%	50%
template_unknown_percent	probability to have an unknown label in a tree variable	70%	70%
Hash Table Parameter			
hash_table_size	size of hash table with respect to *total_label*	25%-125%	100%

5.2 Experiments with Synthetic XML Data

Two sets of experiments are performed on synthetically generated data. The machine used is a Sun UltraSPARC-II with a 440 MHz CPU clock rate and 256 MB main memory.

I. Scale-Up Behavior. We study the scalability of template-guided XML- enabled association rule mining while we increase the database size (*total_tree_in_db*) from 10K to 100K and the tree size (*db_tree_node_num*) from 18 to 22, respectively. Three templates of different lengths (i.e., containing different number of tree variables) are used serving as the mining guidance. The support threshold and hash table size are set to 1% and 100% respectively throughout the experiments. As shown in Figure 10(a), the mining under the guidance of the longest template (*template_length=4*) always performs the best among the three. The reason is obvious: a longer template can better restrict the search space, thus reduce the mining time. For instance, when *tree_num_in_db*=80K, the execution times under templates of length 2, 3, and 4 are 123.6 sec, 30.4 sec, and 18.7 sec, respectively. When a template indicates 3 or more desirable tree variables, the mining time scales quite well with both the database size and tree size.

II. Effect of the Size of the Hash Table. To investigate the impact of the hash table size on content and structure association discovery, we vary the hash table size from 25% to 125%, with respect to the total number of different node labels (*total_label*) in the database. Let support threshold be 1%. Total *tree_in_db* = 10K and *db_tree_node_num* = 20. From the result presented in Figure 10(b), the mining times exhibit a decreasing tendency when we enlarge the hash table. This is because with more hash entries, the problem of hash collision can be alleviated a little more. Different content instantiation combinations have a higher probability to be distributed to different hash buckets, making the support counting process faster.

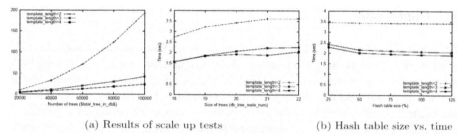

(a) Results of scale up tests   (b) Hash table size vs. time

Fig. 10. Experiments on synthetic data

5.3   Application to Real-Life XML Data

We test the template-guided XML-enabled association mining method on the real-life DBLP data, which contains a huge number of bibliography entries in XML[1]. Suppose we are interested in finding out who publishes frequently together with *Michael J. Franklin* in conference proceedings. Figure 11 is the template we use while mining the DBLP data. To restrict the mining space, we pre-process the original big DBLP file of size 187 MB by running an XQuery to extract in total 284663 fragments enclosed by <inproceedings>......</inproceedings>. After discovering 52 XML segments which structurally contain the two tree variables of the template, i.e., conference papers written by *Michael J. Franklin*, we hash the corresponding co-authors' names into a hash table, and obtain the following rules when the support threshold is set to 0.002%.

Template: Find out who publishes frequently together with "Michael J. Franklin" in conference proceedings.

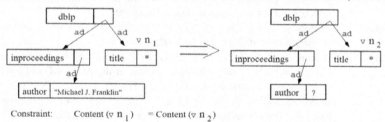

Fig. 11. Template for experiment on DBPL data

Here are some rules, where author is

$$\text{"Stanley B. Zdonik" } (support = \frac{10}{284663} = 0.004\%, confidences = \frac{10}{52} = 19.2\%)$$

$$\text{"Michael J. Franklin" } (support = \frac{7}{284663} = 0.003\%, confidences = \frac{7}{52} = 13.5\%)$$

$$\text{"Samuel Madden" } (support = \frac{6}{284663} = 0.003\%, confidences = \frac{6}{52} = 11.5\%)$$

---

[1] It is available at http://dblp.uni-trier.de/xml/

6   Conclusion

From a structural as well as a semantic point of view, XML-enabled association rule framework is more flexible and powerful than the traditional one in representing both simple and complex structured association relationships. However, mining XML-enabled association relationships poses more challenges for efficient processing than mining traditional association rules. To address the trade-off between the enhanced capabilities on the one side and mining performance on the other side, we present a template model for XML-enabled association mining. We discuss techniques used in mining template-guided XML-enabled association rules, and evaluate the performance on both synthetic and real-life XML data. We are currently investigating properties related to XML-enabled association mining.

References

[AIS93]   R. Agrawal, T. Imielinski, and A. Swami. Mining association rules between sets of items in large databases. In Proc. of the ACM SIGMOD Intl. Conf. on Management of Data, pages 207-216, Washington D.C., USA, May 1993.

[AS94]   R. Agrawal and R. Srikant. Fast algorithms for mining association rules. In Proc. of the 20th Intl. Conf. on Very Large Data Bases, pages 478-499, Santiago, Chile, September 1994.

[AS96a]   R. Agrawal and J.C. Shafer. Parallel mining of association rules. IEEE Transactions on Knowledge and Data Engineering, 8(6):962-969, 1996.

[AS96b]   R. Agrawal and K. Shim. Developing tightly-coupled data mining applications on a relational database system. In Proc. of the 2nd. International Conference on Knowledge Discovery and Data Mining, '96.

[BC00]   A. Bonifati and S. Ceri. Comparative analysis of five XML query languages. SIGMOD Record, 29(1):68-79, 2000.

[BMS97]   S. Brin, R. Motwani, and C. Silverstein. Beyond market basket: generalizing association rules to cor- relations. In Proc. of the ACM SIGMOD Intl. Conf. on Management of Data, pages 265-276, Tucson, Arizona, USA, June 1997.

[BP97]   E. Baralis and G. Psaila. Designing templates for mining association rules. Journal of Intelligent Infor- mation Systems, 9(1):7-32, 1997.

[CDF+00]   E. Cohen, M. Datar, S. Fujiwara, A. Gionis, P. Indyk, R. Motwani, J.D. Ullman, and C. Yang. Finding interesting associations without support pruning. In Proc. Intl. Conf. Data Engineering, pages 489-499, California, USA, March 2000.

[CHNW96]   D. Cheung, J. Han, V. Ng, and C.Y. Wong. Maintenance of discovered association rules in large databases: an incremental updating technique. In Proc. of the Intl. Conf. on Data Engineering, pages 106-114, New Orleans, Louisiana, USA, February 1996.

[Con00]   World Wide Web Consortium. The XML Data Model. http://www.w3.org/XML/ Datamodel.html/, January 2000.

[Con01]   World Wide Web Consortium. Document Object Model (DOM). http://www.w3.org/DOM/, April 2001.

[Con02a]   World Wide Web Consortium. XQuery 1.0: An XML Query Language. http://www.w3.org/TR/ xquery/, April 2002.

[Con02b]	World Wide Web Consortium. XQuery 1.0 and XPath 2.0 Functions and Operators. http://www.w3.org/TR/ xquery-operators/, April 2002.
[CNFF96]	D.W. Cheung, V.T. Ng, A.W. Fu, and Y.J. Fu. Efficient mining of association rules in distributed databases. IEEE Transactions on Knowledge and Data Engineering, 8(6):911-922, 1996.
[CSD98]	S. Chakrabarti, S. Sarawagi, and B. Dom. Mining surprising patterns using temporal description length. In Proc. of the 24th Intl. Conf. on Very Large Data Bases, pages 606-617, New York, USA, August 1998.
[DT99]	L. Dehaspe and H. Toivonen. Discovery of frequent DATALOG patterns. Data Mining and Knowledge Discovery, 3(1):7-36, 1999.
[FDWC03]	L. Feng, T. Dillon, H. Weigand, and E. Chang. An xml-enabled association rule framework. In Proc. of the 14th Intl. Conf. on Database and Expert Systems Applications, pages 88–97, Prague, Czech Republic, September 2003.
[FMMT96a]	T. Fukuda, Y. Morimoto, S. Morishita, and T. Tokuyama. Data mining using two-dimensional optimized association rules: Schema, algorithms, and visualization. In Proc. of the ACM SIGMOD Intl. Conf. on Management of Data, pages 13-23, Montreal, Canada, June 1996.
[FMMT96b]	T. Fukuda, Y. Morimoto, S. Morishita, and T. Tokuyama. Mining optimized association rules for numeric attributes. In Proc. of the 15th ACM SIGACT-SIGMOD-SIGART Symposium on Principles of Database Systems, pages 182-191, Montreal, Canada, June 1996.
[FPSSU95]	U.M. Fayyad, G. Piatetsky-Shapiro, P. Smyth, and R. Uthurusamy, editors. Advances in Knowledge Discovery and Data Mining, chapter Meta-queries for data mining (W. Shen, K. Ong, B. Mitbander and C. Zaniolo). AAAI/MIT Press, 1995.
[FSGM+98]	M. Fang, N. Shivakumar, H. Garcia-Molina, R. Motwani, and J.D. Ullman. Computing iceberg queries efficiently. In Proc. of the 24th Intl. Conf. on Very Large Data Bases, pages 299-310, New York, USA, August 1998.
[HF95a]	J. Han and Y. Fu. Discovery of multiple-level association rules from large databases. In Proc. of the 21st Intl. Conf. on Very Large Data Bases, pages 420-431, Zurich, Switzerland, September 1995.
[HF95b]	J. Han and Y. Fu. Meta-rule-guided mining of association rules in relational databases. In Proc. of the 1st Intl. Workshop on Integration of Knowledge Discovery with Deductive and Object-Oriented Databases, pages 39-46, Singapore, December 1995.
[HFK+96]	J. Han, Y. Fu, K. Koperski, W. Wang, and O. Zaiane. DMQL: a data mining query language for relational databases. In Proc. of the ACM SIGMOD Workshop on Research Issues on Data Mining and Knowledge Discovery, Montreal, Canada, June 1996.
[HK01]	J. Han and M. Kamber. Data Mining: Concepts and Techniques. Morgan Kaufmann Publishers, 2001.
[HKK97]	E.-H. Han, G. Karypis, and V. Kumar. Scalable parallel data mining for association rules. In Proc. of the ACM SIGMOD Intl. Conf. on Management of Data, pages 277-288, Tucson, Arizona, USA, June 1997.
[HS95]	M. Houtsma and A. Swami. Set-oriented mining of association rules. In Proc. of the International Conference on Data Engineering, Taipei, Taiwan, March 1995.

[KHC97]   M. Kamber, J. Han, and J.Y. Chiang. Metarule-guided mining of multi-dimensional association rules using data cubes. In Proc. of the International Conference on Knowledge Discovery and Data Mining, pages 207-210, California, USA, August 1997.

[KMR+94]   M. Klemettinen, H. Mannila, P. Ronkainen, H. Toivonen, and A.I. Verkamo. Finding interesting rules from large sets of discovered association rules. In Proc. of the 3rd Intl. Conf. on Information and Knowledge Management, pages 401-408, Gaithersburg, Maryland, November 1994.

[LHM99]   B. Liu, W. Hsu, and Y. Ma. Mining association rules with multiple minimum supports. In Proc. ACM SIGKDD Intl. Conf. Knowledge Discovery and Dara Mining, pages 125-134, California, USA, August 1999.

[LNHP99]   L.V.S. Lakshmanan, R. Ng, J. Han, and A. Pang. Optimization of constrained frequent set queries with 2-variable constraints. In Proc. of the ACM SIGMOD Intl. Conf. on Management of Data, pages 157-168, USA, June 1999.

[LSW97]   B. Lent, A. Swami, and J. Widom. Clustering association rules. In Proc. of the Intl. Conf. on Data Engineering, pages 220-231, Birmingham, England, April 1997.

[Mor86]   E.J.M. Morgado. Semantic networks as abstract data types. Technical Report Ph.D. thesis, Technical Report 86-1, Department of Computer Science, SUNY at Buffalo, NY, 1986.

[MPC96]   R. Meo, G. Psaila, and S. Ceri. A new SQL-like operator for mining association rules. In Proc. of the 22th Intl. Conf. on Very Large Data Bases, pages 122-133, Mumbai, India, September 1996.

[MU00]   K. Maruyama and K. Uehara. Mining association rules from semi-structured data. In Proc. of the ICDCS Workshop of Knowledge Discovery and Data Mining in the World-Wide Web, Taiwan, April 2000.

[MY97]   R.J. Miller and Y. Yang. Association rules over interval data. In Proc. of the ACM SIGMOD Intl. Conf. on Management of Data, pages 452-461, Tucson, Arizona, USA, June 1997.

[NLHP98]   R. Ng, L.V.S. Lakshmanan, J. Han, and A. Pang. Exploratory mining and pruning optimizations of constrained association rules. In Proc. of the ACM SIGMOD Intl. Conf. on Management of Data, pages 13-24, Seattle, Washington, June 1998.

[ORS98]   B. Ozden, A. Ramaswamy, and A. Silberschatz. Cyclic association rules. In Proc. of the Intl. Conf. on Data Engineering, pages 412-421, Florida, USA, February 1998.

[PCY95a]   J.-S. Park, M.-S. Chen, and P.S. Yu. An effective hash based algorithm for mining association rules. In Proc. of the ACM SIGMOD Intl. Conf. on Management of Data, pages 175-186, San Jose, CA, May 1995.

[PCY95b]   J.-S. Park, M.-S. Chen, and P.S. Yu. Mining association rules with adjustable accuracy. Technical Report IBM Research Report, 1995.

[PCY96]   J.-S. Park, M.-S. Chen, and P.S. Yu. Data mining for path traversal patterns in a web environment. In Proc. of the 16th Conference on Distributed Computing Systems, pages 385-392, Hong Kong, May 1996.

[RMS98]   S. Ramaswamy, S. Mahajan, and A. Silberschatz. On the discovery of interesting patterns in association rules. In Proc. of the 24th Intl. Conf. on Very Large Data Bases, pages 368-379, New York, USA, August 1998.

[RS98]   R. Rastogi and K. Shim. Mining optimized association rules with categorical and numerical attributes. In Proc. of the Intl. Conf. on Data Engineering, pages 503-512, Florida, USA, February 1998.

[SA95]   R. Srikant and R. Agrawal. Mining generalized association rules. In Proc. of the 21st Intl. Conf. on Very Large Data Bases, pages 409-419, Zurich, Switzerland, September 1995.

[SA96]   R. Srikant and R. Agrawal. Mining quantitative association rules in large relational tables. In Proc. of the ACM SIGMOD Intl. Conf. on Management of Data, pages 1-12, Montreal, Canada, June 1996.

[SBMU98]   C. Silverstein, S. Brin, R. Motwani, and J.D. Ullman. Scalable techniques for mining causal structures. In Proc. of the 24th Intl. Conf. on Very Large Data Bases, pages 594-605, New York, USA, August 1998.

[SBMU00]   C. Silverstein, S. Brin, R. Motwani, and J.D. Ullman. Scalable techniques for mining causal structures. Data Mining and Knowledge Discovery, 4(2/3):163-192, 2000.

[SCH+98]   L. Singh, B. Chen, R. Haight, P. Scheuermann, and K. Aoki. A robust system architecture for mining semi-structured data. In Proc. of the 4th. International Conference on Knowledge Discovery and Data Mining, pages 329-333, New York, USA, August 1998.

[SCHS99]   L. Singh, B. Chen, R. Haight, and P. Scheuermann. An algorithm for constrained association rule mining in semi-structured data. In Proc. of the 3rd. Pacific-Asia Conference on Knowledge Discovery and Data Mining, pages 148-158, Beijing, China, April 1999.

[Sha91]   S.C. Shapiro. Cables, paths, and subconscious reasoning in propositional semantic networks (chapter). In Principles of Semantic Networks - Explorations in the Representation of Knowledge, Editor J.F. Sowa, 1991.

[SON95]   A. Savasere, E. Omiecinski, and S. Navathe. An efficient algorithm for mining association rules in large databases. In Proc. of the 21st Intl. Conf. on Very Large Data Bases, pages 432-443, Zurich, Switzerland, Sept '95.

[SSC97]   L. Singh, P. Scheuermann, and B. Chen. Generating association rules from semi-structured documents using an extended concept hierarchy. In Proc. of the 6th. International Conference on Information and Knowledge Management, pages 193-200, Las Vegas, USA, Nov '97.

[STA98]   S. Sarawagi, S. Thomas, and R. Agrawal. Integrating association rule mining with databases: Alternatives and implications. In Proc. of the International Conference on Management of Data, USA, '98.

[SVA97]   R. Srikant, Q. Vu, and R. Agrawal. Mining association rules with item constraints. In Proc. of the 3rd Intl. Conf. on Knowledge Discovery and Data Mining, pages 67-73, Newport Beach, California, August '97.

[SWK+01]   A. Schmidt, F. Waas, M.L. Kersten, D. Florescu, M.J. Carey, I. Manolescu, and R. Busse. Why and how to benchmark XML database. SIGMOD Record, 30(3):27-32, 2001.

[Toi96]   H. Toivonen. Sampling large databases for association rules. In Proc. of the 22th Conference on Very Large Data Bases, pages 134-145, Mumbai, India, September 1996.

[TS98]   S. Thomas and S. Sarawagi. Mining generalized association rules and sequential patterns using SQL queries. In Proc. of the 4th. International Conference on Knowledge Discovery and Data Mining, New York, USA, August 1998.

[TUA+98]   D. Tsur, J.D. Ullman, S. Abitboul, C. Clifton, R. Motwani, and S. Nestorov. Query flocks: a generalization of association-rule mining. In Proc. of the ACM SIGMOD Intl. Conf. on Management of Data, pages 1-12, Seattle, Washington, June 1998.

[WHH00]   K. Wang, Y. He, and J. Han. Mining frequent itemsets using support constraints. In Proc. 26st Intl. Conf. Very Large Data Bases, pages 43-52, Cairo, Egypt, September 2000.

[WPF03]   20. H. Wang, S. Park, W. Fan, and P. Yu. ViST: A dynamic index method for querying XML data by tree structures. In Proc. Of the ACM SIGMOD Intl. Conf. on Management of Data, pages 110–121, California, USA, June 2003.

[WL97]   K. Wang and H. Liu. Schema discovery for semi-structured data. In Proc. of the 3rd. International Conference on Knowledge Discovery and Data Mining, pages 271-274, California, USA, August 1997.

[WL98]   K. Wang and H. Liu. Discovering typical structures of documents: a road map approach. In Proc. Of the ACM SIGIR International Conference on Research and Development in information Retrieval, pages 146-154, Melbourne, Australia, August 1998.

[WL00]   K. Wang and H. Liu. Discovering structural association of semistructured data. IEEE Transactions on Knowledge and Data Engineering, 12(2):353-371, 2000.

[ZPOL97]   M.J. Zaki, S. Parthasarathy, M. Ogihara, and W. Li. New algorithms for fast discovery of association rules. In Proc. of the 3rd International Conference on Knowledge Discovery and Data Mining, pages 283-286, Newport Beach, CA, USA., August 1997.

Database Transposition for Constrained (Closed) Pattern Mining

Baptiste Jeudy[1] and François Rioult[2]

[1] Équipe Universitaire de Recherche en Informatique de St-Etienne,
Université de St-Etienne, France
baptiste.jeudy@univ-st-etienne.fr
[2] GREYC - CNRS UMR 6072,
Université de Caen Basse-Normandie, France
francois.rioult@info.unicaen.fr

Abstract. Recently, different works proposed a new way to mine patterns in databases with pathological size. For example, experiments in genome biology usually provide databases with thousands of attributes (genes) but only tens of objects (experiments). In this case, mining the "transposed" database runs through a smaller search space, and the Galois connection allows to infer the closed patterns of the original database. We focus here on constrained pattern mining for those unusual databases and give a theoretical framework for database and constraint transposition. We discuss the properties of constraint transposition and look into classical constraints. We then address the problem of generating the closed patterns of the original database satisfying the constraint, starting from those mined in the "transposed" database. Finally, we show how to generate all the patterns satisfying the constraint from the closed ones.

1 Introduction

Frequent pattern mining is now well mastered, but these patterns, like association rules, reveal to be too numerous for the experts and very expensive to compute. They have to be filtered or constrained. However, mining and constraining have to be done jointly (pushing the constraint) in order to avoid combinatorial explosion [14]. Mining under complex constraint has become today a hot topic and the subject of numerous works (e.g., [14, 7, 16, 20, 10, 8]). Moreover, new domains are interested in our applications, and data schemes vary consequently. In genome biology, biological experiments are very expensive and time consuming. Therefore, only a small number of these experiments can be processed. However, thanks to new devices (such as biochips), experiments can provide the measurements of the activity of thousands of genes. This leads to databases with lots of columns (the genes) and few rows (the experiments).

Numerous works present efficient algorithms which mine the patterns satisfying a user defined constraint in large databases. This constraint can combine minimum and maximum frequency threshold together with other syntactical

B. Goethals and A. Siebes (Eds.): KDID 2004, LNCS 3377, pp. 89–107, 2005.

constraints. These algorithms are designed for databases with up to several millions of rows. However, their complexity is exponential in the number of columns and thus they are not suited for databases with too many columns, like those encountered in genome biology.

Recently, two propositions were done to solve this problem: instead of mining the original database, these algorithms work on the "transposed" database, i.e., columns of the original database become rows in the "transposed" database and rows becomes columns (this is indeed the same database but with a different representation). Therefore the "transposed" database has significantly less columns than the original one. The CARPENTER algorithm [18] is specifically designed for mining the frequent closed patterns, and our proposition [23, 24] uses a classical algorithm for mining closed patterns with a monotonic (or anti-monotonic) constraint. Both approaches use the transposition principle, however the problem of mining under constraints is not fully studied, specially for complex constraints (i.e., conjunction and disjunction of simple constraints).

In this paper, we study this problem from a theoretical point of view. Our aim is to use classical algorithms (constrained pattern mining algorithms or closed patterns mining algorithms) in the "transposed" database and to use their output to regenerate patterns of the original database instead of directly mining in the original database.

There are several interesting questions which we will therefore try to answer:

1. What kind of information can be gathered in the "transposed" database on the patterns of the original database?
2. Is it possible to "transpose" the constraints? I.e., given a database and a constraint, is it possible to find a "transposed" constraint such that mining the "transposed" database with the "transposed" constraint gives information about the patterns which satisfy the original constraint in the original database?
3. How can we regenerate the closed patterns in the original database from the patterns extracted in the "transposed" database?
4. How can we generate *all* the itemsets satisfying a constraint using the extracted closed patterns.

These questions will be addressed respectively in Sec. 2, 3, 4 and 5.

The organization of the paper is as follows: we start Sec. 2 by recalling some usual definitions related to pattern mining and Galois connection. Then we show in Sec. 3 how to transpose usual and complex constraints. Section 4 is a complete discussion about mining constrained closed patterns using the "transposed" database and in Sec. 5 we show how to use this to compute all (i.e., not only closed) the patterns satisfying a constraint. Finally Sec. 6 is a short conclusion.

2   Definitions

To avoid confusion between rows (or columns) of the original database and rows (columns) of the "transposed" database, we define a database as a relation be-

Table 1. Original and transposed representations of a database. The attributes are $\mathcal{A} = \{a_1, a_2, a_3, a_4\}$ and the objects are $\mathcal{O} = \{o_1, o_2, o_3\}$. We use a string notation for object sets or itemsets, e.g., $a_1 a_3 a_4$ denotes the itemset $\{a_1, a_3, a_4\}$ and $o_2 o_3$ denotes the object set $\{o_2, o_3\}$. This dataset is used in all the examples

object	attribute pattern
o_1	$a_1 a_2 a_3$
o_2	$a_1 a_2 a_3$
o_3	$a_2 a_3 a_4$

attribute	object pattern
a_1	$o_1 o_2$
a_2	$o_1 o_2 o_3$
a_3	$o_1 o_2 o_3$
a_4	o_3

tween two sets : a set of attributes and a set of objects. The set of **attributes** (or items) is denoted $\mathcal{A}$ and the set of **objects** is $\mathcal{O}$. The **attribute space** $2^{\mathcal{A}}$ is the collection of the subsets of $\mathcal{A}$ and the **object space** $2^{\mathcal{O}}$ is the collection of the subsets of $\mathcal{O}$. An **attribute set** (or **itemset** or attribute pattern) is a subset of $\mathcal{A}$. An **object set** (or **object pattern**) is a subset of $\mathcal{O}$. A **database** is a subset of $\mathcal{A} \times \mathcal{O}$.

In this paper we consider that the database has more attributes than objects and that we are interested in mining attributes sets. The database can be represented as an adjacency matrix where objects are rows and attributes are columns (original representation) or where objects are columns and attributes are rows (transposed representation).

2.1 Constraints

Given a database, a **constraint** $\mathcal{C}$ on an attribute set (resp. object set) is a boolean function on $2^{\mathcal{A}}$ (resp. on $2^{\mathcal{O}}$). Many constraints have been used in previous works. One of the most popular is the minimum frequency constraint which requires an itemset to be present in more than a fixed number of objects. But we can also be interested in the opposite, i.e., the maximum frequency constraint. Other constraints are related to Galois connection (see Sect. 2.2), such as closed [2] patterns, free [6], contextual free [7] or key [2] patterns, or even non-derivable [9] or emergent [25, 11] patterns. There are also syntactical constraints, when one focuses only on itemsets containing a fixed pattern (superset constraint), contained in a fixed pattern (subset constraint), etc. Finally, when a numerical value (such as a price) is associated to items, aggregate functions such as sum, average, min, max, etc. can be used in constraints [16].

A constraint $\mathcal{C}$ is **anti-monotonic** if $\forall A, B \ (A \subseteq B \wedge \mathcal{C}(B)) \implies \mathcal{C}(A)$. A constraint $\mathcal{C}$ is **monotonic** if $\forall A, B \ (A \subseteq B \wedge \mathcal{C}(A)) \implies \mathcal{C}(B)$. In both definitions, A and B can be attribute sets or object sets. The frequency constraint is anti-monotonic, like the subset constraint. The anti-monotonicity property is important, because level-wise mining algorithms most of time use it to prune the search space. Indeed, when a pattern does not satisfy the constraint, its specialization neither and can be pruned [1].

Simple composition of constraints has good properties: the conjunction or the disjunction of two anti-monotonic (resp. monotonic) constraints is anti-

monotonic (resp. monotonic). The negation of an anti-monotonic (resp. monotonic) constraints is monotonic (resp. anti-monotonic).

2.2   Galois Connection

The main idea underlying our work is to use the strong connection between
the itemset lattice $2^{\mathcal{A}}$ and the object lattice $2^{\mathcal{O}}$ called the **Galois connection**.
This connection was first used in pattern mining when closed itemset mining
algorithms were proposed [19], while it relates to many works in concept learning [17, 27].
Given a database db, the Galois operators f and g are defined as:

- f, called *intension*, is a function from $2^{\mathcal{O}}$ to $2^{\mathcal{A}}$ defined by

$$f(O) = \{a \in \mathcal{A} \mid \forall o \in O,\ (a, o) \in db\},$$

- g, called *extension*, is a function from $2^{\mathcal{A}}$ to $2^{\mathcal{O}}$ defined by

$$g(A) = \{o \in \mathcal{O} \mid \forall a \in A,\ (a, o) \in db\}.$$

Given an itemset A, $g(A)$ is also called the *support set* of A in db. It is also
the set of objects for which all the attributes of A are true. The **frequency** of
A is $|g(A)|$ and is denoted $\mathcal{F}(A)$.

Both functions enable us to link the attribute space to the object space.
However, since both spaces have not the same cardinality, there is no one to
one mapping between them[1]. This means that several itemsets can have the
same image in the object space and conversely. We thus define two equivalence
relations r_a and r_o on $2^{\mathcal{O}}$ and $2^{\mathcal{A}}$:

- if A and B are two itemsets, $A\,r_a\,B$ if $g(A) = g(B)$,
- if O and P are two sets of objects, $O\,r_o\,P$ if $f(O) = f(P)$.

In every equivalence class, there is a particular element: the largest (for inclusion) element of an equivalence class is unique and is called a **closed attribute
set** (for r_a) or a **closed object set** (for r_o).

The Galois operators f and g lead by composition to two **closure** operators,
namely $h = f \circ g$ and $h' = g \circ f$. They relate to lattice or hypergraph theory and
have good properties [26]. The closed sets are then the fixed points of the closure
operators and the closure of a set is the closed set of its equivalence class. In the
following we will indifferently refer to h and h' with the notation cl. We denote
$\mathcal{C}_{\mathsf{close}}$ the constraint which is satisfied by the itemsets or the object sets which
are closed.

If two itemsets are equivalent, their images are equal in the object space.
There is therefore no mean to distinguish between them if the mining of the
closed patterns is performed in the object space. So, by using the Galois connection to perform the search in the object space instead of the attribute space,

---

[1] This is fortunate since the whole point of transposition is to explore a smaller space.

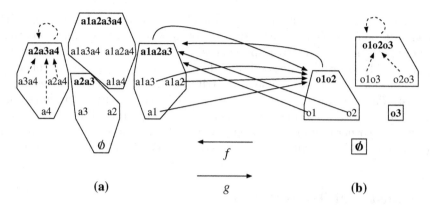

Fig. 1. The equivalence classes for r_a in the itemset lattice (a) and for r_o in the object set lattice (b) built on the database of Tab. 1. The closed sets are in bold face. The arrows represent the f and g operators between the $a_1a_2a_3$ and o_1o_2 equivalence classes. The dotted arrows represent the closure operators h and h'

we will gather information about the equivalence classes of r_a (identified by their closed pattern), not about all individual itemsets. This answers the first question of the introduction, i.e. what kind of information can be gathered in the transposed database on the patterns of the original database. At best, we will only be able to discover closed patterns.

Property 1. Some properties of f and g.

- f and g are decreasing w.r.t. the inclusion order: if $A \subseteq B$ then $g(B) \subseteq g(A)$ (resp. $f(B) \subseteq f(A)$)
- If A is an itemset and O an object set, then $g(A)$ is a closed object set and $f(O)$ a closed itemset
- fixed point: A is closed if and only if $f(g(A)) = \mathsf{cl}(A) = A$ (resp. $g(f(O)) = \mathsf{cl}(O) = O$)
- $f \circ g \circ f = f$ and $g \circ f \circ g = g$
- $A \subseteq \mathsf{cl}(A)$

In the Galois connection framework, the association of a closed pattern of attributes and the corresponding closed pattern of objects is called a *concept*. Concept learning [17, 27] has led to classification tasks and clustering processes. We use this connection in this article through the link it provides between the search spaces 2^A and 2^O.

Example 1. In Fig. 1, the closed objects sets are $\emptyset$, o_3, o_1o_2, and $o_1o_2o_3$. The closed itemsets are a_2a_3, $a_2a_3a_4$, $a_1a_2a_3$ and $a_1a_2a_3a_4$. Since $g(o_1o_2) = a_1a_2a_3$ and $f(a_1a_2a_3) = o_1o_2$, $(a_1a_2a_3, o_1o_2)$ is a concept. The others are $(a_2a_3, o_1o_2o_3)$, $(a_2a_3a_4, o_3)$, $(a_1a_2a_3a_4, \emptyset)$.

Closed sets of attributes are very useful for algorithms with support constraint, because they share, as maximal element of the equivalence class r_a, the same frequency with all patterns in the class. Closed set mining is now well known [12], and frequent closed patterns are known to be less numerous than frequent patterns [5, 9]. Today's approaches relate to closed sets with constraints mining [3]. These patterns are good candidates for constituting relevant concepts, which associate at the same time the attributes and the objects. For example, biologists want to constraint their search to attribute patterns containing some specific genes, with a specified maximum length. They also will be interested in analyzing the other part of the concept. We specifically address here the problem of constrained closed mining in databases with more attributes than objects.

3   Constraint Transposition

Most algorithms extracting closed patterns are search algorithms. The size of the search space strongly determines their performance [12]. In our context, the object space $2^{\mathcal{O}}$ is smaller than the attribute space $2^{\mathcal{A}}$. We therefore choose to search the closed patterns in the smaller space ($2^{\mathcal{O}}$) by transposing the database. In order to mine under constraint, we study in this section how we can adapt constraints to the new transposed database, i.e., how we can transpose constraints. We will therefore answer question 2 of the introduction.

3.1   Definition and Properties

Given an itemset constraint $\mathcal{C}$, we want to extract the collection I of itemsets, $I = \{A \subseteq \mathcal{A} \mid \mathcal{C}(A)\}$. Therefore, we want to find in the transposed database a collection T of object sets (if it exists) such that the image by f of this collection is I, i.e., $\{f(O) \mid O \in T\} = I$. Since $f(O)$ is always a closed itemset, this is only possible if the collection I contains only closed itemsets (i.e., if the constraint $\mathcal{C}$ includes the $\mathcal{C}_{\text{close}}$ constraint). In this case, a solution for T is the collection $\{O \subseteq \mathcal{O} \mid \mathcal{C}(f(O))\}$ which leads to the following definition of a transposed constraint:

Definition 1 (Transposed Constraint). *Given a constraint $\mathcal{C}$, we define the transposed constraint $^t\mathcal{C}$ on a closed pattern O of objects as:*

$$^t\mathcal{C}(O) = \mathcal{C}(f(O)).$$

Example 2. Consider the itemset constraint $\mathcal{C}(A) = (a_1 \in A)$. Its transposed constraint is (by definition) $^t\mathcal{C}(O) = (a_1 \in f(O))$. Using the dataset of Tab. 1, the object sets that satisfy $^t\mathcal{C}$ are $T = \{o_1, o_2, o_1o_2, o_1o_3, o_2o_3, o_1o_2o_3\}$. If we compute $\{f(O) \mid O \in T\}$, we get $\{a_1a_2a_3, a_1a_2a_3a_4\}$ which are exactly the closed itemsets that satisfy $\mathcal{C}$. Theorem 1 will show that this is always the case.

It is interesting to study the effect of transposition w.r.t. the monotonicity or anti-monotonicity of constraints, since many mining algorithms rely on them for efficient pruning:

Proposition 1. *If a constraint C is monotonic (resp. anti-monotonic), the transposed constraint ^tC is anti-monotonic (resp. monotonic).*

Proof: f and g are decreasing (Prop. 1), which inverts monotonicity and anti-monotonicity. □

Since we also want to deal with complex constraints (i.e., constraints built with elementary constraints using boolean operators), we need the following:

Proposition 2. *If C and C' are two constraints then:*

$$^t(C \wedge C') = {}^tC \wedge {}^tC'$$

$$^t(C \vee C') = {}^tC \vee {}^tC'$$

$$^t(\neg C) = \neg {}^tC$$

Proof: For the conjunction: $^t(C \wedge C')(O) = (C \wedge C')(f(O)) = C(f(O)) \wedge C'(f(O)) = ({}^tC \wedge {}^tC')(O)$. The proof is similar for the disjunction and the negation. □

Many algorithms deal with conjunctions of anti-monotonic and monotonic constraints. The two last propositions mean that these algorithms can be used with the transposed constraints since the transposed constraint of the conjunction of a monotonic and an anti-monotonic constraint is the conjunction of a monotonic and an anti-monotonic constraint! The last proposition also helps in building the transposition of a composed constraint. It is useful for the algebraisation [22] of the constraint mining problem, where constraints are decomposed in disjunctions and conjunctions of elementary constraints.

3.2   Transposed Constraints of Some Classical Constraints

In the previous section, we gave the definition of the transposed constraint. In this definition $(^tC(O) = C(f(O)))$, in order to test the transposed constraint on an object set O, it is necessary to compute $f(O)$ (to come back in the attribute space) and then to test C. This means that a mining algorithm using this constraint must maintain a dual context, i.e., it must maintain for each object set O the corresponding attribute set $f(O)$. Some algorithms already do this, for instance algorithms which use the so called *vertical representation* of the database (like CHARM [28]). For some classical constraints however, the transposed constraint can be rewritten in order to avoid the use of $f(O)$. In this section, we review several classical constraints and try to find a simple expression of their transposed constraint in the object space.

Let us first consider the minimum frequency constraint: the transposed constraint of $C_{\gamma\text{-freq}}(A) = (\mathcal{F}(A) > \gamma)$ is, by definition 1, $^tC_{\gamma\text{-freq}}(O) = (\mathcal{F}(f(O)) > \gamma)$. By definition of frequency, $\mathcal{F}(f(O)) = |g(f(O))| = |\text{cl}(O)|$ and if O is a closed object set, $\text{cl}(O) = O$ and therefore $^tC_{\gamma\text{-freq}}(O) = (|O| > \gamma)$. Finally, the transposed constraint of the minimum frequency constraint is the "minimum size" constraint. The CARPENTER [18] algorithm uses this property and mines the closed patterns in a divide-and-conquer strategy, stopping when the length of the object set drops below the threshold.

The next two propositions give the transposed constraints of two other classical constraints : the subset and superset constraints:

Proposition 3 (Subset Constraint Transposition). *Let $\mathcal{C}_{\subseteq E}$ be the constraint defined by: $\mathcal{C}_{\subseteq E}(A) = (A \subseteq E)$ where E is a constant itemset. Then if E is closed (O is an object set):*

$$^t\mathcal{C}_{\subseteq E}(O) \Leftrightarrow g(E) \subseteq \mathsf{cl}(O)$$

and if E is not closed

$$^t\mathcal{C}_{\subseteq E}(O) \Rightarrow g(E) \subseteq \mathsf{cl}(O).$$

Proof: $^t\mathcal{C}_{\subseteq E}(O) \Leftrightarrow \mathcal{C}_{\subseteq E}(f(O)) \Leftrightarrow (f(O) \subseteq E) \Rightarrow (g(E) \subseteq g(f(O))) \Leftrightarrow (g(E) \subseteq \mathsf{cl}(O))$. Conversely (if E is closed): $(g(E) \subseteq g(f(O))) \Rightarrow (f(O) \subseteq \mathsf{cl}(E)) \Rightarrow (f(O) \subseteq E)$.   □

Proposition 4 (Superset Constraint Transposition). *Let $\mathcal{C}_{\supseteq E}$ be the constraint defined by: $\mathcal{C}_{\supseteq E}(A) = (A \supseteq E)$ where E is a constant itemset. Then:*

$$^t\mathcal{C}_{\supseteq E}(O) \Leftrightarrow g(E) \supseteq \mathsf{cl}(O).$$

Proof: $^t\mathcal{C}(O) \Leftrightarrow (E \subseteq f(O)) \Rightarrow (g(f(O)) \subseteq g(E)) \Leftrightarrow (\mathsf{cl}(O) \subseteq g(E))$. Conversely, $(g(f(O)) \subseteq g(E) \Rightarrow (fg(E) \subseteq fgf(O)) \Rightarrow fg(E) \subseteq f(O) \Rightarrow \mathsf{cl}(E) \subseteq f(O) \Rightarrow E \subseteq f(O)$.   □

These two syntactical constraints are interesting because they can be used to construct many other kind of constraints. In fact, all syntactical constraints can be build on top of these using conjunctions, disjunctions and negations. With the proposition 2, it is then possible to compute the transposition of many syntactical constraints. Besides, these constraints have been identified in [13, 4] to formalize dataset reduction techniques.

Table 2 gives the transposed constraints of several classical constraints if the object set O is closed (this is not an important restriction since we will use only closed itemsets extraction algorithms). These transposed constraints are easily obtained using the two previous propositions on the superset and the subset constraints and Prop. 2. For instance, if $\mathcal{C}(A) = (A \cap E \neq \emptyset)$, this can be rewritten $A \not\subseteq \overline{E}$ ($\overline{E}$ denotes the complement of E, i.e. $\mathcal{A} \backslash E$) and then $\neg(A \subseteq \overline{E})$. The transposed constraint is therefore, using Prop. 2 and 3, $\neg(g(\overline{E}) \subseteq O)$ (if $\overline{E}$ is closed) and finally $g(\overline{E}) \not\subseteq O$. If $\overline{E}$ is not closed, then we write $E = \{e_1, ..., e_n\}$ and we rewrite the constraint $\mathcal{C}(A) = (e_1 \in A \vee e_2 \in A \vee ... \vee e_n \in A)$ and then, using Prop. 2 and 4, we obtain the transposed constraint $^t\mathcal{C}(O) = (O \subseteq g(e_1) \vee ... \vee O \subseteq g(e_n))$. These expressions are interesting since they do not involve the computation of $f(O)$. Instead, there are $g(\overline{E})$ or $g(e_i)$ ... However, since E is constant, these values need to be computed only once (during the first database pass, for instance).

Table 2. Transposed constraints of some classical constraints. A is a variable closed itemset, $E = \{e_1, e_2, ..., e_n\}$ a constant itemset, O a variable closed object set and $\overline{E} = A \setminus E = \{f_1, f_2, ..., f_m\}$

Itemset constraint $\mathcal{C}(A)$	Transposed constraint $^t\mathcal{C}(O)$
$\mathcal{F}(A) \, \theta \, \alpha$	$|O| \, \theta \, \alpha$
$A \subseteq E$	if E is closed: $g(E) \subseteq O$
	else: $O \not\subseteq g(f_1) \wedge ... \wedge O \not\subseteq g(f_m)$
$E \subseteq A$	$O \subseteq g(E)$
$A \not\subseteq E$	if E is closed: $g(E) \not\subseteq O$
	else: $O \subseteq g(f_1) \vee ... \vee O \subseteq g(f_m)$
$E \not\subseteq A$	$O \not\subseteq g(E)$
$A \cap E = \emptyset$	if $\overline{E}$ is closed: $g(\overline{E}) \subseteq O$
	else: $O \not\subseteq g(e_1) \wedge ... \wedge O \not\subseteq g(e_n)$
$A \cap E \neq \emptyset$	if $\overline{E}$ is closed: $g(\overline{E}) \not\subseteq O$
	else: $O \subseteq g(e_1) \vee ... \vee O \subseteq g(e_n)$
$\mathrm{SUM}(A) \, \theta \, \alpha$	$\mathcal{F}_p(O) \, \theta \, \alpha$
$\mathrm{MIN}(A) \, \theta \, \alpha$	see text
$\mathrm{MAX}(A) \, \theta \, \alpha$	see text

$$\theta \in \{<, >, \leq, \geq\}$$

Example 3. We show in this example how to compute the transposed constraints with the database of Tab. 1. Let the itemset constraint $\mathcal{C}(A) = (A \cap a_1 a_4 \neq \emptyset)$. In the database of Tab. 1, the itemset $\overline{a_1 a_4} = a_2 a_3$ is closed. Therefore, the transposed constraint is (Tab. 2) $^t\mathcal{C}(O) = (g(a_2 a_3) \not\subseteq O)$. Since $g(a_2 a_3) = o_1 o_2 o_3$, $^t\mathcal{C}(O) = (o_1 o_2 o_3 \not\subseteq O)$. The closed object sets that satisfy this constraint are $T = \{\emptyset, o_1 o_2, o_3\}$. If we apply f to go back to the itemset space: $\{f(O) \mid O \in T\} = \{a_1 a_2 a_3 a_4, a_1 a_2 a_3, a_2 a_3 a_4\}$ which are, as expected (and proved by Th. 1), the closed itemset which satisfy $\mathcal{C}$.

Consider now the constraint $\mathcal{C}(A) = (A \cap a_1 a_2 \neq \emptyset)$. In this case, $\overline{a_1 a_2} = a_3 a_4$ is not closed. Therefore, we use the second expression in Tab. 2 to compute its transposition. $^t\mathcal{C}(O) = (O \subseteq g(a_1) \vee O \subseteq g(a_2))$. Since $g(a_1) = o_1 o_2$ and $g(a_2) = o_1 o_2 o_3$, $^t\mathcal{C}(O) = (O \subseteq o_1 o_2 \vee O \subseteq o_1 o_2 o_3)$ which can be simplified in $^t\mathcal{C}(O) = (O \subseteq o_1 o_2 o_3)$. All the closed object sets satisfy this constraint $^t\mathcal{C}$, which is not surprising since all the closed itemsets satisfy $\mathcal{C}$.

Our last example is the constraint $\mathcal{C}(A) = (|A \cap a_1 a_2 a_4| \geq 2)$. It can be rewritten $\mathcal{C}(A) = ((a_1 a_2 \subseteq A) \vee (a_1 a_4 \subseteq A) \vee (a_2 a_4 \subseteq A))$. Using Prop. 2 and Tab. 2 we get $^t\mathcal{C}(O) = ((O \subseteq g(a_1 a_2)) \vee (O \subseteq g(a_1 a_4)) \vee (O \subseteq g(a_2 a_4)))$ which is $^t\mathcal{C}(O) = ((O \subseteq o_1 o_2) \vee (O \subseteq \emptyset) \vee (O \subseteq o_3))$. The closed object sets satisfying $^t\mathcal{C}$ are $T = \{\emptyset, o_1 o_2, o_3\}$ and $\{f(O) \mid O \in T\} = \{a_1 a_2 a_3 a_4, a_1 a_2 a_3, a_2 a_3 a_4\}$.

Other interesting constraints include aggregate constraints [16]. If a numerical value $a.v$ is associated to each attribute $a \in \mathcal{A}$, we can define constraints of the form $\mathrm{SUM}(A) \, \theta \, \alpha$ for several aggregate operators such as SUM, MIN, MAX or AVG, where $\theta \in \{<, >, \leq, \geq\}$ and α is a numerical value. In this case, $\mathrm{SUM}(A)$ denotes the sum of all $a.v$ for all attributes a in A.

The constraints $\text{MIN}(A)\,\theta\,\alpha$ and $\text{MAX}(A)\,\theta\,\alpha$ are special cases of the constraints of Tab. 2. For instance, if $sup_\alpha = \{a \in \mathcal{A} \mid a.v > \alpha\}$ then $\text{MIN}(A) > \alpha$ is exactly $A \subseteq sup_\alpha$ and $\text{MIN}(A) \leq \alpha$ is $A \not\subseteq sup_\alpha$. The same kind of relation holds for MAX operator: $\text{MAX}(A) > \alpha$ is equivalent to $A \cap sup_\alpha \neq \emptyset$ and $\text{MAX}(A) \leq \alpha$ is equivalent to $A \cap sup_\alpha = \emptyset$. In this case, since α is a constant, the set sup_α can be pre-computed.

The constraints $\text{AVG}(A)\,\theta\,\alpha$ and $\text{SUM}(A)\,\theta\,\alpha$ are more difficult. Indeed, we only found one expression (without $f(O)$) for the transposition of $\text{SUM}(A)\,\theta\,\alpha$. Its transposition is ${}^t\mathcal{C}(O) = (\text{SUM}(f(O))\,\theta\,\alpha)$. In the database, $f(O)$ is a set of attributes, so in the transposed database, it is a set of rows and O is a set of columns. The values $a.v$ are attached to rows of the transposed database, and $\text{SUM}(f(O))$ is the sum of these values for the rows containing O. Therefore, $\text{SUM}(f(O))$ is a pondered frequency of O (in the transposed database) where each row a, containing O, contributes for $a.v$ in the total (we denote this pondered frequency by $\mathcal{F}_p(O)$). It is easy to adapt classical algorithms to count this pondered frequency. Its computation is the same as the classical frequency except that each row containing the counted itemset does contribute with a value different from 1 to the frequency.

4   Closed Itemsets Mining

In a previous work [23] we showed the complementarity of the set of concepts mined in the database, with constraining the attribute patterns, and the set of concepts mined in the transposed database with the *negation* of the transposed constraint, when the original constraint is anti-monotonic. The transposed constraint had to be negated in order to ensure the anti-monotonicity of the constraint used by the algorithm. This is important because we can keep usual mining algorithms which deal with anti-monotonic constraint and apply them in the transposed database with the negation of the transposed constraint. We also showed [24] a specific way of mining under monotonic constraint, by simply mining the transposed database with the transposed constraint (which is anti-monotonic). In this section, we generalize these results for more general constraints.

We define the **constrained closed itemset mining problem**: Given a database db and a constraint $\mathcal{C}$, we want to extract all the closed itemsets (and their frequencies) satisfying the constraint $\mathcal{C}$ in the database db. More formally, we want to compute the collection:

$$\{(A, \mathcal{F}(A, db)) \mid \mathcal{C}(A, db) \wedge \mathcal{C}_{\text{close}}(A, db)\}.$$

The next theorem shows how to compute the above solution set using the closed object patterns extracted in the transposed database, with the help of the transposed constraint.

Theorem 1.

$$\{A \mid \mathcal{C}(A) \wedge \mathcal{C}_{\text{close}}(A)\} = \{f(O) \mid {}^t\mathcal{C}(O) \wedge \mathcal{C}_{\text{close}}(O)\}.$$

Proof: By def. 1, $\{f(O) \mid {}^{t}\mathcal{C}(O) \wedge \mathcal{C}_{\text{close}}(O)\} = \{f(O) \mid \mathcal{C}(f(O)) \wedge \mathcal{C}_{\text{close}}(O)\}$
$= \{A \mid \exists O \ s.t. \ \mathcal{C}(A) \wedge A = f(O)\} = \{A \mid \mathcal{C}(A) \wedge \mathcal{C}_{\text{close}}(A)\}$.   □

This theorem means that if we extract the collection of all closed object patterns satisfying ${}^{t}\mathcal{C}$ in the transposed database, then we can get all the closed patterns satisfying $\mathcal{C}$ by computing $f(O)$ for all the closed object patterns. The fact that we only need the *closed* object patterns and not all the object patterns is very interesting since the closed patterns are less numerous and can be extracted more efficiently (see CHARM [28], CARPENTER [18], CLOSET[21] or [7]). The strategy, which we propose for computing the solution of the constraint closed itemset mining problem, is therefore:

1. Compute the transposed constraint ${}^{t}\mathcal{C}$ using Tab. 2 and Prop. 2. This step can involve the computation of some constant object sets $g(E)$ used in the transposed constraint.
2. Use one of the known algorithms to extract the constrained closed sets of the transposed database. Most closed set extraction algorithms do not use constraints (like CLOSE, CLOSET or CARPENTER). However, it is not difficult to integrate them (by adding more pruning steps) for monotonic or anti-monotonic constraints. In [7], another algorithm to extract constrained closed sets is presented.
3. Compute $f(O)$ for each extracted closed object pattern. In fact, every algorithm already computes this when counting the frequency[2] of O, which is $|f(O)|$. The frequency of $f(O)$ (in the original database) is simply the size of O and can therefore be provided without any access to the database.

The first and third steps can indeed be integrated in the core of the mining algorithm, as it is done in the CARPENTER algorithm (but only with the frequency constraint).

Finally, this strategy shows how to perform constrained closed itemset mining by processing all the computations in the transposed database, and using classical algorithms.

5   Itemsets Mining

In this section, we study how to extract *all* the itemsets that satisfy a user constraint (and not only the closed ones). We define the **constrained itemset mining problem** : Given a database db and a constraint $\mathcal{C}$, we want to extract all the itemsets (and their frequencies) satisfying the constraint $\mathcal{C}$ in the database db. More formally, we want to compute the collection:

$$\{(A, \mathcal{F}(A, db)) \mid \mathcal{C}(A, db)\}.$$

In the previous section, we gave a strategy to compute the *closed* itemsets satisfying a constraint. We will of course make use of this strategy. Solving the

---

[2] This is the frequency in the *transposed database*.

constrained itemset mining problem will involve three steps : Given a database
db and a constraint C,

1. find a constraint C',
2. compute the collection $\{(A, \mathcal{F}(A, db)) \mid C'(A, db) \wedge C_{\mathsf{close}}(A, db)\}$ of closed sets
   satisfying C' using the strategy of Sec. 4,
3. compute the collection $\{(A, \mathcal{F}(A, db)) \mid C(A, db)\}$ of all the itemsets satisfying
   C from the closed ones satisfying C'.

We will study the first step in the next subsection and the third one in
Sec. 5.2, but first we will show why it is necessary to introduce a new constraint
C'. Indeed, it is not always possible to compute all the itemsets that satisfy C
from the closed sets that satisfy C. Let us first recall how the third step is done
in the classical case where C is the frequency constraint [19]:

The main used property is that all the itemsets of an equivalence class have
the same frequency than the closed itemset of the class. Therefore, if we know
the frequency of the closed itemsets, it is possible to deduce the frequency of
non-closed itemsets provided we are able to know in which class they belong.
The regeneration algorithm of [19] use a top down approach. Starting from the
largest frequent closed itemsets, it generates their subsets and assign them their
frequencies, until all the itemsets have been generated.

Now, assume that the constraint C is not the frequency constraint and that we
have computed all the closed itemsets (and their frequencies) that satisfy C. If an
itemset satisfies C, it is possible that its closure does not satisfies it. In this case,
it is not possible to compute the frequency of this itemset from the collection
of the closed itemsets that satisfy C (this is illustrated in Fig. 2). Finally, the
collection of the closed itemsets satisfying C is not sufficient to generate the
non-closed itemsets. In the next section, we show how the constraint C can be
relaxed to enable the generation all the non-closed itemsets satisfying it.

5.1   Relaxation of the Constraint

In order to be able to generate all the itemsets from the closed ones, it is necessary
to have at least the collection of closed itemsets of all the equivalence classes
that contain an itemset satisfying the constraint C. This collection is also the
collection of the closures of all itemsets satisfying C : $\{\mathsf{cl}(A) \mid C(A, db)\}$.

We must therefore find a constraint C' such that $\{\mathsf{cl}(A) \mid C(A, db)\}$ is included
in $\{A \mid C'(A, db) \wedge C_{\mathsf{close}}(A)\}$. We call such a C' constraint a **good relaxation**
of C (see Fig. 3). If we have an equality instead of the inclusion, we call C' an
optimal relaxation of C. For example, the constant "true" constraint (which
is true on all itemset) is a good relaxation of any constraint, however it is not
very interesting since it will not provide any pruning opportunity during the
extraction of step 2.

If the closed itemsets (and their frequencies) satisfying an optimal relaxation
of C are computed in step 2, we will have enough information for regenerating
all itemsets satisfying C in step 3. However it is not always possible to find such
an optimal relaxation. In this case, we can still use a good relaxation in step 2.

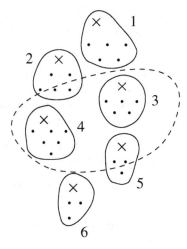

Fig. 2. The dots represent itemsets, the x are closed itemsets, the lines enclose the equivalence classes. The itemsets inside the region delimited by the dashed line satisfy the constraint $\mathcal{C}$ and the others do not. The closed sets satisfying $\mathcal{C}$ are the closed sets of classes 3, 4 and 5. They will enable to generate the itemsets of these three classes. However, to get the two itemsets of class 2, we need the closed itemset of this class which does not satisfy $\mathcal{C}$. Therefore, in this case, having the closed itemsets satisfying $\mathcal{C}$ is not enough to generate all itemsets satisfying $\mathcal{C}$

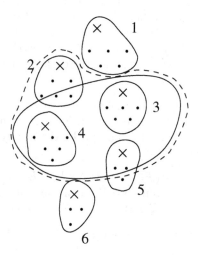

Fig. 3. An optimal relaxation of $\mathcal{C}$. The constraint $\mathcal{C}$ is represented by the solid line and an optimal relaxation is represented by the dashed line

In this case, some superfluous closed itemsets will be present in the collection and will have to be filtered out in step 3.

We will now give optimal relaxation for some classical constraints, and we start with two trivial cases:

Proposition 5. *The optimal relaxation of a monotonic constraint is the constraint itself and the optimal relaxation of the frequency constraint is the frequency constraint itself.*

Proof: Let $\mathcal{C}$ be a monotonic constraint or a frequency constraint. We only have to prove that if an itemset A satisfy $\mathcal{C}$ then $\mathsf{cl}(A)$ also. If $\mathcal{C}$ is monotonic, this is true since $S \subseteq \mathsf{cl}(S)$ (Prop. 1. If $\mathcal{C}$ is a minimum frequency constraint, it is true because A and $\mathsf{cl}(A)$ have the same frequency.   □

The next proposition is used to compute the relaxation of a complex constraint from the relaxation of simple constraints.

Proposition 6. *If $\mathcal{C}_1$ and $\mathcal{C}_2$ are two constraints and $\mathcal{C}_1'$ and $\mathcal{C}_2'$ are optimal relaxation of them, then :*

- *$\mathcal{C}_1' \vee \mathcal{C}_2'$ is an optimal relaxation of $\mathcal{C}_1 \vee \mathcal{C}_2$ and*
- *$\mathcal{C}_1' \wedge \mathcal{C}_2'$ is a good relaxation of $\mathcal{C}_1 \wedge \mathcal{C}_2$.*

Proof: A constraint $\mathcal{C}'$ is a good relaxation of a constraint $\mathcal{C}$ if and only if $\forall A, \mathcal{C}(A) \Rightarrow \mathcal{C}'(\mathsf{cl}(A))$. To prove that it is an *optimal* relaxation, we must also prove that if A is closed and satisfies $\mathcal{C}'$ then there exists an itemset B satisfying $\mathcal{C}$ such that $\mathsf{cl}(B) = A$ (cf. definitions). We will use this two facts in our proofs.

Let A be an itemset satisfying $\mathcal{C}_1 \wedge \mathcal{C}_2$. This means that A satisfies $\mathcal{C}_1$ and $\mathcal{C}_2$. Therefore, $\mathsf{cl}(A)$ satisfies $\mathcal{C}_1'$ and $\mathcal{C}_2'$, i.e., $cl(A)$ satisfies $\mathcal{C}_1' \wedge \mathcal{C}_2'$. This means that $\mathcal{C}_1' \wedge \mathcal{C}_2'$ is a good relaxation of $\mathcal{C}_1 \wedge \mathcal{C}_2$.

We can prove similarly that $\mathcal{C}_1' \vee \mathcal{C}_2'$ is a good relaxation of $\mathcal{C}_1 \vee \mathcal{C}_2$. Let us now prove that it is optimal: Let A be a closed itemset satisfying $\mathcal{C}_1' \vee \mathcal{C}_2'$. Then A satisfies $\mathcal{C}_1'$ or $\mathcal{C}_2'$, suppose that it satisfies $\mathcal{C}_1'$. Since $\mathcal{C}_1'$ is an optimal relaxation of $\mathcal{C}_1$, there exists B satisfying $\mathcal{C}_1$ such that $\mathsf{cl}(B) = A$. Therefore B satisfies $\mathcal{C}_1 \vee \mathcal{C}_2$ and $\mathsf{cl}(B) = A$.   □

We found no relaxation for the negation of a constraint but this is not a problem. If the constraint is simple (i.e., in Tab. 2) its negation is also in the table and if it is complex, then we can "push" the negation into the constraint as shown in the next example.

Example 4. Let $\mathcal{C}(A) = (\neg(((\mathcal{F}(A) > 3) \wedge (A \not\subseteq E)) \vee (A \cap F = \emptyset)))$ where E and F are two constant itemsets. We can push the negation and we get: $\mathcal{C}(A) = ((\neg(\mathcal{F}(A) > 3) \vee \neg(A \not\subseteq E)) \wedge \neg(A \cap F = \emptyset))$, and finally :

$$\mathcal{C}(A) = (((\mathcal{F}(A) \leq 3) \vee (A \subseteq E)) \wedge (A \cap F \neq \emptyset)).$$

Then with Prop. 5, 6 and Tab. 3, we can compute a good relaxation $\mathcal{C}'$ of $\mathcal{C}$:

$$\mathcal{C}'(A) = (((\mathcal{F}(A) \leq 3) \vee (A \subseteq \mathsf{cl}(E))) \wedge (A \cap F \neq \emptyset)).$$

Table 3 gives good relaxation of the other constraints of Tab. 2 which are not covered by the previous proposition (i.e., which are not monotonic) except for the non-monotonic constraints involving SUM for which we did not find any interesting (i.e., other than the constant true constraint) good relaxation.

Table 3. Good relaxation of some classical constraints. A is a variable closed itemset, $E = \{e_1, e_2, ..., e_n\}$ a constant itemset

Itemset constraint $\mathcal{C}(A)$	Good relaxation $\mathcal{C}'(A)$
$A \subseteq E$	$A \subseteq \mathsf{cl}(E)$
$E \not\subseteq A$	$A \subseteq \mathsf{cl}(\overline{e_1}) \vee A \subseteq \mathsf{cl}(\overline{e_2}) \vee ... \vee A \subseteq \mathsf{cl}(\overline{e_n})$
$A \cap E = \emptyset$	$A \subseteq \mathsf{cl}(\overline{E})$
$\mathrm{MIN}(A) > \alpha$	$A \subseteq \mathsf{cl}(sup_\alpha)$
$\mathrm{MAX}(A) < \alpha$	$A \subseteq \mathsf{cl}(\overline{supeq_\alpha})$

Proof: We prove here the results given in Tab. 3.

$\mathcal{C}(A) = (A \subseteq E)$, $\mathcal{C}'(A) = (A \subseteq \mathsf{cl}(E))$: If $A \subseteq E$ then $\mathsf{cl}(A) \subseteq \mathsf{cl}(E)$. This means that $\mathcal{C}(A) \Rightarrow \mathcal{C}'(\mathsf{cl}(A))$ therefore $\mathcal{C}'$ is a good relaxation of $\mathcal{C}$.

$\mathcal{C}(A) = (A \cap E = \emptyset)$: $\mathcal{C}$ can be rewritten $\mathcal{C}(A) = (A \subseteq \overline{E})$ and the previous case applies with $\overline{E}$ instead of E.

$\mathcal{C}(A) = (E \not\subseteq A)$: If $E = \{e_1, e_2, ..., e_n\}$, this constraint can be rewritten $\{e_1\} \not\subseteq A \vee \{e_2\} \not\subseteq A \vee ... \vee \{e_n\} \not\subseteq A$ which is also $A \subseteq \overline{\{e_1\}} \vee ... \vee A \subseteq \overline{\{e_n\}}$. Then the first case and Prop 6 give the result.

$\mathcal{C}(A) = (\mathrm{MIN}(A) > \alpha)$ and $\mathcal{C}(A) = (\mathrm{MAX}(A) < \alpha)$: $\mathcal{C}(A) = (\mathrm{MIN}(A) > \alpha)$ can be rewritten $A \subseteq sup_\alpha$ with $sup_\alpha = \{a \in \mathcal{A} \mid a.v > \alpha\}$ and we are in the first case. $\mathcal{C}(A) = (\mathrm{MAX}(A) < \alpha)$ can be rewritten $A \cap supeq_\alpha = \emptyset$ with $supeq_\alpha = \{a \in \mathcal{A} \mid a.v \geq \alpha\}$ and we are in the second case. □

5.2 Regeneration

Given a database db and a constraint $\mathcal{C}$, we suppose in this section that a collection $\{(A, \mathcal{F}(A, db)) \mid \mathcal{C}'(A, db) \wedge \mathcal{C}_{\mathrm{close}}(A, db)\}$ of closed itemsets (and their frequencies) satisfying a good relaxation $\mathcal{C}'$ of $\mathcal{C}$ is available. The aim is to compute the collection $\{(A, \mathcal{F}(A, db)) \mid \mathcal{C}(A, db)\}$ of all itemset satisfying $\mathcal{C}$ (and their frequencies).

If $\mathcal{C}$ is a minimum frequency constraint, $\mathcal{C}$ is an optimal relaxation of itself, therefore we take $\mathcal{C}' = \mathcal{C}$. The regeneration algorithm is then the classical algorithm 6 of [19]. We briefly recall this algorithm:

We suppose that the frequent closed itemsets (and their frequencies) of size i are stored in the list $\mathcal{L}_i$ for $0 < i \leq k$ where k is the size of the longest frequent closed itemset. At the end of the algorithm, each $\mathcal{L}_i$ contains all the frequent itemsets of size i and their frequencies.

```
1 for (i = k; i > 0; i − −)
2   forall A ∈ L_i
3     forall subset B of size (i − 1) of A
4       if B ∉ L_{i−1}
5         B.freq = A.freq
6         L_{i−1} = L_{i−1} ∪ {B}
```

7   endif
8   end
9   end
10 end

If $\mathcal{C}'$ is not the frequency constraint, this algorithm generates all the subsets of the closed itemsets satisfying $\mathcal{C}'$ and two problems arise:

1. Some of these itemsets do not satisfy $\mathcal{C}$. For instance, in Fig. 3, all the itemsets of classes 2, 3, 4, 5 and 6 are generated (because they are subsets of closed itemsets that satisfy $\mathcal{C}'$) and only those of classes 3 and 4 and some of classes 2 and 5 satisfy $\mathcal{C}$.
2. The frequency computed in step 5 of the above algorithm for B is correct only if the closure of B is in the collection of the closed sets at the beginning of the algorithm. If it is not, then this computed frequency is smaller than the true frequency of B. In Fig. 3, this means that the computed frequency of the itemsets of class 6 are not correct.

However, the good news is that all the itemsets satisfying $\mathcal{C}$ are generated (because $\mathcal{C}'$ is a good relaxation of $\mathcal{C}$) and their computed frequencies are correct (because their closures belongs to the $\mathcal{L}_i$ at the beginning).

A last filtering phase is therefore necessary to filter out all the generated itemsets that do not satisfy $\mathcal{C}$. This phase can be pushed inside the above generation algorithm if the constraint $\mathcal{C}$ has good properties (particularly if it is a conjunction of a monotonic part and an anti-monotonic one). However, we will not detail this point here.

We are still facing a last problem: to test $\mathcal{C}(A)$, we can need $\mathcal{F}(A)$. However, if $\mathcal{C}(A)$ is false, it is possible that the computed frequency of A is not correct. To solve this problem, we propose the following strategy.

We assume that the constraint $\mathcal{C}$ is a Boolean formula built using the atomic constraints listed in Tab. 2 and using the two operators $\wedge$ and $\vee$ (if the $\neg$ operator appears, it can be pushed inside the formula as shown in Ex. 4). Then, we rewrite this constraint in disjunctive normal form (DNF), i.e., $\mathcal{C} = \mathcal{C}_1 \vee \mathcal{C}_2 \vee \ldots \vee \mathcal{C}_n$ with $\mathcal{C}_i = \mathcal{A}_{m_{i-1}+1} \wedge \ldots \wedge \mathcal{A}_{m_i}$ where each $\mathcal{A}_i$ is a constraint listed in Tab. 2.

Now, consider an itemset A whose computed frequency is f (with $f \leq \mathcal{F}(A)$). First, we consider all the conjunction $\mathcal{C}_i$ that we can compute, this include those where $\mathcal{F}(A)$ does not appear and those of the form $\mathcal{F}(A) > \alpha$ or $\mathcal{F}(A) < \alpha$ where $\alpha < f$ (in this two cases we can conclude since $\mathcal{F}(A) \geq f$). If one of them is true, then $\mathcal{C}(A)$ is true and A is not filtered out.

If all of them are false, we have to consider the remaining conjunctions of the form $\mathcal{A}_1 \wedge \ldots \wedge (\mathcal{F}(A) > \alpha) \wedge \ldots$ with $\alpha \geq f$. If one of the $\mathcal{A}_i$ is false, then the conjunction is false. If all are true, we suppose that $\mathcal{F}(A) > \alpha$: in this case $\mathcal{C}(A)$ is true and therefore $\mathcal{F}(A) = f$ which contradict $\alpha \geq f$. Therefore, $\mathcal{F}(A) > \alpha$ is false and also the whole conjunction.

If it is still impossible to answer, it means that all the conjunctions are false, and that there are conjunction of the form $\mathcal{A}_1 \wedge \ldots \wedge (\mathcal{F}(A) < \alpha) \wedge \ldots$ with

$\alpha \geq f$. In this case, it is not possible to know if $\mathcal{C}(A)$ is true without computing the frequency $\mathcal{F}(A)$.

Finally, all this means that if there is no constraints of the form $\mathcal{F}(A) < \alpha$ in the DNF of $\mathcal{C}$, we can do this last filtering phase efficiently. If it appears, then the filtering phase can involve access to the database to compute the frequency of some itemsets. Of course, all these frequency computation should be made in one access to the database.

Example 5. In this example, we illustrate the complete process of the resolution of the constrained itemset mining problem on two constraints (we still use the dataset of Tab. 1):

$$\mathcal{C}(A) = ((\mathcal{F}(A) > 1) \vee (a_1 \in A)).$$

This constraint is its own optimal relaxation (cf. Prop. 5 and 6). According to Tab. 2 and Prop. 2, its transposed constraint is ${}^t\mathcal{C}(O) = ((|O| > 1) \vee (O \subseteq g(a_1)))$ and $g(a_1) = o_1 o_2$. The closed objects sets that satisfy this constraints are $T = \{o_1 o_2, o_1 o_2 o_3, \emptyset\}$. If we apply f to go back to the itemset space: $\{f(O) \mid O \in T\} = \{a_1 a_2 a_3 a_4, a_1 a_2 a_3, a_2 a_3\}$. Since this set contains $a_1 a_2 a_3 a_4$, all the itemsets are generated. However, the generated frequency for the itemsets of the class of $a_2 a_3 a_4$ is 0. The other generated frequencies are correct. $\mathcal{C}$ is in DNF with two simple constraints $(\mathcal{F}(A) > 1)$ and $(a_1 \in A)$. During the filtering step, when considering the itemsets of $a_2 a_3 a_4$'s class, the second constraint is always true. Since the generated frequency f is 0 and α is 1, $\alpha > f$ and therefore these itemsets must be filtered out. Finally, the remaining itemsets are exactly those that satisfy $\mathcal{C}$.

$$\mathcal{C}(A) = ((\mathcal{F}(A) > 1) \wedge (A \subseteq a_2 a_4)).$$

A good relaxation of $\mathcal{C}$ is $\mathcal{C}'(A) = ((\mathcal{F}(A) > 1) \wedge (A \subseteq \text{cl}(a_2 a_4))) = ((\mathcal{F}(A) > 1) \wedge (A \subseteq a_2 a_3 a_4))$. The corresponding transposed constraint is ${}^t\mathcal{C}'(O) = ((|O| > 1) \wedge (g(a_2 a_3 a_4) \subseteq O)) = ((|O| > 1) \wedge (o_3 \subseteq O))$ since $a_2 a_3 a_4$ is closed. The closed objects sets that satisfy this constraints are $T = \{o_1 o_2 o_3\}$. If we apply f to go back to the itemset space: $\{f(O) \mid O \in T\} = \{a_2 a_3\}$. Then all the subsets of $a_2 a_3$ are generated and only $\emptyset$ and a_2 remains after the filtering step.

6   Conclusion

In order to mine constrained closed patterns in databases with more columns than rows, we proposed a complete framework for the transposition: we gave the expression in the transposed database of the transposition of many classical constraints, and showed how to use existing closed set mining algorithms (with few modifications) to mine in the transposed database.

Then we gave a strategy to use this framework to mine all the itemset satisfying a constraint when a constrained closed itemset mining algorithm is available.

This strategy consists of three steps: generation of a relaxation of the constraint, extraction of the closed itemset satisfying the relaxed constraint and, finally, generation of all the itemsets satisfying the original constraint.

We can therefore choose the smallest space between the object space and the attribute space depending on the number of rows/columns in the database. Our strategy gives new opportunities for the optimization of mining queries (also called inductive queries) in contexts having a pathological size. This transposition principle could also be used for the optimization of sequences of queries: the closed object sets computed in the transposed database during the evaluation of previous queries can be stored in a cache and be re-used to speed up evaluation of new queries in a fashion similar to [15].

References

1. R. Agrawal, H. Mannila, R. Srikant, H. Toivonen, and A. I. Verkamo. Fast discovery of association rules. In *Advances in Knowledge Discovery and Data Mining*, 1996.
2. Y. Bastide, N. Pasquier, R. Taouil, G. Stumme, and L. Lakhal. Mining minimal non-redundant association rules using frequent closed itemsets. In *Proc. Computational Logic*, volume 1861 of *LNAI*, pages 972–986, 2000.
3. J. Besson, C. Robardet, and J.-F. Boulicaut. Constraint-based mining of formal concepts in transactional data. In *Proc. PAKDD*, 2004. to appear.
4. F. Bonchi, F. Giannotti, A. Mazzanti, and D. Pedreschi. Exante: Anticipated data reduction in constrained pattern mining. In *PKDD'03*, 2003.
5. E. Boros, V. Gurvich, L. Khachiyan, and K. Makino. On the complexity of generating maximal frequent and minimal infrequent sets. In *Symposium on Theoretical Aspects of Computer Science*, pages 133–141, 2002.
6. J.-F. Boulicaut, A. Bykowski, and C. Rigotti. Free-sets : a condensed representation of boolean data for the approximation of frequency queries. *DMKD*, 7(1), 2003.
7. J.-F. Boulicaut and B. Jeudy. Mining free-sets under constraints. In *Proc. IDEAS*, pages 322–329, 2001.
8. C. Bucila, J. Gehrke, D. Kifer, and W. White. Dualminer: a dual-pruning algorithm for itemsets with constraints. In *Proc. SIGKDD*, pages 42–51, 2002.
9. T. Calders and B. Goethals. Mining all non-derivable frequent itemsets. In *Proc. PKDD*, volume 2431 of *LNAI*, pages 74–85, 2002.
10. L. de Raedt and S. Kramer. The levelwise version space algorithm and its application to molecular fragment finding. In *Proc. IJCAI*, pages 853–862, 2001.
11. G. Dong and J. Li. Efficient mining of emerging patterns : discovering trends and differences. In *Proc. SIGKDD*, pages 43–52, 1999.
12. H. Fu and E. M. Nguifo. How well go lattice algorithms on currently used machine learning testbeds ? In *1st Intl. Conf. on Formal Concept Analysis*, 2003.
13. B. Goethals and J. V. den Bussche. On supporting interactive association rule mining. In *DAWAK'00*, 2000.
14. B. Jeudy and J.-F. Boulicaut. Optimization of association rule mining queries. *Intelligent Data Analysis*, 6(4):341–357, 2002.
15. B. Jeudy and J.-F. Boulicaut. Using condensed representations for interactive association rule mining. In *Proc. PKDD*, volume 2431 of *LNAI*, 2002.
16. R. Ng, L. V. Lakshmanan, J. Han, and A. Pang. Exploratory mining and pruning optimizations of constrained associations rules. In *SIGMOD*, 1998.

17. E. M. Nguifo and P. Njiwoua. GLUE: a lattice-based constructive induction system. *Intelligent Data Analysis*, 4(4):1–49, 2000.
18. F. Pan, G. Cong, A. K. H. Tung, J. Yang, and M. J. Zaki. CARPENTER: Finding closed patterns in long biological datasets. In *Proc. SIGKDD*, 2003.
19. N. Pasquier, Y. Bastide, R. Taouil, and L. Lakhal. Efficient mining of association rules using closed itemset lattices. *Information Systems*, 24(1):25–46, Jan. 1999.
20. J. Pei, J. Han, and L. V. S. Lakshmanan. Mining frequent itemsets with convertible constraints. In *Proc. ICDE*, pages 433–442, 2001.
21. J. Pei, J. Han, and R. Mao. CLOSET an efficient algorithm for mining frequent closed itemsets. In *Proc. DMKD workshop*, 2000.
22. L. D. Raedt, M. Jaeger, S. Lee, and H. Mannila. A theory of inductive query answering (extended abstract). In *Proc. ICDM*, pages 123–130, 2002.
23. F. Rioult, J.-F. Boulicaut, B. Crémilleux, and J. Besson. Using transposition for pattern discovery from microarray data. In *DMKD workshop*, 2003.
24. F. Rioult and B. Crémilleux. Optimisation of pattern mining : a new method founded on database transposition. In *EIS'04*, 2004.
25. A. Soulet, B. Crémilleux, and F. Rioult. Condensed representation of emerging patterns. In *Proc. PAKDD*, 2004.
26. B. Stadler and P. Stadler. Basic properties of filter convergence spaces. *J. Chem. Inf. Comput. Sci.*, 42, 2002.
27. R. Wille. Concept lattices and conceptual knowledge systems. In *Computer mathematic applied, 23(6-9):493-515*, 1992.
28. M. J. Zaki and C.-J. Hsiao. CHARM: An efficient algorithm for closed itemset mining. In *Proc. SDM*, 2002.

An Efficient Algorithm for Mining String Databases Under Constraints*

Sau Dan Lee and Luc De Raedt

Institute for Computer Science,
University of Freiburg, Germany
{danlee, deraedt}@informatik.uni-freiburg.de

Abstract. We study the problem of mining substring patterns from string databases. Patterns are selected using a conjunction of monotonic and anti-monotonic predicates. Based on the earlier introduced version space tree data structure, a novel algorithm for discovering substring patterns is introduced. It has the nice property of requiring only one database scan, which makes it highly scalable and applicable in distributed environments, where the data are not necessarily stored in local memory or disk. The algorithm is experimentally compared to a previously introduced algorithm in the same setting.

1 Introduction

In recent years, the number of string databases (particularly, in bioinformatics) has grown enormously [1]. One of the motivations for constructing and maintaining these databases is the desire to discover new knowledge from these databases using data mining techniques. While more traditional data mining techniques, such as frequent itemset mining [2] and frequent sequence mining [3], can be adapted to mine string databases, they do not take advantage of some properties specific to strings to accelerate the mining process. By specifically targeting string databases, it should be possible to devise more effective algorithms for discovering string patterns.

The most important contribution of this paper is the introduction of a novel algorithm, called FAVST, for mining string patterns from string databases. This algorithm combines ideas from data mining with string processing principles. More specifically, we employ ideas from suffix trees [4,5] to represent and compute the set of patterns of interest. The data structure used is that of Version Space Trees (VST, introduced by [6]) to organize the set of substring patterns being discovered. We have observed that a suffix trie can be treated as a deterministic automata so that we can visit all the substring patterns contained in a data string efficiently. We exploit this property of the suffix trie in VST and devised the FAVST algorithm (see Sect. 5.2). This algorithm performs frequency

---

* This work was supported by the EU IST FET project cInQ, contract number IST-2000-26469.

B. Goethals and A. Siebes (Eds.): KDID 2004, LNCS 3377, pp. 108–129, 2005.

counting in only one database scan. It is thus is especially efficient when database access is slow (e.g. over the internet). We also compare FAVST with a more traditional level-wise data mining algorithm, called VST, that we developed earlier [6]. As it employs the same data structure VST and the same setting as FAVST, this provides an appropriate setting for comparison. Although FAVST consumes more memory than VST our experiments (Sect. 6) show that the memory requirements are relatively cheap by today's hardware standards. Furthermore, as we will show, it can be controlled by imposing an upper bound on the length of patterns to be discovered, making FAVST very attractive in practice.

The two algorithms FAVST and VST discover all patterns that satisfy a conjunctive constraint or inductive query of the form $A_1 \wedge \ldots \wedge A_m \wedge M_1 \wedge \cdots \wedge M_n$ where the A_i's and M_j's are anti-monotonic and monotonic predicates, respectively.

1.1   Related Works

The present work is to a large extent motivated by the earlier MolFea system [7, 8], in which conjunctive queries (over anti-monotonic and monotonic predicates) for molecular features were solved using a version space approach. MolFea features are essentially strings that represent sequences of atoms and bonds.

On the theoretical side, we have previously introduced a general theory [6, 9] for mining of general patterns (not restricted to strings) satisfying a complicated predicate, which is composed of anti-monotonic and monotonic ones using Boolean algebra (negation, conjunction and disjunction). In this theoretical framework, one key component is an algorithm for efficiently discovering patterns satisfying the conjunction of a set of anti-monotonic and monotonic predicates. It is this component that we are addressing in this paper.

Furthermore, we have also generalized the concept of version spaces for performing usual set operations [10]. This results in an algebraic framework for handling general predicates composed of anti-monotonic and monotonic predicates.

There has been a lot of work in frequent itemset mining under constraints. In [11], a method for combining monotone and anti-monotone constraints is presented. In [12], the database is filtered and compressed into a compact *prefix tree* structure called the FP-tree and then frequent itemsets are computed directly from the data structure. This is not to be confused with our approach, in which we base on a general theoretical framework that works not only itemsets, but also many other pattern spaces. We do not only mine frequent patterns, but any patterns in the pattern space that satisfy a conjunction of monotonic and antimonotonic constraints. Moreover, our implemenation uses a suffix tree rather than a prefix tree. The tree stores the string patterns being mined, rather than (filtered) data items from the database. In [13], the use of the FP-tree with several monotonic and anti-monotonic constraints is discussed. However, that approach is specific for itemset patterns.

This work is also related to that of [14], which addresses the same setting as VST and FAVST, i.e. mining strings under conjunctive constraints using the

VST data structure. However, whereas VST and FAVST aim at minimizing the number of scans of the string database, the approach of [14] aims at minimizing the number of tests whether a string pattern covers an example. To this aim, [14] employs cost functions and the resulting algorithm is entirely different. Also, the algorithm by [14] is targeted at situations where testing whether a pattern covers an example is computationally expensive and the underlying data sets relatively small. These situations arise in e.g. graph mining, cf. [7].

The rest of this paper is organized as follows. Important definitions are introduced in Sect. 2. We take a closer look into the search space of the problem in Sect. 3 and describe a data structure to handle it in Sect. 4. Two algorithms are devised to construct this data structure. They're presented in Sect. 5. Our approach are verified by experiments presented in Sect. 6. Finally, we come up with conclusions in Sect. 7.

2   Definitions

2.1   Strings

Definition 1. *A string s over an alphabet Σ is a sequence of symbols from Σ. The length of a string s, denoted $|s|$, is the number of symbols in that sequence. The unique string of length zero is called the empty string, denoted ϵ. The set of all strings over an alphabet Σ is denoted Σ^*.*

Definition 2. *A substring s' of s is a sequence of consecutive symbols taken from s. We denote this relation as $s' \sqsubseteq s$. We also say that s is a superstring of s', or $s \sqsupseteq s'$.*

Example 3. With an alphabet of $\Sigma = \{a, b, c, d\}$, the following sequences are valid strings: ϵ, "ab", "abac", "dbacd". But "ae" is not a valid string over this alphabet, as $e \notin \Sigma$.

Note that $\sqsubseteq$ is a partial order relation. This fact is exploited in the design of our algorithms in Sect. 5.

2.2   Database and Substring Patterns

Since our goal is to mine substring patterns from a database, we have to define these two terms first. Further, not all substring patterns are interesting. We express the interestingness of the patterns using a predicate. Patterns not satisfying the predicate are considered to be uninteresting, and hence should not to be generated.

Definition 4. *A database D over an alphabet Σ is a bag (i.e. multi-set) of strings over Σ.*

Definition 5. *A pattern s over an alphabet Σ is a string over Σ.*

Definition 6. *A predicate $\mathcal{P}$ for substring patterns over Σ is a boolean function on a substring pattern $s \in \Sigma^*$ and (sometimes) a database D.*

We include D into the definition of predicates because our focus is mining patterns in databases, although it turns out that database-independent predicates are also useful in expressing the interestingness more precisely. In this latter case, we can simply treat D as a dummy parameter of our predicate. When D is a dummy parameter, we omit it for brevity.

Definition 7. *Define two predicates:*

$$\textsf{substring\_of}(s;t) \equiv s \sqsubseteq t$$
$$\textsf{superstring\_of}(s;t) \equiv s \sqsupseteq t$$

where $t \in \Sigma^*$ is a constant string.

Example 8. Using $\Sigma = \{a, b, c, d\}$, substring_of(ab; abc) and superstring_of(bcd; bc) evaluate to *true* whereas substring_of(cd; abc) and superstring_of(b; bc) evaluate to *false*.

Note that a predicate may have other parameters, such as a constant string as illustrated above, or a frequency threshold as shown below. We require these extra parameters to be independent of the database D, so that they can be fitted into our framework by the syntactic transformation $\mathcal{P}(s, D; x_1, x_2, \ldots, x_k) \mapsto \mathcal{P}_{x_1, x_2, \ldots, x_k}(s, D)$.

Analogous to frequent itemset mining, we may express our interestingness in frequent substring patterns by imposing a minimum occurrence frequency.

Definition 9. *Given a database D over an alphabet Σ and a pattern string $s \in \Sigma^*$, we define the frequency $freq(s; D)$ to be the number of strings in D that is a superstring of s. i.e.*

$$freq(s, D) = |\{d \in D | s \sqsubseteq d\}|$$

We define two predicates related to frequency.

Definition 10. *Given a database D and an integer θ, define*

$$\textsf{minimum\_frequency}(s, D; \theta_{\min}) \iff freq(s, D) \geq \theta_{\min}$$

$$\textsf{maximum\_frequency}(s, D; \theta_{\max}) \iff freq(s, D) \leq \theta_{\max}$$

When context is clear, we omit s and D and simply write minimum_frequency(θ) and maximum_frequency(θ).

Example 11. Let $\Sigma_1 = \{a, b, c, d\}$ and $D = \{abc, abd, cd, d, cd\}$. With this database, we have $freq(abc) = 1$, $freq(cd) = 2$, $freq(c) = 3$, $freq(abcd) = 0$. And trivially, $freq(\epsilon) = |D| = 5$. Thus, the following predicates evaluate to true: minimum_frequency(c, D; 2), minimum_frequency(cd, D; 2), maximum_frequency(abc, D; 2), maximum_frequency(cd, D; 2).

In some applications (e.g. MolFea [7]), it is useful to partition the database D into different subsets $D_1, \ldots, D_n$ and define frequency predicates that counts only a subset of D. e.g. $\mathcal{A}_1 = \mathsf{minimum\_frequency}(s, D_1; \theta_1)$ and $\mathcal{M}_2 = \mathsf{maximum\_frequency}(s, D_2; \theta_2)$. Then, we can construct a compound predicate $\mathcal{P} = \mathcal{A}_1 \wedge \mathcal{M}_2$ to mine the patterns that are frequent in the subset D_1 but not in D_2. Our experiments in Sect. 6 make use of such a setting extensively.

2.3   The Substring Mining Problem

Definition 12. *Given an alphabet Σ, a database D, and a predicate $\mathcal{P}$, the problem of* Mining Substring Patterns *is to find the set of substring patterns over Σ satisfying $\mathcal{P}$:*

$$Sol(\mathcal{P}, D, \Sigma^*) = \{s \in \Sigma^* \mid \mathcal{P}(s; D)\}$$

Example 13. Continuing from Example 11, let $P_1(s, D) \equiv \mathsf{minimum\_frequency}(s, D_1; 2) \wedge \mathsf{superstring\_of}(s; \mathsf{d})$. Then, we have $Sol(\mathcal{P}_1, D_1, \Sigma_1^*) = \{\mathsf{d}, \mathsf{cd}\}$.

3   The Search Space

To solve the problem of Mining Substring Patterns, one naïve approach is of course a brute-force search: check all the substrings over Σ^* against $\mathcal{P}$ and print out the satisfying ones. However, since Σ^* is countably infinite, one can never exhaust the whole pattern space, although one can enumerate them in a certain order.

A much better idea, as in itemset mining, is to exploit the structure of the search space. It has already been mentioned in Sect. 2.1 that $\sqsubseteq$ is a partial order relation. We will restrict the predicates to one of the following two types, or a conjunction of any number of them.

Definition 14. *An* anti-monotonic *predicate $\mathcal{A}$ is a predicate that satisfies:*

$$\forall s_1, s_2 \in \Sigma^* \text{ such that } s_1 \sqsubseteq s_2, \quad \mathcal{A}(s_2) \Rightarrow \mathcal{A}(s_1)$$

Definition 15. *A* monotonic *predicate $\mathcal{M}$ is a predicate that satisfies:*

$$\forall s_1, s_2 \in \Sigma^* \text{ such that } s_1 \sqsubseteq s_2, \quad \mathcal{M}(s_1) \Rightarrow \mathcal{M}(s_2)$$

Example 16. $\mathsf{substring\_of}$ and $\mathsf{minimum\_frequency}$ are anti-monotonic predicates whereas $\mathsf{superstring\_of}$ and $\mathsf{maximum\_frequency}$ are monotonic predicates.

With a compound query $\mathcal{P} = (\mathcal{A}_1 \wedge \cdots \wedge \mathcal{A}_m) \wedge (\mathcal{M}_1 \wedge \cdots \wedge \mathcal{M}_k)$, we can rewrite it as $\mathcal{P} = \mathcal{A} \wedge \mathcal{M}$, where $\mathcal{A} = \mathcal{A}_1 \wedge \cdots \wedge \mathcal{A}_m$ and $\mathcal{M} = \mathcal{M}_1 \wedge \cdots \wedge \mathcal{M}_k$. Note that $\mathcal{A}$ is anti-monotonic and $\mathcal{M}$ is monotonic. Therefore, we only need to consider predicates of the form $\mathcal{A} \wedge \mathcal{M}$.

While confining ourselves to predicates of this form may appear restrictive, we should note that in most formulations of data mining problems in the past years, an even more restrictive form of the predicate is used. For example, in most frequent-itemset, frequent-sequence mining problems, only a minimum-frequency predicate (anti-monotonic) is used. The consideration of using monotonic predicates has appeared only recently, and is still a rarity. [15, 16] The general conjunction of an arbitrary number of monotonic and anti-monotonic predicate is seldom seen, either. Thus, our restricted form $\mathcal{P} = \mathcal{A} \wedge \mathcal{M}$ is already quite expressive.

In previous works [6, 9], we suggested how to support queries that are arbitrary boolean functions of anti-monotonic and monotonic predicates. As shown in those papers, mining patterns under of these arbitrary boolean predicates can be reduced to the mining of predicates of the form $\mathcal{P} = \mathcal{A} \wedge \mathcal{M}$ as well as some set manipulation operations. The latter can be done efficiently (see Sect. 4.1). The former is non-trivial, and is the most time-consuming step. So, in this paper, we concentrate on the algorithms and performance issues, and restrict ourselves mainly to the form $\mathcal{P} = \mathcal{A} \wedge \mathcal{M}$.

3.1 Version Space

Restricting the predicate to the form $\mathcal{P} = \mathcal{A} \wedge \mathcal{M}$, the set of solutions to the Subsection Mining Problem $Sol(\mathcal{P}, D, \Sigma^*)$ turns out to be a version space [17] under the $\sqsubseteq$ relation. This means that there exists two sets $S, G \subseteq \Sigma^*$ with the following properties.

- $S = \{p \in Sol(\mathcal{P}, D, \Sigma^*) \mid \nexists q \in Sol(\mathcal{P}, D, \Sigma^*) \text{ such that } p \sqsubseteq q\}$
- $G = \{p \in Sol(\mathcal{P}, D, \Sigma^*) \mid \nexists q \in Sol(\mathcal{P}, D, \Sigma^*) \text{ such that } q \sqsubseteq p\}$
- $\forall p \in Sol(\mathcal{P}, D, \Sigma^*), \exists s \in S \wedge g \in G \text{ such that } g \sqsubseteq p \sqsubseteq s$
- $\forall p, q, r \in \Sigma^* \text{ such that } p \sqsubseteq q \sqsubseteq r, \text{ we have: } p, r \in Sol(\mathcal{P}, D, \Sigma^*) \Rightarrow q \in Sol(\mathcal{P}, D, \Sigma^*)$

Example 17. For $Sol(\mathcal{P}_1, D_1, \Sigma_1^*)$ from Example 13, we have $S = \{\texttt{cd}\}$ and $G = \{\texttt{d}\}$.

The set S is called the maximally *specific* set and G is called the maximally *general* set. For more details on how this mining problem relates to version spaces, please refer to our previous works [6, 9]. In this paper, we focus on the algorithms and optimizations.

4 Version Space Trees

To facilitate mining of string patterns, we have devised a data structure, which we called the version space tree (VST). We have already described the VST in other publications [6, 9]. So, we will give a brief overview of it here.

The VST data structure is inspired by the suffix tree, which is well studied [4, 5]. Instead of using a suffix tree, the VST is based on a less compact form, called suffix trie.

A trie is a tree with each edge labelled with a symbol from the alphabet Σ concerned. Moreover, the labels on every edge emerging from a node must be unique. Each node n in a trie thus uniquely represents the string $s(n)$ containing the characters on the path from the root r to the node n. The root node itself represents the empty string ϵ.

A suffix trie is a trie with the following properties:

- For each node n in the trie, and for each suffix t of $s(n)$, there is also a node n' in the trie representing t, i.e. $t = s(n')$.
- Each node n has as a *suffix link* $suffix(n) = n'$ where $s(n')$ is the suffix obtained from $s(n)$ obtained by dropping the first symbol. Note that $|s(n')| = |s(n)| - 1$. The root node is special because it represents ϵ, which has no suffixes. We define $suffix(root) = \perp$, where $\perp$ is a virtual node, acting as a null pointer.

Example 18. The VST for $Sol(\mathcal{P}_1, D_1, \Sigma_1^*)$ from Example 13 is depicted in Fig. 1. The numbers in each node n shows $freq(s(n), D_1)$. The label of each node is shown to the left of the node. The dashed arrows show the suffix links. The suffix links of the first level of nodes have been omitted for clarity. They all point to the root node. Note that this diagram is for illustrative purpose. In practice, we would prune away all branches containing only $\ominus$ nodes to save memory.

What makes VST unique is that we make two major deviations from the main stream approach in the suffix tree culture. The first one is that instead of building a suffix trie on all the suffixes of a *single* string, we are indexing all the suffixes of a *set of strings* in a database D. This means multiple strings are stored in the tree. As intermediate computation results, we even keep a count of occurrences of each such substring. In addition to a count, we also store a label on each node of the VST. The label $\oplus$ indicates that the represented string pattern is in our solution $Sol(\mathcal{P}, D, \Sigma^*)$. Otherwise, it is $\ominus$. Our algorithms in Sect. 5 exploit this label to store intermediate mining results. By contrast, theoretical works in the literature normally handle multiple strings by reducing the problem to a single string formed from concatenating the original strings, using a new delimiter symbol. While this is elegant in theory, it is impractical.

A second difference is that most studies on suffix trees usually consider a more compact form of suffix trie in which a chain of nodes with only one out-going edges are coalesced into one edge label with the string containing the symbols involved. We are not using this representation, as our algorithms need to keep flags and counts with each substring represented in the tree.

One interesting property of a VST tree is that one can compute the sets S and G (see Sect. 3.1) easily by a tree traversal. The S set consists of the strings $s(n)$ represented by the $\oplus$ nodes n who have no $\oplus$ descendants and no other $\oplus$ nodes n' with $suffix(n') = n$. The G set consists of the strings represented by the $\oplus$ nodes n whose parent is $\ominus$ and $suffix(n)$ is labelled $\ominus$.

Example 19. It can be easily checked from Fig. 1 with the above method that for $Sol(\mathcal{P}_1, D_1, \Sigma_1^*)$ from Example 13, $S = \{\text{cd}\}$ and $G = \{\text{d}\}$. This is consistent with Example 17.

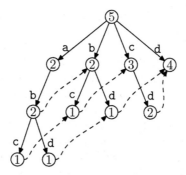

Fig. 1. A Version Space Tree

4.1   Beyond Version Spaces

The algorithms to be presented in Sect. 5 are designed to build VSTs that represent sets of strings that form a version space under $\sqsubseteq$. This restriction to version spaces is only needed for the algorithms to build the VSTs efficiently. Once the trees are built, we can perform other operations on them, treating the VSTs as representations of sets only.

Indeed, once the VSTs are built, we can use tree merging algorithms to compute the unions, intersections and set differences of them. No access to the database D is needed for these operations. Therefore, they can be performed completely in memory. We will see in section 6.4 that these operations generally takes little time when compared to the VST building, because the latter involves database scans.

With the possibility of performing general set operations on the resulting VSTs, we can actually handle more complicated predicates than the form $\mathcal{P} = \mathcal{A} \wedge \mathcal{M}$. The problem is how to break down a general predicate $\mathcal{P}$ into sub-predicates of the form $\mathcal{P}_i = \mathcal{A}_i \wedge \mathcal{M}_i$, so that $Sol(\mathcal{P}, D, \Sigma^*)$ can be computed from the intermediate results $Sol(\mathcal{P}_i, D, \Sigma^*)$ using set operations (e.g. union, intersection, set difference). We have made an elaborated study on this problem in previous publications [6, 9]. So, we are not repeating it here. In this paper, we give the details of the VST algorithm, as well as a new, faster algorithm FAVST.

5   The Algorithms

In this section, we present two algorithms to build a version space tree, given as input an alphabet Σ, a database D, and a predicate $\mathcal{P}$ of the form $\mathcal{A} \wedge \mathcal{M}$. Algorithm VST is a level-wise algorithm based on the well-known Apriori [18] algorithm. It was first introduced in [6]. The other algorithm, FAVST is new and is based on techniques in the suffix-tree literature [4], which is much faster when the database size is large and the database access time is not negligible.

We require that $\mathcal{A}$ be a non-trivial anti-monotonic predicate[1], as the version space and hence the corresponding tree with a trivial $\mathcal{A}$ will be infinite: There would be a finite integer k such that all strings on Σ with length greater than k will satisfy $\mathcal{M}$. There is no such restriction on $\mathcal{M}$, though.

In the algorithms, the alphabet Σ being used is restricted to the subset of "interesting symbols", i.e. those symbols that we want to appear in the discovered patterns. Uninteresting or irrelevant symbols are dropped. The algorithms effectively ignores symbols in the database D which do not belong to this restricted Σ. This deviates a bit from the previous theoretical section. However, in practice, this can significantly prune down the search space, esp. when the original alphabet is very large. This is because, like suffix tries, the size of a VST depends on the alphabet size, which affects the search space of our algorithms. Using a smaller alphabet improves the performance of both algorithms to be introduced.

5.1   Algorithm VST

The VST (Version Space Tree) algorithm is based on Agrawal's Apriori [18] algorithm. It consists of two phases:

1. Top-down growing of the version space tree using the anti-monotonic predicate $\mathcal{A}$.
2. Bottom-up marking of the version space tree using the monotonic predicate $\mathcal{M}$.

Both phases are designed to minimise the number of database scans. As such, they both exhibit the cyclic pattern: candidate generation, candidate testing (database scan) and pruning. The cycle terminates when no more new candidates patterns are generated.

Since only the anti-monotonic predicate is handled in phase 1, we can reuse the idea of Apriori. This is presented as the DESCEND algorithm (Algorithm 1). This algorithm searches the strings satisfying $\mathcal{A}$ in a top-down, breath-first manner. At each depth level k (corresponding to the k-th iteration in Apriori), the algorithm first expands the nodes from the previous level. The nodes resulting from expansion is the set C_k. These candidate nodes are then tested against predicate $\mathcal{A}$. The testing involves one database scan. The candidate patterns that satisfy the predicate are put into L_k. Those that do not are pruned away from the tree. This is repeated for $k = 1, 2, \ldots$ until C_k is empty. All generated nodes are labelled with $\oplus$ and the suffix links are set up during the process as illustrated in Algorithm 1.

Note that the sets C_k and L_k are the same as the candidate sets and "large" (i.e. frequent) sets in the Apriori algorithm. Moreover, the generation of C_k from L_{k-1} also mimics the Apriori-join operation in the Apriori algorithm.[2]

---

[1] A trivial anti-monotonic predicate is one that always evaluates to true.

[2] There are some differences here since we are dealing with strings instead of sets. E.g., while Apriori-join generates generate itemset {a, b, c} from {a, b} and {a, c}, the DESCEND algorithm generates abc from ab and bc, because these are the *only* immediately shorter *substrings* of abc.

Algorithm 1 DESCEND

Input: D = a database
  Σ = the alphabet of interesting symbols
  $\mathcal{A}$ = an anti-monotonic predicate
Output: T = a version space tree with nodes for all strings on Σ satisfying $\mathcal{A}$, and
  all nodes labelled with $\oplus$.
Body:
  Create version space tree T with root node r.
  $suffix(r) \leftarrow \bot$; $label(r) \leftarrow \oplus$
  // 1st iteration
  for all $l \in \Sigma$ **do** // Candidate Generation
5:    Add child node c to r with edge label l.
    $suffix(c) \leftarrow r$; $label(c) \leftarrow \oplus$; Add c to C_1, which is initially empty.
  end for
  $L_1 = \{c \in C_1 \mid \mathcal{A}(c, D)\}$. // Database Scan
  Remove from T all nodes $n \in C_1 \setminus L_1$. // Pruning
10:
  $k \leftarrow 2$
  loop // k-th iteration
    for all node $n \in L_{k-1}$ **do** // Candidate Generation
      for all child node c' of $n' - suffix(n)$ **do**
15:        Add child node c to n with the same edge label as that from n' to c'.
        $suffix(c) \leftarrow c'$; $label(c) \leftarrow \oplus$; Add c to C_k, which is initially empty.
      end for
    end for
    if C_k is empty **then**
20:      return T
    end if
    $L_k = \{c \in C_k \mid \mathcal{A}(c, D)\}$. // Database Scan
    Remove from T all nodes $n \in C_k \setminus L_k$. // Pruning
    $k \leftarrow k + 1$
25: **end loop**

DESCEND makes use of the suffix link and parent-child relationship of a suffix trie to perform the join efficiently (line 15). The major difference between DE-SCEND and Apriori is that the former also organizes the discovered strings into a suffix trie, facilitating the join operation and the second phase of the VST algorithm.

The second phase is implemented with algorithm ASCEND. This phase handles the monotonic predicate $\mathcal{M}$. Here we assume that we have the set F_0 of leave nodes in the tree T generated by DESCEND. F_0 can be easily obtained by a tree traversal. Actually, it can also be computed during algorithm DESCEND. While DESCEND works top-down, ASCEND starts from the leaves and works upwards. It first checks the leave nodes against $\mathcal{M}$. If any of these nodes n does not satisfy $\mathcal{M}$, its label is changed to $\ominus$. In addition, all its ancestors are also labelled as $\ominus$, due to the monotonicity. So, we can propagate this $\ominus$ mark upwards until we have marked the root with $\ominus$. Actually, we can stop as soon as we reach an ancestor already marked with $\ominus$, as another such leave node n' may share some ancestors with n. So, all the ancestors from that point upwards have already been marked with $\ominus$. This is repeated for all n not satisfying $\mathcal{M}$. For nodes p in F_0 that satisfy $\mathcal{M}$, they should remain labelled $\oplus$. We enter the parent of p into the set F_1 (with duplication removed), which are to be considered in the next iteration. This is to be repeated until we have an empty F_k.

Algorithm 2 ASCEND

Input: T = the version space tree from DESCEND
    D = the database being mined
    $\mathcal{M}$ = the monotonic predicate
    F_1 = the set of leaf nodes in T
Output: T = the tree from input, with all nodes for strings not satisfying the predicate $\mathcal{M}$ labelled with $\ominus$.
Body:
    $k \leftarrow 1$
    while F_k is non-empty **do** // *sweep upwards, starting from leaves*
        $P_k = \{f \in F_k \mid \mathcal{M}(f, D)\}$ // *Database Scan*
        for all $q \in F_k \setminus P_k$ **do** // *Pruning*
            $label(q) \leftarrow \ominus$
            while q is not root $\wedge label(parent(q)) \neq \ominus$ **do** // *mark upwards*
                $q \leftarrow parent(q)$
                $label(q) \leftarrow \ominus$
            end while
        end for
        $F_{k+1} = \{parent(p) \mid p \in P_k \wedge p \text{ is not root}\}$ // *Candidate Generation*
        $k \leftarrow k + 1$
    end while

So, after these two phases, namely DESCEND and then ASCEND, both $\mathcal{A}$ and $\mathcal{M}$ have been handled. With a simply tree traversal, we can prune away branches which now contains only $\ominus$ children. We have a resulting tree T that is a pruned suffix trie representing all the strings satisfying $\mathcal{P} = \mathcal{A} \wedge \mathcal{M}$.

Theorem 20. *The VST algorithm performs at most $2m$ database scans, where m is the longest string satisfying $\mathcal{A}$.*

Proof. The proof is quite straight-forward. Firstly, DESCEND is just the Apriori algorithm with modifications to handle the suffix trie structure. Therefore, it does the same number of database scans as Apriori, which is m. For ASCEND, we note that it starts with F_1 containing all the leaves of the resulting T from DESCEND. So, the deepest one has depth m. The $(k-1)$-th iteration of ASCEND generates a new F_k containing only parents of the previous F_{k-1} (less the pruned ones). As a result, nodes in F_k has at most depth $m - k + 1$. Since the depth of a non-root node[3] must be positive, we have $m - k + 1 \geq 1$, i.e. $k \leq m$. Thus, ASCEND makes at most m iterations and hence at most m database scans. $\square$

---

[3] The root node represents the empty string, which needs not be checked against any database.

Algorithm 3 FAVST

Input: $D = D_1, \ldots, D_n$ the database (divided into subsets)
$\quad \Sigma = $ the pattern alphabet
$\quad \mathcal{A} = \bigwedge_{i=1}^n$ minimum_frequency$(s, D_i, \theta_{\min_i})$ the anti-monotonic predicate
$\quad \mathcal{M} = \bigwedge_{i=1}^n$ maximum_frequency$(s, D_i, \theta_{\max_i})$ the monotonic predicate $\text{len}_{\max} = $
maximum length of substring pattern
Output: $T = $ version space tree representing strings satisfying $\mathcal{P} = \mathcal{A} \wedge \mathcal{M}$.
Body:
$\quad T \leftarrow \mathsf{InitTree}(D_1, \Sigma, \theta_{\min_1}, \theta_{\max_1}, \text{len}_{\max})$
$\quad$ Prune away branches in T with only $\ominus$ nodes.
$\quad$ **for all** $i = 2, \ldots, n$ **do**
$\quad\quad \mathsf{CountAndUnmark}(T, D_i, \Sigma, \theta_{\min_i}, \theta_{\max_i})$
$\quad\quad$ Prune away branches in T with only $\ominus$ nodes.
$\quad$ **end for**

5.2   Algorithm **FAVST**

The drawback of the previous algorithm is that it still has to scan the database $2m$ times, where m is the length of the longest string satisfying $\mathcal{A}$. Actually, strings exhibit some properties not exhibited by itemsets. Therefore, there is still room for improvements. Our next algorithm, FAVST[4] makes use of techniques from the suffix-tree literature to improve performance. It is well-known in that literature that the suffix-tree of a string can be built in linear time. Some of these ideas are employed in the FAVST algorithm to make it possible to build the version space tree with just a single database scan. We show here only how frequency-based predicates are handled. Database-independent predicates can be handled efficiently without database scanning. For other types of database-dependent predicates, predicate-specific adaptations would be needed.

The FAVST algorithm is shown in Algorithm 3. It first calls InitTree to process the first minimum_frequency predicate and scan the first database subset (see Sect. 2.2) to build an initial VST. Then, it invokes CountAndUnmark to process the remaining database subsets and the corresponding minimum_frequency predicates. Note that CountAndUnmark will not grow the VST. It will only count the frequency of the patterns in the corresponding database subset and mark those not satisfying the thresholds $\theta_{\min_i}$ and $\theta\max_i$ with $\ominus$. Branches with only $\ominus$ are pruned away immediately after the the scanning of each database subset to reduce the number of patterns that need to be checked against the subsequent subsets.

The parameter $\text{len}_{\max}$ specifies an upper bound on the length of the substring patterns to be discovered. When set appropriately, this parameter makes FAVST to be very efficient both in terms of computation time and memory usage (see Sect. 6). FAVST is presented here as if we must specify a minimum and maximum frequency threshold for every database subset. This is indeed not the case. If we are not interested in specify a minimum frequency for subset i, we can simply

---

set $\theta_{\min_i} = 0$. Similarly, a maximum frequency can be set to $\theta_{\min_i} = \infty$ to "disable" it. The algorithm in Algorithm 3 is presented in a way to simplify the pseudo-code.

We will later see that each of the subalgorithms InitTree and CountAndUnmark scans the specified database subset only once. So, the whole FAVST algorithm scans each database subset only once. If the database subsets are disjoint, then we can in implementation scan only the subset of data being processed. In that case, FAVST completes in only one scan of the whole database. So, FAVST is a single-scan algorithm.

Algorithm InitTree is shown in Algorithm 4. It scans each string in the database subset symbol for symbol, going down the tree as it proceeds. If a node does not have a suitable child for it to go downward, one such child is created with CreateChild, so that we can go down the tree. Note that this "going down" increases the length of the string pattern represented by the current node (n) by one. To handle the upper bound on the pattern length ($\text{len}_{\max}$), the algorithm checks the depth of the current node before actually going down. If the length limit is reached, the algorithm "backs up" by following the suffix link. Essentially, if the current node represents string aw where a is a symbol and w is a string so that $|aw| = \text{len}_{\max}$, then the next substring to be counted would be "$aw\varsigma$", which exceeds the length limit. So, we continue with the suffix "$w\varsigma$", which is achieved by changing the current node n to $suffix(n)$, because this latter represents string w. Next, InitTree increments the count of the destination of this going down, as well as all its suffixes. Then, the next symbol is processed, continuing from this destination. When an uninteresting symbol (i.e. $\notin \Sigma$) or the end of a string is encountered, it starts the downward travel from the root node again.

This is basically a suffix tree building algorithm, with four modifications. The first is that we do frequency counting on the way as we go. The second is that we put an upper bound on the length of the substring patterns, or the depth of the trie. Thirdly, we jump back to the root when we encounter uninteresting symbols, saving the need to process any strings containing such symbols. Last but not least, we handle multiple strings, instead of a concatenation of these strings. In the traditional and theoretical approach, multiple strings are handled by building a suffix trie T_{all} on a single string $s_1\$s_2\$\ldots\$s_m$ (where m is the number of strings in D) obtained by concatenating all strings in D, with a special character "$\$$" not occurring in the database as delimiter. While this approach is a convenient tool for theoretical analysis of complexity, it is costly in implementation as it increases the amount of memory required multifold. It also multiples the depth of the trie, making a complete traversal expensive. Our approach, instead, overlays all the strings s_k onto a suffix trie with the same root, maintaining multiplicity with the frequency $count(n)$. Note that our trie T can be obtained by taking T_{all}, cutting it at all the "$\$$" nodes to obtain a forest of smaller tries, and then merging all these smaller tries at the root to produce a single trie. Uninteresting symbols are handled similarly. Therefore, we have the following theorem.

Algorithm 4 InitTree

Input: D_i = a database subset
    Σ = the pattern alphabet
    $\theta_{\min}$ = minimum frequency threshold
    $\theta_{\max}$ = maximum frequency threshold
    $\text{len}_{\max}$ = maximum length of substring pattern
Output: T = version space tree representing strings in D_i satisfying $\mathcal{P} = \mathcal{A} \wedge \mathcal{M}$.
Body:
  Create version space tree T with root nod r.
  $suffix(r) = \bot$; $label(r) = \oplus$
  $count(n) \leftarrow 0$; $last\text{-}id(n) \leftarrow$ undefined
  for all string $s \in DB_i$ with unique id id **do**
    $n \leftarrow r$
    for all symbol $\varsigma \in s$ **do**
      if $\varsigma \in \Sigma$ **then** // *an interesting symbol*
        if depth of $n \geq \text{len}_{\max}$ **then**
          $n \leftarrow suffix(n)$
        end if
        if node n has no child c on outgoing edge labeled ς **then**
          $c \leftarrow$ CreateChild(n, ς)
          add child c to n with edge label ς
        end if
        while $x \neq \bot \wedge last\text{-}id(c) \neq id$ **do** // *not counted yet*
          $count(c) \leftarrow count(c) + 1$
          $last\text{-}id(c) = id$
          $x \leftarrow suffix(c)$ // *count also all suffixes*
        end while
        $n \leftarrow c$ // *process next symbol from here (i.e. longer string)*
      else // *an uninteresting symbol*
        $n \leftarrow r$ // *break string; continue from root*
      end if
    end for
  end for
  for all node n in T **do** // *traverse the trie T*
    if $count(n) < \theta_{\min} \vee count(n) > \theta_{\max}$ **then**
      $label(n) \leftarrow \ominus$
    end if
    $count(n) \leftarrow 0$ // *reset for next invocation*
    $last\text{-}id(n) \leftarrow$ undefined // *reset for next invocation*
  end for

Theorem 21. *The suffix trie T obtained as described above is a sub-trie of the suffix trie T_{all}. Moreover, it takes the same time complexity to build as T_{all}.*

After scanning the database, InitTree performs a traversal of the trie and checks if the counts satisfy the specified thresholds. If not, it labels that node with "$\ominus$". Meanwhile, the algorithm also resets $count(n)$ and $last\text{-}id(n)$ for every node to prepare for the next invocation.

Algorithm 5 CreateChild

Input: $p =$ the parent node
$\varsigma =$ the edge label to use
Output: $c =$ the newly created node
Body:
  Create new node c.
  $count(c) \leftarrow 0$
  $last\text{-}id(c) =$ undefined
  $label(c) = \oplus$
  $sn \leftarrow suffix(p)$
  if $sn = \perp$ **then** // p is root
    $suffix(c) \leftarrow p$
  else
    if sn has a child sc on outgoing edge labelled ς **then**
      $suffix(c) \leftarrow sc$
    else // *create recursively*
      $sc \leftarrow$ InitTree(sn, ς)
      Add sc to sn with edge label ς
      $suffix(c) \leftarrow sc$
    end if
  end if

The subroutine CreateChild (Algorithm 5) is relatively straight-forward. It creates and initializes a new node. The most tricky part is to establish the suffix link, recursively creating the node for the suffix if it is not already there. The suffix node can be located by following the parent's suffix. This is because if the parent node p represents the string aw (where a is a symbol and w is a string) and the new child node represents string $aw\varsigma$, then the suffix of the new child must represent $w\varsigma$, which is represented by a node whose parent represents w—the suffix of p.

Algorithm 6 show the CountAndUnmark algorithm, which is similar to InitTree except that it does not create new nodes. For any node n already present in T, we need not recreate it or re-calculate the suffix link. We only need to increase the support count $count(n)$ for that node. If the node n is not in T as we do the downward walk, we know that s that it would represent is not present in T, and hence it is not a pattern we are looking for (because it doesn't satisfy the predicate a_0 used to build the initial trie). So, there is no need to create that node. Neither do we need to care about the length limit on the substring patterns, because InitTree has avoided creating the nodes for substrings exceeding the length limit. However, we should continue counting by considering the immediate suffix s' of s. This is done by following the suffix link of p, i.e. $p' = suffix(p)$, which represents the string $t' = suffix(t)$. The node n' representing s' would be a child of p'. If it is there, then we have located the node for s' and we continue. If not, then we repeat the above method of following suffix links until we have $t' = \perp$. The support counts are thus counted in this manner. Again, as we visit a node n, we increment the counter on that node to count the occurrence of the corresponding substring pattern.

Algorithm 6 CountAndUnmark

Input: T = a version space tree
  D_i = a database subset
  Σ = the alphabet of interesting symbols
  $\theta_{\min}$ = the lower support threshold
  $\theta_{\max}$ = the upper threshold threshold
Output: T = the input T with nodes that have support counts in database subset D_i
  not satisfying the threshold labeled with "$\ominus$"
Require: $count(n) = 0 \wedge label(n) =$ undefined $\forall$ node $n \in T$
Body:
  for all string $s \in D_i$ with unique id id **do**
    $n \leftarrow r$, where r is the root node of T
    for all symbol $\varsigma \in s$ **do**
      if $\varsigma \in \Sigma$ **then** // *an interesting symbol*
        while $n \neq \bot \wedge$ node n has no child c on outgoing edge labeled ς **do** //
        substring is not in T
          $n \leftarrow suffix(n)$ // *try a suffix (a shorter string)*
        end while
        if $n \neq \bot$ **then** // *found a suffix in* T
          $x \leftarrow c$
          while $x \neq \bot \wedge last\text{-}id(c) \neq id$ **do** // *not counted yet*
            $count(c) \leftarrow count(c) + 1$
            $last\text{-}id(c) = id$
            $x \leftarrow suffix(c)$ // *count also all suffixes*
          end while
          $n \leftarrow c$ // *process next symbol from here (i.e. longer string)*
        end if
      else // *an uninteresting symbol*
        $n \leftarrow r$ // *break string; continue from root*
      end if
    end for
  end for
  for all node n in T **do** // *traverse the trie* T
    if $count(n) < \theta_{\min} \vee count(n) > \theta_{\max}$ **then**
      $label(n) \leftarrow \ominus$
    end if
    $count(n) \leftarrow 0$ // *reset for next invocation*
    $last\text{-}id(n) \leftarrow$ undefined // *reset for next invocation*
  end for

In order to avoid double-counting a node for the same string[5] in both InitTree and CountAndUnmark, we also record the string id $last\text{-}id(n) \leftarrow k$ after incrementing the count. The support count is incremented only if $last\text{-}id(n) \neq k$. The nodes are labeled with "$\oplus$" when they are created.

---

[5] This can happen e.g. for $s_t =$ ababc and a node n representing string ab. This is because ab occurs twice in s_t. However, the frequency is defined in terms of number of strings in DB_r containing a string, irrelevant of how many times it occurs in the same string.

The major efficiency improvement of FAVST comes from the single database scan. Firstly, note that the algorithm does not work level-wise in the style of Apriori. Rather, it examine the predicates one by one and invokes InitTree and CountAndUnmark to scan the concerned database subsets.

On the space efficiency, since the suffix trie is $O(|D|^2)$ in size (where $|D|$ is the total number of symbols in D), FAVST is less space-efficient than VST. Nevertheless, in practice, we can specify a relatively small upper bound d on the length of the longest substring pattern we are going to find. This can effectively limit the depth of the VST to d, reducing the amount of memory that FAVST would need. Of course, a minor modification to FAVST, which is not shown here, is needed.

6   Experiments

The algorithms VST and FAVST have been implemented in C. The experiments are performed on PC computer with a Pentium-4 2.8GHz processor, 2GB main memory, and running Linux operating system (kernel 2.4.19, glibc 2.2.5).

6.1   Unix Command History Database

The database DB used in the experiments are command history collected from 168 Unix users over a period of time. [19] The users are divided into four groups: computer scientists, experienced programmers, novice programmers and non-programmers. The corresponding data subsets are denoted "sci", "exp", "nov" and "non", respectively. Each group has a number of users. When each users accesses the Unix system, he first logs in, then type in a sequence of commands, and finally logs out. Each command is taken as a symbol in the database, The sequence of commands from log in to log out constitutes a login session, which is mapped to a string in our experiment. Each user contributes to many login sessions in the database. Table 1 gives some summary data on the database. To study the effectiveness of the $\text{len}_{\max}$ parameter to FAVST, we repeated FAVST twice for each experiment: once with $\text{len}_{\max} = \infty$, essentially disabling the length limit; and once with $\text{len}_{\max} = 10$. These are denoted "FAVST" and "FAVST^{ml}", respectively, in all the tables and the figures.

Table 1. Summary statistics of the data

Subset (D_i)	no. of users	no. of strings	$\theta_{\min}$	frequent substrings	time (milliseconds) VST	FAVST	FAVST^{ml}
nov	55	5164	24	294*	770	1040	330
exp	36	3859	80	292	700	950	530
non	25	1906	80	293	180	280	110
sci	52	7751	48	295	1170	2310	1010

*Of these 294 patterns, 36 have length > 10. They are thus dropped in FAVST^{ml}.

6.2   Performance—Minimum_Frequency Only

The first set of experiments are done with only one minimum_frequency predicate. The thresholds used are shown in Table 1. These thresholds are selected so that they produce around 300 frequent string patterns in each database subset. The time taken (wall-clock time) by the two algorithms are noted and given in the same table.

It is promising that FAVST[ml] is the fastest in all cases. With an upper bound on the length of the substring patterns, FAVST works much more efficiently, because of the reduction of the size of the trie structure. The drawback is that 36 patterns are pruned away by this length limit.

On the other hand, it seems disappointing that FAVST takes longer time to finish than VST, despite our claim of a single database scan. Our explanation is that the data files are stored in local harddisk, and hence are extremely fast to access. Thus, the single-scan advantage of FAVST is suppressed. Moreover, the disk caching effect also diminishes the advantage of a single database scan. However, this is only valid for small databases which can be accessed quickly (e.g. local drive). Much larger databases that do not fit into main memory or that are

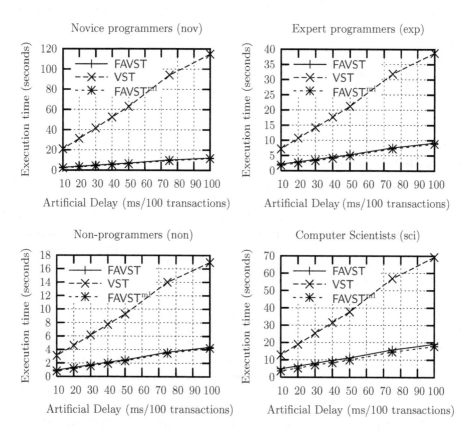

Fig. 2. Performance comparison with database access delays

Table 2. Memory usage of the two algorithms

Data sub-set(D_i)	Max. mem. usage (bytes)			Ratio	
	VST	FAVST	FAVST^{ml}	FAVST/VST	FAVST^{ml}/VST
nov	57158	17456767	3573695	305	63.5
exp	88870	14439604	5367732	162	60.4
non	59918	6797462	2081558	113	34.7
sci	94454	23107503	8997455	245	95.3

stored on much slower storage devices (e.g. on CDROM, on a file server accessed via a LAN, or even over a web server) can benefit from the single database scan. To simulate this idea, we modified the programs to introduce a delay in the database reading routine. The delay is parameter-controlled. It inserts m milliseconds of delay for every 100 transactions (i.e. strings) read. Repeating the above experiment with different values of m gives the results in Figure 2. We plot the result of each data set separately, comparing the two algorithms in each case.

It is clear from the figure that FAVST out-performs VST once the database access delay becomes non-trivial. The former is consistently 3 times faster than the latter. For the "nov" data set, the speed up ratio even reaches 6. Evidently, the single database scan algorithm FAVST scales much better with large database with slow access than the simpler algorithm VST. The effect of the limit on pattern length does not appear significant here. The curves for FAVST and FAVST^{ml} almost overlap for all four data sets. This is because the dominant factor in execution time is the number of database scans, which is always 1, whether or not we specify a length limit on the patterns.

6.3   Memory Footprints

The speed up is a trade off with memory usage. Table 2 shows the maximum amount of memory consumed by the two algorithms for the data structures. VST has a memory footprint in the order of tens of kilobytes, whereas that of FAVST is in megabytes. With today's computing equipments, the memory consumption of FAVST is absolutely affordable. Imposing a limit on the length of patterns makes FAVST^{ml} build a much smaller trie than FAVST, significantly reducing the memory consumption by a factor of 2–5.

It should be noted that the memory consumption of the algorithms has no direct relation to the database sizes. From Table 1, we can see that the data set "nov" is larger than "exp" and "non". However, it turns out to cause the algorithms to consume less memory than the other two data sets. Our explanation is that the "nov" data set has more repeated string patterns. Since our algorithm uses the same trie node for the same pattern, the fewer the number of distinct string patterns, the fewer nodes are created, and hence the less memory consumed. In other words, the memory consumption is related to the number of distinct string patterns, but not the database size. Thus, our algorithms exhibits very nice properties for data mining applications. They scale well with database

Table 3. An experiment on compound predicates

Trie	$\mathcal{P} = \mathcal{A} \wedge \mathcal{M}$
T_1	minimum_frequency(non; 24) $\wedge$ maximum_frequency(sci; 60)
T_2	minimum_frequency(nov; 80) $\wedge$ maximum_frequency(exp; 36)
U	$T_1 \cup T_2$

Table 4. Results on finding the union of two version spaces

Trie	Time (seconds)			number of nodes		
	VST	FAVST	FAVST^{ml}	labeled $\oplus$	labeled $\ominus$	total
T_1	0.56	0.39	0.19	166	40	206
T_2	1.23	1.19	0.37	237*	18	255
U		negligible		401*	47	448

*Of these $\oplus$ nodes, 36 are at depth > 10, representing patterns of length > 10. These are pruned away in the FAVST^{ml} case.

size, and use an amount of memory depending on the amount of interesting patterns that will be discovered.

6.4   Performance—Compound Predicates

The above experiments only makes use of the minimum_frequency predicate. No monotonic predicates are specified. Thus, the full features of our algorithms has not been utilized. The following experiment uses the algorithms VST and FAVST to compute two version space trees T_1 and T_2, each representing a set of strings satisfying a predicate of the form $\mathcal{P} = \mathcal{A} \wedge \mathcal{M}$, where $\mathcal{A}$ is minimum_frequency and $\mathcal{M}$ is maximum_frequency. The details are tabulated in Table 3. The database used is the same as described above. The thresholds for the minimum_frequency predicate are copied from Table 1, where as those for the maximum_frequency are from Table 1 less 25%. After computing these trees, the union of them, U is computed by a naïve tree-merging operation. Note that U is no longer a version space tree, as it represents a subsets of Σ^* which is not a version space anymore.

The results of the experiments are shown in Table 4. Each row shows the time that either algorithm used to build that tree. The time taken to compute U in either case is negligible, as it is done completely in memory. It takes so little time (less than 0.01 second) that we cannot reliably measure because of the granularity of the time-measurement program we are using.

It is encouraging that in this general case, FAVST runs faster than VST, even though we did not add the artificial database access delay into the programs. FAVST^{ml} takes even less time to compute the result, although 36 patterns are not discovered due to the length limit.

The longest pattern found (represented by the deepest node in U having a $\oplus$ label) was "pix umacs pix umacs pix umacs pix umacs pix umacs pix umacs pix umacs pix umacs pix umacs pix", which has a length of 19. The deepest $\ominus$ node in U represented the string "cd ls cd ls", of length 4, which has an interesting (labelled $\oplus$) child representing the string "cd ls cd ls e". If we did not have any monotonic predicates (i.e. maximum_frequency in this case), "cd ls cd ls" would have been considered interesting because it is frequent enough. However, with the monotonic predicates, this string is now *too* frequent and hence it is considered uninteresting and marked with $\ominus$ in U. This illustrates the increased power and expressiveness of using both anti-monotonic and monotonic predicates together in data mining. The ability to compute U efficiently by manipulating the results T_1 and T_2 shows the power of these algorithms in combination with the results in [6, 9].

7   Conclusions

In this paper, we have addressed the problem of Mining Substring Patterns under conjunctive constraints. This is a core component of a more general data mining framework in a couple of related works [6, 9, 10].

The main contribution of this paper was the FAVST algorithm, which employs the VST data structure of [6, 9] and combines principles of constraint based mining with those of suffix-trees. This algorithm has the very nice property of requiring only one database scan, at the expense of very affordable memory overheads. Such overheads can be significantly reduced by imposing an upperbound on the length of patterns. The data structure and algorithms have been empirically proved to be practical and useful for finding substring patterns in a unix user command database.

One direction for further research is concerned with data streams. It might be possible to combine the present framework with that proposed by Han et al.

References

1. Creighton, C., Hanash, S.: Mining gene expression databases for association rules. Bioinformatics **19** (2003) 79–86
2. Agrawal, R., Imielinski, T., Swami, A.N.: Mining association rules between sets of items in large databases. In Buneman, P., Jajodia, S., eds.: Proceedings of the 1993 ACM SIGMOD International Conference on Management of Data, Washington, D.C., U.S.A. (1993) 207–216
3. Agrawal, R., Srikant, R.: Mining sequential patterns. In Yu, P.S., Chen, A.S.P., eds.: Eleventh International Conference on Data Engineering, Taipei, Taiwan, IEEE, IEEE Computer Society Press (1995) 3–14
4. Ukkonen, E.: On-line construction of suffix trees. Algorithmica **14** (1995) 249–260
5. Weiner, P.: Linear pattern matching algorithm. In: Proc. 14 IEEE Symposium on Switching and Automata Theory. (1973) 1–11
6. De Raedt, L., Jaeger, M., Lee, S.D., Mannila, H.: A theory of inductive query answering (extended abstract). In Kumar, V., Tsumoto, S., Zhong, N., Philip S. Yu, X.W., eds.: Proc. The 2002 IEEE International Conference on Data Mining (ICDM'02), Maebashi, Japan (2002) 123–130 ISBN 0-7695-1754-4.

7. Kramer, S., De Raedt, L., Helma, C.: Molecular feature mining in HIV data. In: KDD-2001: The Seventh ACM SIGKDD International Conference on Knowledge Discovery and Data Mining, Association for Computing Machinery (2001) ISBN: 158113391X.
8. De Raedt, L., Kramer, S.: The levelwise version space algorithm and its application to molecular fragment finding. In: IJCAI01: Seventeenth International Joint Conference on Artificial Intelligence. (2001)
9. De Raedt, L., Jaeger, M., Lee, S.D., Mannila, H.: A theory of inductive query answering. (2003) (submitted to a journal).
10. Lee, S.D., De Raedt, L.: An algebra for inductive query evaluation. [20] 147–154
11. Grahne, G., Lakshmanan, L.V.S., Wang, X.: Efficient mining of constrained correlated sets. In: Proceedings of the 16th International Conference on Data Engineering, IEEE Computer Society (2000) 512–521
12. Han, J., Pei, J., Yin, Y.: Mining frequent patterns without candidate generation. In Chen, W., Naughton, J.F., Bernstein, P.A., eds.: Proceedings of the 2000 ACM SIGMOD International Conference on Management of Data, Dallas, Texas, U.S.A., ACM Press (2000) 1–12
13. Pei, J., Han, J.: Can we push more constraints into frequent pattern mining? In: Proceedings of the Sixth ACM SIGKDD International Conference on Knowledge Discovery and Data Mining (KDD 2000), Boston, MA, USA (2000) ISBN: 1-58113-233-6.
14. Fischer, J., De Raedt, L.: Towards optimizing conjunctive inductive queries. In: Proc. The Eighth Pacific-Asia Conference on Knowledge Discovery and Data Mining (PAKDD2004), Carlton Crest Hotel, Sydney, Australia (2004)
15. Boulicaut, J.F., Jeudy, B.: Using constraints during set mining: Should we prune or not? In: Actes des Seizième Journées Bases de Données Avancées (BDA'00), Blois, France (2000) 221–237
16. Bonchi, F., Giannotti, F., Mazzanti, A., Pedreschi, D.: ExAMiner: Optimized level-wise frequent pattern mining with monotone constraints. [20] 11–18
17. Mitchell, T.M.: Generalization as search. Artificial Intelligence 18 (1982) 203–226
18. Agrawal, R., Srikant, R.: Fast algorithms for mining association rules. In Bocca, J.B., Jarke, M., Zaniolo, C., eds.: Proceedings of the 20th International Conference on Very Large Databases, Santiago, Chile, Morgan Kaufmann (1994) 487–499
19. Greenberg, S.: Using unix: Collected traces of 168 users. Research Report 88/333/45, Department of Computer Science, University of Calgary, Alberta, Canada. (1988)
20. Wu, X., Tuzhilin, A., Shavlik, J., eds.: Proceedings of The Third IEEE International Conference on Data Mining (ICDM'03). In Wu, X., Tuzhilin, A., Shavlik, J., eds.: Proceedings of The Third IEEE International Conference on Data Mining (ICDM'03), Melbourne, Florida, USA, Sponsored by the IEEE Computer Society (2003)

An Automata Approach to Pattern Collections

Taneli Mielikäinen

HIIT Basic Research Unit,
Department of Computer Science,
University of Helsinki, Finland
Taneli.Mielikainen@cs.Helsinki.FI

Abstract. Condensed representations of pattern collections have been recognized to be important building blocks of inductive databases, a promising theoretical framework for data mining, and recently they have been studied actively. However, there has not been much research on how condensed representations should actually be represented.

In this paper we study how condensed representations of frequent itemsets can be concretely represented: we propose the use of deterministic finite automata to represent pattern collections and study the properties of the automata representation. The automata representation supports visualization of the patterns in the collection and clustering of the patterns based on their structural properties and interestingness values. Furthermore, we show experimentally that finite automata provide a space-efficient way to represent itemset collections.

1 Introduction

One of the most important approaches to mine data is *pattern discovery* which aims to extract *interesting patterns* (possibly with some *interestingness values* associated to each of them) from data. The most prominent example of a pattern discovery task is the *frequent itemset mining* problem [1]:

Problem 1 (Frequent Itemset Mining). Given a multi-set $d = \{d_1 \ldots d_n\}$ (a *transaction database*) of subsets (*transactions*) of a set $\mathcal{I}$ of *items* and a *minimum frequency threshold* $\sigma \in [0,1]$, find the *collection of σ-frequent itemsets* in d, i.e., the collection

$$\mathcal{F}(\sigma, d) = \{X \subseteq \mathcal{I} : fr(X, d) \geq \sigma\}$$

where

$$fr(X, d) = \frac{supp(X, d)}{n},$$

$$supp(X, d) = |cover(X, d)|$$

and

$$cover(X, d) = \{i : X \subseteq d_i, 1 \leq i \leq n\}.$$

There exist techniques to find all frequent itemsets reasonably efficiently [2]. A major advantage of frequent itemsets is that they can be computed from data

B. Goethals and A. Siebes (Eds.): KDID 2004, LNCS 3377, pp. 130–149, 2005.

without much domain knowledge: any transaction database determines an empirical joint probability distribution over the item combinations and the marginal probabilities of the combinations with high probability can be considered as a reasonable way to summarize the empirical joint probability distribution determined by the data. The generality of this summarization approach causes also troubles: the frequent itemset collections that describe data quite well tend to be quite large. Although the frequent itemsets might be found efficiently enough even from very large transaction databases, it is not certain that an enormously large collection of frequent itemsets is very concise summary of the data.

The problem of discovering too large frequent itemset collections to comprehend has been tried to solve by finding small sub-collections of the frequent itemsets that are sufficient to determine which itemsets are frequent and what are the frequencies of the frequent itemsets. Such sub-collections are often called the *condensed representations* of frequent itemsets. (In general, the condensed representations do not have to be sub-collections of patterns but just some data structures from which it is possible to answer queries of certain kind accurately and efficiently enough. In fact, the condensed representations were originally introduced in this broader context [3].) The condensed representations of frequent itemsets (and interesting patterns, in general) have been recognized to have an important role in *inductive databases* which seems to be a promising theoretical model for data mining [4, 5, 6]. Furthermore, many condensed representations of itemset collections are readily applicable to several other collections of interesting patterns.

The condensed representations of frequent itemsets have studied actively and several condensed representations, such as *maximal itemsets* [7], *closed itemsets* [8], *free itemsets* [9], *disjunction-free itemsets* [10], *disjunction-free generators* [11], *k-free itemsets* [12] *non-derivable itemsets* [13], *condensed pattern bases* [14], *pattern orderings* [15] and *pattern chains* [16], have been proposed. However, not much has been done on how the condensed representations should actually be represented although it is an important question: the representation of the knowledge can drastically affect the efficiency of the inductive database but it also affects the data analyst to comprehend or not to comprehend the mining results.

In this paper we study how pattern collections can be represented explicitly. (Two other alternatives to represent pattern collections would be the represent the collection implicitly or represent it partly implicitly and partly explicitly. These representations have been studied in [17] and in [18], respectively.) We suggest using deterministic finite automata as condensed representations of pattern collections. For brevity, we focus on itemset collections. The automata representations of itemset collections are space-efficient, allow efficient ad-hoc queries of frequencies, support exploratory data analysis, can be used to cluster the patterns, and have very natural visualizations. The approach can be adapted also to other kinds of pattern collections such as subsequences and subgraphs.

The paper is organized as follows. Section 2 concerns pros and cons of describing a pattern collection by listing the patterns explicitly. In Section 3 we define the automata terminology used in this paper, describe the currently used automata approach for pattern collections (that is, representing pattern collections as tries) and study their properties. In Section 4 and Section 5 we propose two more refined automata approaches to express the condensed representations of frequent itemset collections. In Section 6 the visualization and clustering possibilities of the automata representations are discussed and in Section 7 the conciseness of the proposed approaches is experimentally evaluated. The work is concluded in Section 8.

2   Listing Patterns

A straightforward way to describe a pattern collection is to list the patterns and their interestingness values. In the case of frequent itemsets (or any other itemset collection), each itemset can be expressed as a bit vector of length $|\mathcal{I}|$.

A fundamental assumption in frequent itemset mining is that the frequent itemsets are quite small compared to the number of items. Partly this is a practical necessity as an itemset of cardinality k has 2^k subsets but the property has been observed in many real data sets (for sufficiently high minimum frequency threshold values), too. Thus, it is often more appropriate to represent each itemset as a list of items rather than as a binary vector. An itemset collection can then be represented as a list of these lists. In practice, the frequent itemsets are usually represented to the user and stored this way.

Representing an itemset collection as a list of itemsets is quite comprehensible representation. However, retrieving the frequency of a certain itemset X can take time proportional to $\Omega(|\mathcal{S}|\,|X|)$ as each itemset in a collection $\mathcal{S}$ might have to be compared with X and the comparison can take time proportional to $\Omega(|X|)$. Also, the representation needs $\Omega(|\mathcal{S}|\,|\mathcal{I}|)$ space. On the bright side, it can be checked easily in space $\mathcal{O}(|X|)$ whether or not an itemset X is in $\mathcal{S}$, and if $X \in \mathcal{S}$ the frequency of X can be retrieved in space $\mathcal{O}(|X|)$, too. It is possible to ask also many other kinds of itemset queries to the list in space $\mathcal{O}(|X|)$ and time $\mathcal{O}(|\mathcal{S}|\,|\mathcal{I}|)$.

Note that throughout the paper we charge unit cost (instead of, e.g., $\log |\mathcal{I}|$ cost) for representing an item. Usually in practice the items fit into computer words (e.g., 2^{64}) and thus this is a reasonable assumption. If more concise representation for the items is desired and the number of items is greater than the word size, then one could use, for example, Huffman codes [19] that emphasize as a side product the typicalness of the items in the database.

3   Patterns in Tries

Another very popular representations of itemset collections are *tries*, also called as *prefix trees* and *itemset trees*, see e.g. [20, 21, 22]. A trie is an $|\mathcal{I}|$-ary tree representing a prefix-free collection of strings over alphabet $\mathcal{I}$ such that each string in the collection corresponds to a (unique) path from the root to some leaf. To make the collection of strings prefix-free an end symbol $ (that is not in $\mathcal{I}$) is concatenated to the end of each string.

Thus, an itemset collection $\mathcal{S} \subseteq 2^{\mathcal{I}}$ can be represented in a trie by fixing some ordering $A_1, \ldots, A_{|\mathcal{I}|}$ of the items in $\mathcal{I}$ as follows: each itemset $X = \{A_{i_1}, \ldots, A_{i_{|X|}}\} \in \mathcal{S}$ ($1 \leq i_1 < \ldots < i_{|X|} \leq |\mathcal{I}|$) in the collection is represented as a string $A_{i_1} \ldots A_{i_{|X|}}\$$. The size of the trie is the number of its nodes including the leaves. The prefix tries can be seen also as a special case of *deterministic finite automata*:

Definition 1 (Deterministic Finite Automaton [23]). *A deterministic finite automaton (DFA) is a 5-tuple $A = (Q, \Sigma, \delta, r, F)$ where*

1. *Q is a finite set of states,*
2. *Σ is a finite set of input symbols,*
3. *$\delta : \Sigma \times Q \to Q$ is a transition function,*
4. *$r \in Q$ is a start state, and*
5. *$F \subseteq Q$ is a finite set of final states.*

The automaton A accepts a string $x \in \Sigma^*$ if and only if $\delta(x, r) \in F$ where the transition function is defined for strings recursively as follows:

$$\delta(x, r) = \delta(x_1 \ldots x_{|x|}, r)$$
$$= \delta(x_2 \ldots x_{|x|}, \delta(x_1, r)) = \ldots$$
$$= \delta(x_{|x|}, \delta(x_1 \ldots x_{|x|-1}, r)) = \ldots$$
$$= \delta(x_{|x|}, \delta(x_{|x|-1}, \ldots, \delta(x_1, r))).$$

Similarly to the deterministic finite automata, also the prefix tries offer efficient retrieval of frequencies. Namely, the frequency $fr(X, d)$ of an itemset $X = \{A_{i_1}, \ldots, A_{i_{|X|}}\}$ can be retrieved in time $\mathcal{O}(|X|)$ by traversing from the initial state r (i.e., the root r of the trie) to an end state $q = \delta(A_{i_1} \ldots A_{i_{|X|}}\$, r)$ (i.e., the leaf q) and reporting the frequency corresponding to q if it exists, or decide that the itemset X is infrequent.

The size of the trie representation can be considerably smaller than than representing the itemset collection $\mathcal{S} \subseteq 2^{\mathcal{I}}$ explicitly.

Proposition 1. *Let $\mathcal{S} = 2^{\mathcal{I}}$. Then the size of the explicit representation (i.e., the number of items) of $\mathcal{S}$ is*

$$|\mathcal{I}| \, 2^{|\mathcal{I}|-1}$$

and the size of the trie representing $\mathcal{S}$ is

$$2^{|\mathcal{I}|+1}.$$

Proof. The number of itemsets in $\mathcal{S}$ containing an item $A \in \mathcal{I}$ is

$$\frac{1}{2}|\mathcal{S}| = 2^{|\mathcal{I}|-1}.$$

Thus, the total number of items in all itemsets of $\mathcal{S}$ is

$$\sum_{X \in \mathcal{S}} |X| = \sum_{A \in \mathcal{I}} 2^{|\mathcal{I}|-1} = |\mathcal{I}| \, 2^{|\mathcal{I}|-1}.$$

The trie representation of $\mathcal{S}$ consists of one root node, inner nodes and $|\mathcal{S}|$ leaf nodes. The number of inner nodes is as follows. Let $<_\mathcal{I}$ be the ordering of the items in $\mathcal{I}$ and let $A_1, \ldots, A_{|\mathcal{I}|}$ be the items in $\mathcal{I}$ in ascending order in $<_\mathcal{I}$. The number of itemsets having $A_{|\mathcal{I}|}$ as their last item is $|\mathcal{S}|/2$. The number of itemsets having $A_{|\mathcal{I}|-1}$ as their last item is $|\mathcal{S}|/4$. In general, the number of itemsets having $A_{|\mathcal{I}|-k}$ as their last item is $|\mathcal{S}|/2^k$ for all $k < |\mathcal{I}|$. Thus, the total number of inner nodes is

$$\sum_{i=1}^{|\mathcal{I}|} 2^{|\mathcal{I}|}/2^i = \sum_{i=1}^{|\mathcal{I}|} 2^{|\mathcal{I}|-i} = \sum_{i=0}^{|\mathcal{I}|-1} 2^i = 2^{|\mathcal{I}|} - 1$$

Each inner node and the root node have exactly one leaf attached to them. Thus, the total number of nodes in the trie representing $\mathcal{S} = 2^{\mathcal{I}}$ is

$$2\left(1 + 2^{|\mathcal{I}|} - 1\right) = 2^{|\mathcal{I}|+1}$$

as claimed.   □

Note that the itemset trie can be transformed into a binary tree where in each node it is decided whether some particular item A is in the itemset or not. The size of the binary tree is less than two times the size of the itemset trie since each edge in the itemset trie induces at most two edges to the binary tree.

As the itemsets in the trie are represented by strings instead of itemsets, we must be able to fix an ordering for the items. It is easy to fix some ordering for the items. However, it is not clear what ordering would be most desirable. For example, it is natural to ask how the size of the trie depends on the ordering.

3.1   Downward Closed Itemset Collections

Let us first consider *downward closed* itemset collections, i.e., itemset collections $\mathcal{S}$ such that $X \in \mathcal{S}$ implies that also all subsets of X are in $\mathcal{S}$. Many itemset collections in data mining are downward closed. Maybe the most well-known examples of this kind of itemset collections are the collections of frequent itemsets. A downward closed itemset collection $\mathcal{S}$ can be described by its *maximal itemsets* [24]:

Definition 2 (Maximal Itemsets). *An itemset $X \subseteq \mathcal{I}$ is maximal in $\mathcal{S} \subseteq 2^{\mathcal{I}}$ if no proper superset of X is in $\mathcal{S}$.*

The collection maximal σ-frequent itemsets in d is denoted by

$$\mathcal{M}(\sigma, d) = \{X \in \mathcal{F}(\sigma, d) : Y \in \mathcal{F}(\sigma, d) \Rightarrow Y \not\supseteq X\}.$$

The collection of maximal itemsets in $\mathcal{S}$ is also the smallest sub-collection of a downward closed itemset collection $\mathcal{S}$ that determines the whole collection $\mathcal{S}$.

Example 1. The collection $\mathcal{M}(\sigma, d)$ of maximal σ-frequent itemsets determine the collection $\mathcal{F}(\sigma, d)$ (but not usually the frequencies of the itemsets in $\mathcal{F}(\sigma, d)$) in the following way:

$$\mathcal{F}(\sigma, d) = \{X \subseteq \mathcal{I} : X \subseteq Y \in \mathcal{M}(\sigma, d)\}.$$

Downward closed itemset collections are very desirable with respect to the orderings of the items. Namely, all orderings are equally good for downward closed itemset collections as shown by the following theorem:

Theorem 1. *If the itemset collection $\mathcal{S}$ is downward closed then the ordering of the items does not affect the size of the trie.*

Proof. Let $\mathcal{M}$ denote the maximal itemsets in $\mathcal{S}$ and let $X_1, \ldots, X_{|\mathcal{M}|}$ be an arbitrary ordering of the itemsets in $\mathcal{M}$. We proceed by induction in the number k of maximal itemsets in $\mathcal{S}$.

The claim holds when $k = 1$. Assume that the result holds the downward closed collection determined by the maximal itemsets $X_1, \ldots, X_k, k \geq 1$. We will show that then it holds also for $X_1, \ldots X_{k+1}$. The maximal set X_{k+1} is charged for the nodes it creates to the trie of determined by the maximal itemsets $X_1, \ldots, X_k$. Let us, w.l.o.g., insert the subsets of X_{k+1} to the trie from smallest to largest and charge the cost of creating a node from the itemset that caused it creation. This way each set in a downward closed set collection has a cost at most 1. Inserting the subsets of X_{k+1} that are contained in some $X_i, 1 \leq i \leq k$, cost nothing. Let the subset Y of X_{k+1} have cost one. This means that Y is not contained in any set $X_i, 1 \leq i \leq k$. Thus Y would have cost one anyway.

Thus the ordering of the items does not affect the size of the trie representing a downward closed set collection over the items. □

3.2   Arbitrary Itemset Collections

In the case of arbitrary itemset collections the ordering of the items can drastically affect the size of the trie.

Example 2. Let $\mathcal{I} = \{1, \ldots, n\}$ and let $\mathcal{S} = \{\{1, \ldots, n\}, \{2, \ldots, n\}, \ldots, \{n\}\}$. If the items are in ascending order, the number of edges in the tree would be $\Theta(|\mathcal{I}|^2)$ whereas all itemsets fit into one branch and thus size of the tree would be $\mathcal{O}(|\mathcal{I}|)$ if the ordering is descending.

Usually items are ordered to increasing or decreasing order with respect to their frequencies. Neither of these provide the optimal ordering in the size of the trie. Thus, there is a need for better criteria.

There are two immediate approaches to look at the problem: from the root to the leaves and from the leaves to the root. The trie can be partitioned into sub-tries considering the prefixes of the itemsets. The sub-trie of the node corresponds to the itemsets in the collections with the prefix equal to the edge labels from the root to the that node. Similarly, the common suffixes of the itemsets determine partitions of the itemset trie.

Finding an ordering that produces a small itemset trie has similarity to the problems of ordering the variables in OBDDs and finding a small equivalent decision tree, which both are known to be NP-hard [25, 26]. (Ordered Binary-Decision Diagrams (OBDDs) represent Boolean functions as acyclic graphs, see [27] for more details.) So, finding a desirable ordering for items is also a good candidate of being NP-hard. This does not mean much in practice since it is sufficient to find orderings that are *good enough*.

An efficient approach to avoid pathological item orderings is construct the trie for several random permutations of the items and choosing the one with the smallest trie. This can be done in time $\mathcal{O}(k\,|\mathcal{S}|\,|\mathcal{I}|)$ where k is the number of random permutations tried, since the trie of $\mathcal{S}$ for a given permutation can be constructed in time $|\mathcal{S}|\,|\mathcal{I}|$. Random permutations of the items are also in line with the fact that data mining is exploratory, since different permutations can reveal different properties of the pattern collections.

A standard approach to solve combinatorial optimization problems is to systematically evaluate potential solutions, and detect and prune regions of the search space that cannot have the optimum solution. For example, most of the pattern discovery techniques, including the famous APRIORI algorithm [20], are based on that approach. Evaluating a given ordering can be done relatively easily by just constructing the trie. The systematic evaluation of different orderings can be done faster by modifying the current trie rather than constructing the trie from scratch for each ordering. Furthermore, the search space can be pruned by detecting unpromising prefixes of the orderings by computing the lower bounds for the sizes of the tries for a given prefix.

The simplest lower bound is the size of the trie for the itemset collection projected on the prefix, i.e., neglecting all items that are not in the ordering yet. To improve this lower bound, we have to be able to bound the sizes of the sub-tries induced by the unordered items. First, all itemsets containing only those items that are already ordered, can be neglected. The rest of the itemsets are partitioned into equivalence classes with respect to their ordered prefixes. Each equivalence class corresponds to the itemsets in a sub-trie of still unordered items. The sizes of the sub-tries can be bounded by the number of itemsets in the sub-trie and the cardinality distributions of the itemsets in the sub-trie.

The ordered representations of itemsets would benefit on having different orderings in different parts of the representation. A varying ordering, however, can cause serious efficiency problems to ad-hoc queries to the pattern collection and making it more difficult to understand the collection. Finding a good varying ordering seems to be also computationally very difficult problem.

4   Automata Representations Based on Trie Refinements

The trie for an itemset collection has quite redundant structure if we are interested only to decide whether certain itemset is frequent, and if it is, what is its frequency. For example, trie has a separate final state for each itemset in the collection although the number of different frequencies in the itemset collection is usually smaller. If we interpret the trie as an automaton we can reduce the size of the representation without sacrificing the understandability. In fact, it can be argued that the simplified automaton is even more understandable representation than the trie (although also the opposite can be argued). Let us remark that that the automaton representing a finite number of strings is always an acyclic graph.

The most obvious improvement is to replace the final states by one final state for each different frequency. In addition to reducing the size of the representation, this optimization also represents the clustering of the itemsets based on their frequencies, see Section 6. This improvement can be further developed by merging the identical paths from the leaves of the trie, similarly to the standard itemset construction.

Example 3. Let the collection S consists of itemsets $\{A_1, A_i, A_{|\mathcal{I}|}\}$ for all $1 < i < |\mathcal{I}|$. Then the automaton representation of the itemset collection S consists of one state for each item in $\mathcal{I}$ and one end state but the trie representation of S contain $|\mathcal{I}| - 2$ states for $A_{|\mathcal{I}|}$ and $|\mathcal{I}| - 2$ end states. Thus, the total number of states in the trie is

$$1 + 3\left(|\mathcal{I}| - 2\right) = 3\,|\mathcal{I}| - 5$$

for all $|\mathcal{I}| \geq 3$.

In general, as any automaton representing an itemset collection is acyclic, it can be minimized in linear time in the number of states [28, 29]. Automata representations of itemset collections can be reduced even further due to the special structure of the input strings: itemsets are represented by subsequences of $A_1 \ldots A_{|\mathcal{I}|}$ extended with the end symbol $\$$.

The minimum automata representations can be considerably smaller than the trie representations. Namely, the automata representations can be exponentially smaller than the trie representations:

Example 4. Let $\mathcal{I}$ be the set of items and let the itemset collection be $2^{\mathcal{I}}$. Then the number of states in the automaton representation of $2^{\mathcal{I}}$ is $|\mathcal{I}| + 1$ whereas the trie representing the collection $2^{\mathcal{I}}$ is of size $2^{|\mathcal{I}|+1}$ as shown in Proposition 1.

Similarly to the item ordering in the case of tries, we suspect the computational complexity of finding the best ordering for the automata representation to be high too.

5   Commutative Automata

Although the automata constructions described in Section 4 enable efficient queries and compact representations of the itemset collections, the ordering of the items might sometimes conceal some relevant aspects of the itemset collection since the language defined by the itemset collection is actually commutative: there is no evident reason (without any additional information about the itemset collection and the items) why some of the strings 123, 132, 213, 231, 312 and 321 should be favored to be the true representation of the itemset $\{1, 2, 3\}$.

One way to avoid this problem of item orderings but still compressing the itemset collection is to find a minimum chain partition for the collection [16]. Minimum chain partitions of pattern collections are appealing also because only a partial ordering for the pattern collection is needed in order to find the partition. Although being potentially smaller, the chain partitions share strengths and weaknesses with lists of patterns.

Another downside of the representations described in Section 3 and Section 4 is that it is not easy to decide whether a given itemset Y is contained in some itemset in the itemset collection $\mathcal{S}$. In the worst case one has to transverse essentially the whole trie or generate all strings accepted by the automaton to assure that the itemset Y is not contained in any of the itemsets in the itemset collection $\mathcal{S}$.

As data mining is inherently iterative and exploratory process, a good condensed representation should reflect and support the exploration process. This goal can be achieved by a *commutative automaton*, i.e., an automaton that accepts an itemset of the collection (and expresses the frequencies) regardless of the order the items are revealed to the automaton.

Definition 3 (Commutative Automaton). *The commutative automaton for an itemset collection $\mathcal{S}$ is the following deterministic finite automaton:*

1. *The state space Q consists of all subsets of each itemset X in $\mathcal{S}$ and the frequencies of the itemsets in $\mathcal{S}$.*
2. *The set Σ of input symbols is the set $\mathcal{I} \cup \{\$\}$.*
3. *There is a transition from a state $X \in Q$ to a state $Y \in Q$ by A if and only if $Y = X \cup \{A\}$ and a transition from a state $X \in Q$ to a state $fr(X,d) \in Q$ by $\$$ if and only if $X \in \mathcal{S}$.*
4. *The initial state r corresponds to the empty set $\emptyset$.*
5. *The set F of final states are the frequencies of the itemsets in the itemset collection $\mathcal{S}$.*

Usually there is also some additional information associated to each final state. For example, in the case of the frequent itemsets the additional information is typically the frequency of the itemset.

Note that in the commutative automaton representing the collection $\mathcal{S}$ there is one state for each itemset in the downward closure of $\mathcal{S}$, i.e., the collection

$$cl(\mathcal{S}) = \{X \subseteq \mathcal{I} : X \subseteq Y \in \mathcal{S}\}.$$

Many popular itemset collections are downward closed but there are important itemset collections that are not. Thus, this basic version of commutative automaton can actually blow up the representation.

Still, the commutative automaton for a frequent itemset collection can be minimized in linear time using the same algorithms as in the previous section. The number of states can be reduced also by exploiting the structure of the itemset collection and the frequencies of the itemsets. For example, the state space Q consisting of the frequent itemsets can be replaced by the closed frequent itemsets:

Definition 4 (Closed Itemsets). *an itemset $X \in \mathcal{S}$ is closed with respect to a transaction database d if its frequency is higher than the maximum of the frequencies of its supersets, i.e., if*

$$X \subset Y \subseteq \mathcal{I} \Rightarrow fr(X, d) > fr(Y, d).$$

The collection closed σ-frequent itemsets in d is denoted by

$$\mathcal{C}(\sigma, d) = \{X \in \mathcal{F}(\sigma, d) : Y \supset X \Rightarrow fr(X, d) > fr(Y, d)\}.$$

The great virtue of closed itemsets is their natural interpretation as intersections of transactions [8, 11].

Definition 5 (Closures). *A closure of X in a transaction database d, denoted by $cl(X, d)$, is the (unique) largest superset $cl(X, d) = Y$ of X that $fr(X, d) = fr(Y, d)$. (Thus, $cover(X, d) = cover(Y, d)$.) The closure of X is equal to the intersection of the transactions containing X, i.e.,*

$$cl(X, d) = \bigcap_{i \in cover(X, d)} d_i.$$

All maximal σ-frequent itemsets are closed σ-frequent itemsets too, but the number of closed σ-frequent itemsets can be exponentially larger than the number maximal σ-frequent itemsets.

Example 5. Let the transaction database d consist of transactions $\mathcal{I} \setminus \{A\}$ for all $A \in \mathcal{I}$ and $\lceil \sigma/(1 - \sigma) \rceil$ transactions $\mathcal{I}$. Then all subsets of $\mathcal{I}$ are closed but only $\mathcal{I}$ is maximal. The number of subsets of $\mathcal{I}$ is $2^{|\mathcal{I}|}$.

On the other hand, the collection of closed σ-frequent itemsets is a subcollection of the collection of σ-frequent itemsets and the number closed σ-frequent itemsets can be exponentially smaller than the number of all σ-frequent itemsets.

Example 6. Let the transaction database d consist of an itemset $\mathcal{I}$. Then the only closed itemset is $\mathcal{I}$ but all subsets of $\mathcal{I}$ are σ-frequent for all $\sigma \in [0, 1]$.

We can define the commutative automaton also for the closures of the itemsets. The commutative automaton for the closures in the itemset collection $\mathcal{S}$ differs from the commutative automaton represented above only by the state space and the transition function:

- The state space consists of closures of the itemsets in $\mathcal{S}$, the intersections of the closures of the itemsets in $\mathcal{S}$, and the frequencies of the itemsets in $\mathcal{S}$.
- There is a transition from the state $cl(X, d), X \in \mathcal{S}$ to the state $cl(Y, d), Y \in \mathcal{S}$ by A if and only if

$$cl(Y, d) = cl(cl(X, d) \cup \{A\}, d) = cl(X \cup \{A\}, d).$$

- There is a transition from the state $cl(X, d), X \in \mathcal{S}$, to the state $fr(X), X \in \mathcal{S}$ by $\$$ if and only if $X = cl(X, d)$.

The intersection of the closures of the itemsets in $\mathcal{S}$ are needed to ensure the uniqueness of the closures in $\mathcal{S}$, i.e., to ensure the automaton being deterministic. In the case of σ-frequent itemsets, the intersections of the σ-frequent closed itemsets are also σ-frequent closed itemsets. Thus, the state space of the commutative automaton represented by the closures of σ-frequent itemsets consists of the closed σ-frequent itemsets and their frequencies. The commutative automaton of an itemset collection $\mathcal{S}$ based on closures accepts all subsets of itemsets in $\mathcal{S}$ that have unique closures. In the case of σ-frequent itemsets, this means that the automaton accepts all σ-frequent itemsets.

Queries to this automaton traverse in the closures of the itemsets in the itemset collection. The automata minimization algorithm described in [28] can be implemented to run in linear time also for this kind of automata since the cycles in the automaton are only self-loops. A commutative automaton can efficiently answer frequency queries for all frequent itemsets. Note that this is not the case with itemset tries and automata of the previous section.

6   Clustering and Visualization of Automata

The automata representations of frequent itemset collections can be useful in visual data mining of frequent itemset collections as there are advanced techniques to visualize automata. An example of visualization of itemset collection

$$2^{\{A,B,C\}} = \{\emptyset, \{A\}, \{B\}, \{C\}, \{A,B\}, \{A,C\}, \{B,C\}, \{A,B,C\}\}$$

with supports equal to $4 - |X|$ for each itemset $X \in 2^{\{A,B,C\}} \setminus \{\emptyset\}$ and support equal to 3 for $\emptyset$ is shown in Figure 1.

A simplest approach is to cluster the patterns is to group them by their end states. An automaton representation for each cluster can be found from the automaton representations by reversing the edges of the underlying graph

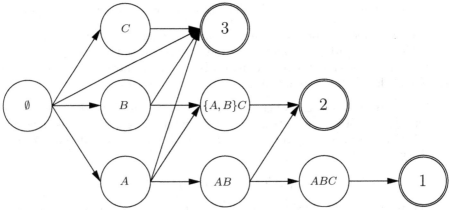

Fig. 1. An automata visualization of the itemset collection $2^{\{A,B,C\}}$

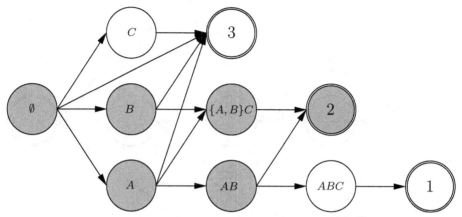

Fig. 2. An automata visualization of the itemset collection $2^{\{A,B,C\}}$ emphasizing the itemset cluster with supports equal to two by color

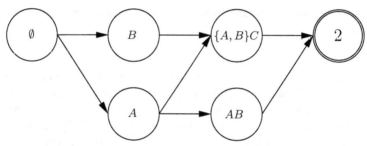

Fig. 3. The sub-automaton of Figure 1 corresponding to the itemsets with supports equal to two

and computing which nodes are reachable from the corresponding final state. This can be done in time linear in the number of transitions. There are several possibilities how the clusterings can be visualized by the automata. For example, the nodes can be colored based on which clusters they belong. If a state belongs to several clusters, its color can be a mixture of the colors of the clusters. For an illustration of highlighting the clusters, see Figure 2.

Alternatively each cluster can be represented as its own sub-automaton (that could be interactively highlighted from the visualization of the original automaton). The sub-automaton of the automaton of Figure 1 is shown in Figure 3. Note automata minimization can be applied also to sub-automaton. For example, the automaton of Figure 3 can be reduced by one third, i.e., to four states. However, the automaton might change considerably by the minimization process and thus make exploratory data analysis more difficult.

If approximate frequencies would suffice, the number of final states could be further reduced by discretizing the frequencies [30]. As the most extreme case of the frequency discretization we get only the information whether the itemset is frequent or not. Thus, by a hierarchical discretization of the frequencies we get a

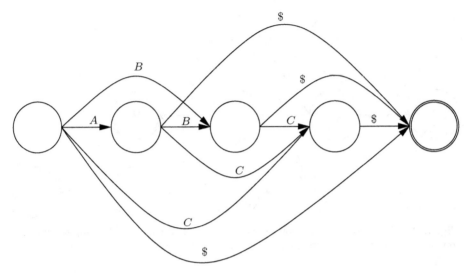

Fig. 4. The automaton of Figure 1 after discretizing (i.e., merging end states) and minimizing

refining series of automata. The minimized automaton for the itemset collection $2^{\{A,B,C\}}$ when all frequencies are discretized to be the same is shown in Figure 4.

In addition to clustering by frequencies, the patterns could be clustered also based on the structural properties of the patterns and the pattern collection. For example, the pattern collection could be partitioned in such way that the patterns that share many states with each other in the automaton would be in the same group. Also this naturally gives rise of a hierarchical clustering of patterns as refining partition of automata.

7   Experiments

To evaluate the applicability of the automata approach to represent itemset collections we experimented with two data sets from UCI KDD Repository:[1] Internet Usage data set consisting of 10104 transactions and 10674 items, and IPUMS Census data set consisting of 88443 transactions and 39954 items.

In particular, we wanted to know how much the automata representation described in Section 3 could reduce the space consumption compared to the straightforward listing of the itemsets and their frequencies. We were interested to see also how much the ordering of the items affects the sizes of the automata. We computed tries, automata and minimum automata from closed σ-frequent itemset collections with different minimum frequency threshold values σ and several random permutations of the items.

---

[1] http://kdd.ics.uci.edu

Table 1. The sizes of closed itemsets and tries on Internet Usage data

	closed itemsets		trie		
σ	the number of itemsets	size	minimum size	mean size	maximum size
0.20	1856	8493	3713	3713	3713
0.19	2228	10345	4457	4457	4457
0.18	2667	12559	5335	5335	5335
0.17	3246	15552	6493	6493	6493
0.16	4013	19571	8027	8027	8027
0.15	4983	24738	9967	9967	9967
0.14	6290	31805	12581	12581	12582
0.13	7998	41178	15997	15998	15999
0.12	10472	55017	20945	20947	20949
0.11	13802	74167	27605	27608	27616
0.10	18594	102152	37189	37196	37210
0.09	25686	144392	51373	51382	51415
0.08	36714	211617	73429	73443	73496
0.07	54550	323187	109101	109147	109287
0.06	84873	435804	169748	169844	170141
0.05	141568	893400	283137	283515	284508
0.04	260076	1705361	520157	521014	524750

Table 2. The sizes of automata on Internet Usage data

	automaton			minimum automaton		
σ	minimum size	mean size	maximum size	minimum size	mean size	maximum size
0.20	2927	2927	2927	2315	2431	2537
0.19	3398	3398	3398	2557	2723	2848
0.18	3937	3937	3937	2821	3046	3227
0.17	4617	4617	4617	3078	3460	3697
0.16	5485	5485	5485	3559	3876	4150
0.15	6556	6556	6556	3860	4447	4818
0.14	7964	7964	7965	4207	5073	5520
0.13	9773	9774	9775	4703	5878	6651
0.12	12348	12350	12352	5626	6888	7893
0.11	15779	15782	15790	6562	8515	9618
0.10	20672	20679	20693	8528	10329	11852
0.09	27865	27874	27907	9770	13040	15050
0.08	38994	39008	39061	12607	17558	20101
0.07	56931	56977	57117	18726	25003	28936
0.06	87355	87451	87748	25977	34694	38919
0.05	144151	144529	145522	46814	58581	70426
0.04	262764	263621	267357	67080	102552	121889

The results are shown in Table 1 and Table 2 for the Internet Usage data, and in Table 3 and Table 4 for the Census IPUMS data. The columns of Table 1 and Table 3 correspond to the number of closed frequent itemsets, the number of elements (including one extra element representing the frequency) in the rep-

Table 3. The sizes of closed itemsets and tries on Census IPUMS data

	closed itemsets		trie		
σ	the number of itemsets	size	minimum size	mean size	maximum size
0.30	1335	8933	2882	3531	4655
0.29	1505	10216	3112	3884	5073
0.28	1696	11639	3635	4345	5854
0.27	1948	13626	4160	5067	6768
0.26	2293	16318	5004	6198	8373
0.25	2577	18514	5480	6669	9935
0.24	3006	21849	6368	7854	10475
0.23	3590	26532	7766	9370	12359
0.22	4271	31928	9231	11173	14273
0.21	5246	39941	11461	14058	18632
0.20	6689	52229	14112	18019	24998
0.19	8524	68826	18035	23103	29896
0.18	10899	91171	23702	29091	35668
0.17	13435	114705	28202	35351	47138
0.16	16907	138415	36867	45059	59808
0.15	22185	199791	48485	60630	85813
0.14	29194	274170	63282	78036	100977

Table 4. The sizes of automata on Census IPUMS data

	automaton			minimum automaton		
σ	minimum size	mean size	maximum size	minimum size	mean size	maximum size
0.30	2821	3470	4594	2780	3432	4534
0.29	3035	3807	4996	2998	3759	4919
0.28	3541	4251	5760	3513	4196	5666
0.27	4034	4941	6642	4010	4861	6524
0.26	4807	6001	8176	4665	5863	7982
0.25	5235	6424	9690	5086	6265	9446
0.24	6031	7517	10138	5828	7311	9913
0.23	7283	8887	11876	7089	8587	11403
0.22	8533	10475	13575	8252	10028	12887
0.21	10379	12976	17550	9789	12241	16468
0.20	12279	16186	23165	11493	14930	21332
0.19	15149	20217	27010	13489	18271	24124
0.18	19259	24648	31225	16873	21773	28004
0.17	22051	29200	40987	18506	25376	34836
0.16	28108	36300	51049	23135	29617	39889
0.15	35331	47476	72659	28517	38919	59756
0.14	44003	58757	81698	33280	46004	67153

resentations of the itemsets as a list, and minimum, average and maximum sizes
of the tries over 50 random orderings of the items. The columns of Table 2 and
Table 4 correspond to minimum, average and maximum sizes of the automata
and minimized automata, over the same random orderings than for the tries.

Table 5. The sizes of commutative automata on Internet Usage data

	itemset collection	automaton	minimum automaton
σ	the number of itemsets	the number of states	the number of states
0.20	2927	2927	1665
0.19	3398	3398	1866
0.18	3937	3937	2112
0.17	4617	4617	2368
0.16	5485	5485	2680
0.15	6556	6556	3046
0.14	7965	7964	3520
0.13	9775	9773	4014
0.12	12352	12348	4799
0.11	15790	15779	5716
0.10	20693	20672	7137
0.09	27908	27865	9095
0.08	39092	38994	11872
0.07	57174	56931	16695
0.06	87974	87355	24700
0.05	145974	144151	39600
0.04	268543	262760	70370

Table 6. The sizes of commutative automata on IPUMS Census data

	itemset collection	automaton	minimum automaton
σ	the number of itemsets	the number of states	the number of states
0.30	9481	2610	2133
0.29	11071	2934	2389
0.28	13047	3299	2729
0.27	15667	3771	3159
0.26	19601	4390	3617
0.25	22357	4910	4000
0.24	26574	5676	4623
0.23	34900	6698	5471
0.22	56778	7845	6368
0.21	68897	9411	7493
0.20	91737	11546	9124
0.19	157549	14163	11156
0.18	256899	17356	13732
0.17	387431	20720	16484
0.16	532833	25056	19389
0.15	863202	31217	23453
0.14	1854484	39110	29260

The automata and minimum automata representations show clear improvement over direct listing of itemsets and their frequencies or the trie representations in terms of the space consumption. Also, the minimization seems to simplify the automata a reasonable amount.

We experimented with commutative automata, too. More specifically, we constructed commutative automata based on closures for σ-frequent itemsets with several minimum frequency threshold values σ and minimized the automata. The results of these commutative automata experiments for the Internet Usage data and the IPUMS Census data are shown in Table 5 and Table 6, respectively. Again, the automata representation and the minimization of the automata show clear improvement in the number of states needed in the representation.

8   Conclusions

In this paper we have described how finite automata could be used to support pattern discovery, in particular, to help the analysis of the σ-frequent itemset collections. We suggested representations of itemset collections based on deterministic finite automata that enable time-efficient queries, space-efficient representation, and quite understandable description of the itemset collections. An additional benefit of this kind of representations is that automata can be visualized as graphs. We described how the automata approach can be used to express clusterings of the itemsets and how the itemset collection can be hierarchically described by a refining series of automata.

The automata approach seems to be promising also for use in inductive databases and there are several interesting questions related to representing condensed representations of itemset collections by automata:

- How itemset collections could and should be represented by automata? The approaches described in this paper seem to be quite reasonable but other kinds of representations could suitable when there is some domain knowledge available.
- What kinds of patterns are decent for automata representations? Many kinds of patterns can be represented as strings. However, it is not always clear how the patterns should be represented as strings most conveniently. Although some patterns could not be represented as strings very naturally, the automata approach might still have something to offer the patterns of that kind.
- How to find the best ordering for the items? Even in the case of tries this seems to be a challenging problem. Finding the ordering that produces the smallest automaton for a pattern collection seems to be computationally even more difficult due to more complicated dependencies between the states. Still, there might exist accurate approximation algorithms and efficient heuristics to at least locally improving the item orderings. Random orderings are also reasonable way to reorder items as each random permutation emphasizes different aspects of the pattern collection which supports the exploratory nature of data mining. There might be, however, more useful ways to generate permutations than uniformly. An important question for finding the best ordering is what is the best ordering.

Acknowledgments. I wish to thank the anonymous reviewers for their constructive comments and illuminating insights.

References

1. Agrawal, R., Imielinski, T., Swami, A.N.: Mining association rules between sets of items in large databases. In Buneman, P., Jajodia, S., eds.: Proceedings of the 1993 ACM SIGMOD International Conference on Management of Data, Washington, D.C., May 26-28, 1993. ACM Press (1993) 207–216
2. Goethals, B., Zaki, M.J., eds.:   Proceedings of the Workshop on Frequent Itemset Mining Implementations (FIMI-03), Melbourne Florida, USA, November 19, 2003.   Volume 90 of CEUR Workshop Proceedings.   (2003) http://CEUR-WS.org/Vol-90/.
3. Mannila, H., Toivonen, H.: Multiple uses of frequent sets and condensed representations. In Simoudis, E., Han, J., Fayyad, U.M., eds.: Proceedings of the Second International Conference on Knowledge Discovery and Data Mining (KDD-96). AAAI Press (1996) 189–194
4. De Raedt, L.: A perspective on inductive databases. SIGKDD Explorations **4** (2003) 69–77
5. Imielinski, T., Mannila, H.: A database perspective on knowledge discovery. Communications of The ACM **39** (1996) 58–64
6. Mannila, H.: Inductive databases and condensed representations for data mining. In Maluszynski, J., ed.: Logic Programming, Proceedngs of the 1997 International Symposium, Port Jefferson, Long Island, N.Y., October 13-16, 1997. MIT Press (1997) 21–30
7. Gunopulos, D., Khardon, R., Mannila, H., Saluja, S., Toivonen, H., Sharma, R.S.: Discovering all most specific sentences. ACM Transactions on Database Systems **28** (2003) 140–174
8. Pasquier, N., Bastide, Y., Taouil, R., Lakhal, L.: Discovering frequent closed itemsets for association rules. In Beeri, C., Buneman, P., eds.: Database Theory - ICDT '99, 7th International Conference, Jerusalem, Israel, January 10-12, 1999, Proceedings. Volume 1540 of Lecture Notes in Computer Science. Springer (1999) 398–416
9. Boulicaut, J.F., Bykowski, A., Rigotti, C.: Free-sets: a condensed representation of Boolean data for the approximation of frequency queries. Data Mining and Knowledge Discovery **7** (2003) 5–22
10. Bykowski, A., Rigotti, C.: A condensed representation to find frequent patterns. In: Proceedings of the Twentieth ACM SIGACT-SIGMOD-SIGART Symposium on Principles of Database Systems, May 21-23, 2001, Santa Barbara, California, USA. ACM (2001)
11. Kryszkiewicz, M.: Concise representation of frequent patterns based on disjunction-free generators. In Cercone, N., Lin, T.Y., Wu, X., eds.: Proceedings of the 2001 IEEE International Conference on Data Mining, 29 November - 2 December 2001, San Jose, California, USA. IEEE Computer Society (2001) 305–312
12. Calders, T., Goethals, B.: Minimal k-free representations of frequent sets. [31] 71–82

13. Calders, T., Goethals, B.: Mining all non-derivable frequent itemsets. In Elomaa, T., Mannila, H., Toivonen, H., eds.: Principles of Data Mining and Knowledge Discovery, 6th European Conference, PKDD 2002, Helsinki, Finland, August 19-23, 2002, Proceedings. Volume 2431 of Lecture Notes in Artificial Intelligence. Springer (2002) 74–865

14. Pei, J., Dong, G., Zou, W., Han, J.: On computing condensed pattern bases. In Kumar, V., Tsumoto, S., eds.: Proceedings of the 2002 IEEE International Conference on Data Mining (ICDM 2002), 9-12 December 2002, Maebashi City, Japan. IEEE Computer Society (2002) 378–385

15. Mielikäinen, T., Mannila, H.: The pattern ordering problem. [31] 327–338

16. Mielikäinen, T.: Chaining patterns. In Grieser, G., Tanaka, Y., Yamamoto, A., eds.: Discovery Science, 6th International Conference, DS 2003, Sapporo, Japan, October 17–19, 2003, Proceedings. Volume 2843 of Lecture Notes in Computer Science. Springer (2003) 232–243

17. Mielikäinen, T.: Implicit enumeration of patterns. In Goethals, B., Siebes, A., eds.: Knowledge Discovery in Inductive Databases, 3rd International Workshop, KDID 2004, Pisa, Italy, September 20, 2004, Revised Papers. Volume 3377 of Lecture Notes in Computer Science. Springer (2004)

18. Mielikäinen, T.: Separating structure from interestingness. In Dai, H., Srikant, R., Zhang, C., eds.: Advances in Knowledge Discovery and Data Mining, 8th Pacific-Asia Conference, PAKDD 2004, Sydney, Australia, May 26-28, 2004, Proceedings. Volume 3056 of Lecture Notes in Artificial Intelligence. Springer (2004) 476–485

19. Vitter, J.S.: Design and analysis of dynamic huffman codes. Journal of the Association for Computing Machinery 34 (1987) 825–845

20. Agrawal, R., Mannila, H., Srikant, R., Toivonen, H., Verkamo, A.I.: Fast discovery of association rules. In Fayyad, U.M., Piatetsky-Shapiro, G., Smyth, P., Uthurusamy, R., eds.: Advances in Knowledge Discovery and Data Mining. AAAI/MIT Press (1996) 307–328

21. Hafez, A., Deogun, J., Raghavan, V.V.: The item-set tree: A data structure for data mining. In Mohania, M.K., Tjoa, A.M., eds.: Data Warehousing and Knowledge Discovery, First International Conference, DaWaK '99, Florence, Italy, August 30 - September 1, 1999, Proceedings. Volume 1676 of Lecture Notes in Artificial Intelligence. Springer (1999) 183–192

22. Zaki, M.J.: Scalable algorithms for association mining. IEEE Transactions on Knowledge and Data Engineering 12 (2000) 372–390

23. Hopcroft, J.E., Motwani, R., Ullman, J.D.: Introduction to Auotmata Theory, Languages and Computation. 2nd edn. Addison-Wesley (2001)

24. Mannila, H., Toivonen, H.: Levelwise search and borders of theories in knowledge discovery. Data Mining and Knowledge Discovery 1 (1997) 241–258

25. Bollig, B., Wegener, I.: Improving the variable ordering of OBDDs is NP-complete. IEEE Transactions on Computers 45 (1996) 993–1002

26. Zantema, H., Bodlaender, H.L.: Finding small equivalent decision trees is hard. International Journal of Foundations of Computer Science 11 (2000) 343–354

27. Bryant, R.E.: Symbolic boolean manipulation with ordered binary-decision diagrams. ACM Computing Surveys 24 (1992) 293–318

28. Revuz, D.: Minimisation of acyclic deterministic automata in linear time. Theoretical Computer Science 92 (1992) 181–189

29. Watson, B.W.: A new algorithm for the construction of minimal acyclic DFAs. Science of Computer Programming 48 (2003) 81–97

30. Mielikäinen, T.: Frequency-based views to pattern collections. In Hammer, P.L., ed.: Proceedings of the IFIP/SIAM Workshop on Discrete Mathematics and Data Mining, SIAM International Conference on Data Mining (2003), May 1-3, 2003, San Francisco, CA, USA. SIAM (2003)

31. Lavrac, N., Gamberger, D., Blockeel, H., Todorovski, L., eds.: Knowledge Discovery in Databases: PKDD 2003, 7th European Conference on Principles and Practice of Knowledge Discovery in Databases, Cavtat-Dubrovnik, Croatia, September 22-26, 2003, Proceedings. Volume 2838 of Lecture Notes in Artificial Intelligence. Springer (2003)

Implicit Enumeration of Patterns

Taneli Mielikäinen

HIIT Basic Research Unit,
Department of Computer Science,
University of Helsinki, Finland
Taneli.Mielikainen@cs.Helsinki.FI

Abstract. Condensed representations of pattern collections have been recognized to be important building blocks of inductive databases, a promising theoretical framework for data mining, and recently they have been studied actively. However, there has not been much research on how condensed representations should actually be represented.

In this paper we study implicit enumeration of patterns, i.e., how to represent pattern collections by listing only the interestingness values of the patterns. The main problem is that the pattern classes are typically huge compared to the collections of interesting patterns in them. We solve this problem by choosing a good ordering of listing the patterns in the class such that the ordering admits effective pruning and prediction of the interestingness values of the patterns. This representation of interestingness values enables us to quantify how surprising a pattern is in the collection. Furthermore, the encoding of the interestingness values reflects our understanding of the pattern collection. Thus the size of the encoding can be used to evaluate the correctness of our assumptions about the pattern collection and the interestingness measure.

1 Introduction

One of the most important approaches to mine data is *pattern discovery* which aims to extract *interesting patterns* (possibly with some *interestingness values* associated to each of them) from data. The most prominent example of a pattern discovery task is the *frequent itemset mining* problem [1]:

Problem 1 (Frequent Itemset Mining). Given a multi-set $d = \{d_1 \ldots d_n\}$ (a *transaction database*) of subsets (*transactions*) of a set $\mathcal{I}$ of *items* and a *minimum frequency threshold* $\sigma \in [0, 1]$, find the *collection of σ-frequent itemsets* in d, i.e., the collection

$$\mathcal{F}(\sigma, d) = \{X \subseteq \mathcal{I} : fr(X, d) \geq \sigma\}$$

where

$$fr(X, d) = \frac{supp(X, d)}{n},$$

$$supp(X, d) = |cover(X, d)|$$

and

$$cover(X, d) = \{i : X \subseteq d_i, 1 \leq i \leq n\}.$$

B. Goethals and A. Siebes (Eds.): KDID 2004, LNCS 3377, pp. 150–172, 2005.

There exist techniques to find all frequent itemsets reasonably efficiently [2]. The techniques for frequent itemset mining have been adapted to mine also other kinds of frequent patterns such as graphs [3, 4, 5, 6] and sequences [7, 8, 9]. Also other measures of interestingness have been considered [10]. In general, the problem can be formulated as the discovery of interesting patterns as follows:

Problem 2 (Discovery of Interesting Patterns). Given a pattern class $\mathcal{P}$, an interestingness measure $\phi : \mathcal{P} \to [0, 1]$ and a minimum interestingness threshold $\sigma \in [0, 1]$ find the collection of σ-interesting patterns. That is, find the collection

$$\mathcal{P}(\sigma, \phi) = \{p \in \mathcal{P} : \phi(p) \geq \sigma\}.$$

A major advantage of frequent itemsets is that they can be computed from data without much domain knowledge: any transaction database determines an empirical joint probability distribution over the item combinations and the marginal probabilities of the combinations with high probability can be considered as a reasonable way to summarize the empirical joint probability distribution determined by the data. The generality of this summarization approach causes also troubles: the frequent itemset collections that describe data quite well tend to be quite large. Although the frequent itemsets might be found efficiently enough even from very large transaction databases, it is not certain that an enormously large collection of frequent itemsets is very concise summary of the data.

The problem of discovering too large frequent itemset collections to comprehend has been tried to solve by finding small sub-collections of the frequent itemsets that are sufficient to determine which itemsets are frequent and what are the frequencies of the frequent itemsets. Such sub-collections are often called the *condensed representations* of frequent itemsets. (In general, the condensed representations do not have to be sub-collections of patterns but just some data structures from which it is possible to answer queries of certain kind accurately and efficiently enough. In fact, the condensed representations were originally introduced in this broader context [11].) The condensed representations of frequent itemsets (and other interesting patterns) have been recognized to have an important role in *inductive databases* which seems to be a promising theoretical model for data mining [12, 13, 14]. Furthermore, many condensed representations of itemset collections are readily applicable to several other collections of interesting patterns.

The condensed representations of frequent itemsets have studied actively and several condensed representations, such as *maximal itemsets* [15], *closed itemsets* [16], *free itemsets* [17], *disjunction-free itemsets* [18], *disjunction-free generators* [19], *k-free itemsets* [20] *non-derivable itemsets* [21], *condensed pattern bases* [22], *pattern orderings* [23] and *pattern chains* [24], have been proposed. However, not much has been done on how the condensed representations should actually be represented although it is an important question: the representation of the knowledge can drastically affect the efficiency of the inductive database but it also affects the data analyst to comprehend or not to comprehend the mining results.

In this paper we study how pattern collections and their interestingness values can be represented by listing only the interestingness values of the patterns (and not the actual patterns) in some suitable order. We describe how the pattern enumeration space can be pruned by some structural properties of the pattern collections and how the interestingness values can be deduced from the interestingness values of the patterns earlier in the enumeration. This approach to represent pattern collections suggests also an approach to quantify how surprising a pattern is with respect to the interestingness values of previously seen patterns. The quantification of surprisingness seems to have some interest independent from implicit enumerations. Furthermore, the size of the representation reflects also how accurate our assumptions about the pattern collections are and thus it could support us in the exploration of the collection.

The rest of the paper is organized as follows. In Section 2 we propose the idea of implicitly enumerating all interesting patterns and their interestingness values by listing the values in some convenient order. We discuss why this approach should be considered at all as a reasonable way to represent pattern collections. In Section 3 we describe different strategies to prune the pattern enumeration space. In Section 4 we examine different ways to encode the interestingness values based on the interestingness values of patterns seen previously in the enumeration. In Section 5 we describe how the binary encodings of the interestingness values give us a convenient way to quantify the surprisingness of the pattern with respect to our knowledge about the interesting patterns obtained earlier in the implicit enumeration of the pattern class. In Section 6 we experimentally evaluate the space consumptions of the suggested implicit representations of pattern collections. Section 7 is a short conclusion.

2   Implicit Pattern Enumeration

Usually it is not sufficient to discover only the interesting patterns but also their interestingness values are needed. This is the case, for example, with frequent itemsets: An important use of frequent itemsets is to find accurate association rules.

Example 1 (Association Rules). Association rules are rules of form $X \Rightarrow Y$ where X and Y are itemsets. The accuracy $acc(X \Rightarrow Y, d)$ of the rule $X \Rightarrow Y$ in a transaction database d is the fraction of transactions containing X that contain also Y. That is,

$$acc(X \Rightarrow Y, d) = \frac{fr(X \cup Y, d)}{fr(X, d)}.$$

Thus, it would usually make more sense to compute $\phi|_{\mathcal{P}(\sigma,\phi)}$, the restriction of the interestingness measure ϕ to the collection $\mathcal{P}(\sigma, \phi)$ of σ-interesting patterns, instead of a pattern collection $\mathcal{P}(\sigma, \phi)$ and the interestingness values of the patterns in $\mathcal{P}(\sigma, \phi)$.

Most of the condensed representations of pattern collections are based on listing some sub-collection of the interesting patterns (and their interestingness values) that is sufficient to determine the whole collection of interesting patterns (and their interestingness values). However, it is not clear whether this is always the best way to describe the collections of interesting patterns.

If the collection of interesting patterns is dense, then listing all interesting patterns with their interestingness values explicitly might not be very effective. First, the object is not a relation but a function. Representations of the collection as a list of pattern-interestingness pairs does not take this into account. Second, the patterns often share some parts with each other. For example, a collection of frequent itemsets contain all subsets of the largest itemset in the collection. These observations, in fact, have already been exploited, for example, in trie presentations of pattern collections [25, 26], in pattern automata [27], and in pattern chains [24]. Using these approaches the sizes of the pattern collection representations can be reduced considerably.

A further step to avoid listing all pattern explicitly, even by tries or automata, is to describe the pattern collection and the interestingness values separately [28]. This sometimes leads to considerably small representations of the collections, especially when approximate interestingness values suffice.

The natural next step is to consider how pattern collections and their interesting values completely implicitly, i.e., by listing the interestingness values of the patterns in the given pattern class. For example, the pattern class in the case of frequent itemsets is all subsets of $\mathcal{I}$ and the interesting patterns in that class are those subsets of $\mathcal{I}$ that are frequent enough in the given transaction database. Unfortunately the whole pattern class can be very large even if the number of interesting patterns is assumed to be relatively small. For example, in the case of frequent itemset the whole pattern collection consists of $2^{|\mathcal{I}|}$ itemsets. Thus, at first glance, this approach to describe pattern collections might seem to be quite useless and uninteresting. However, the applicability of finding interesting patterns relies on the assumption that the interestingness values have to be evaluated only for relatively few patterns in the pattern collection. Hence the collection of potentially interesting patterns can be usually pruned very effectively. Also, when considering the encoding of the interestingness values, the next interestingness value in the enumeration can sometimes be predicted very accurately from the previous values and thus only a small number of bits are needed to correct that prediction. The implicit enumeration of σ-interesting patterns can be formulated as follows.

Definition 1 (Implicit Enumeration of Patterns). *An implicit enumeration of σ-interesting patterns in a pattern class $\mathcal{P}$ with respect to an interestingness measure ϕ consists of*

- *a minimum interestingness threshold $\sigma \in [0, 1]$,*
- *a sequence $s \in [0, 1]^*$ of interestingness values from the range of $\phi|_{\mathcal{P}(\sigma, \phi)}$, and*
- *an algorithm $A_{\mathcal{P}, \Phi}$ for the collection $\mathcal{P}$ of patterns and for the class Φ of interestingness measures that computes the mapping $\phi|_{\mathcal{P}(\sigma, \phi)}$ given the sequence s and the minimum interestingness value threshold $\sigma \in [0, 1]$.*

The intuition behind this definition is as follows. The interestingness values needed to represent to describe $\phi|_{\mathcal{P}(\sigma,\phi)}$ are listed as a sequence $s \in [0,1]^*$. The algorithm $A_{\mathcal{P},\Phi}$ is defined to the pattern collection $\mathcal{P}$ and some particular class Φ of interestingness measures and it decodes s to $\phi|_{\mathcal{P}(\sigma,\phi)}$ with the additional information of the minimum interestingness value threshold $\sigma \in [0,1]$. An example of such pattern classes is the collection of all itemsets over $\mathcal{I}$. A natural class of interestingness measures for itemsets are the frequencies induced by different transaction databases.

In the next two sections we consider how the pattern collection pruning and binary encoding of interestingness values can be realized as implicit representations of pattern collections. For the sake of brevity, we describe the methods using frequent itemsets instead of general interesting pattern collections but the methods can be adapted to several other pattern classes and interestingness measures.

3   Enumeration Space Pruning

Possibilities to prune infrequent itemsets from the collection $2^{\mathcal{I}}$ of all subsets of the set $\mathcal{I}$ of items depend strongly on the order in which the frequencies of the itemsets are determined. At least in principle the ordering can be used to reflect the viewpoint of the data analyst to the data besides describing the patterns in a small space. Let $<_{\mathcal{I}}$ be an ordering over the items in $\mathcal{I}$ and let $A_1, \ldots, A_{|\mathcal{I}|}$ be the items in $\mathcal{I}$ in ascending order in $<_{\mathcal{I}}$. (For example, the items can be assumed to be integers $1, \ldots, |\mathcal{I}|$.) For rest of the paper we use the following ordering for itemsets $X, Y \subseteq \mathcal{I}$:

$$X \prec Y \iff |X| < |Y| \vee (|X| = |Y| \wedge \min(Y \setminus X) <_{\mathcal{I}} \min(X \setminus Y)). \quad (1)$$

Using this ordering for itemsets, we shall next consider different strategies to prune the enumeration space.

3.1   Implicit Frequent Itemset Representation

A very natural way to prune infrequent itemsets is to evaluate frequencies of itemsets levelwise from the smallest to the largest itemset, i.e., from the most general to the most specific itemset. This ordering enables effective pruning due to two most well-known pruning properties of frequent itemsets: the *anti-monotonicity of frequencies* (Proposition 1) and the *downward-closedness of the collection of frequent itemsets* (Proposition 2). The anti-monotonicity property says that the frequency of an itemset is never greater than the frequency of its subset:

Proposition 1 (Anti-monotonicity). *Let $X, Y \subseteq \mathcal{I}$ such that $X \subseteq Y$. Then $fr(X, d) \geq fr(Y, d)$.*

In fact, the anti-monotonicity of the frequencies implies also the downward-closedness of frequent itemsets: all subsets of a frequent itemset are frequent and all supersets of an infrequent itemset are infrequent.

Proposition 2 (Downward-Closedness). *The collection $\mathcal{F}(\sigma, d)$ of frequent itemsets is downward closed, i.e., for all $X \in \mathcal{F}(\sigma, d)$ hold $Y \subseteq X \Rightarrow Y \in \mathcal{F}(\sigma, d)$.*

For example, the efficiency of the famous APRIORI algorithm is mostly due to these pruning rules [25]. It is immediate that the number of frequencies to be listed using the rules is at most $|\mathcal{I}| \, |\mathcal{F}(\sigma, d)|$. This bound is also tight: if the empty itemset is the only frequent itemset then we have to evaluate the frequencies of all singleton subsets of $\mathcal{I}$.

Thus, by listing frequencies from the smallest to the largest itemset as defined by Equation 1, and pruning the enumeration space by the rules of Proposition 1 and Proposition 2, it is sufficient to determine frequencies for all frequent itemsets and the itemsets whose all proper subsets are frequent, i.e., the collection of *minimal infrequent itemsets*, denoted by

$$\mathcal{F}(\sigma, d)^- = \{X \subseteq \mathcal{I} : X \notin \mathcal{F}(\sigma, d), Y \in \mathcal{F}(\sigma, d) \forall Y \subset X\}.$$

Furthermore, as the frequency of the empty itemset is always 1, it is not needed in the sequence of frequencies. Thus, the whole collection sufficient for the implicit enumeration is

$$\mathcal{F}(\sigma, d)^* = \big(\mathcal{F}(\sigma, d) \cup \mathcal{F}(\sigma, d)^-\big) \setminus \{\emptyset\}.$$

Let $X_0, X_1, \ldots, X_{|\mathcal{F}(\sigma, d)^*|}$ be the itemsets in $\mathcal{F}(\sigma, d)^* \cup \{\emptyset\}$ ordered in ascending order with respect to $\prec$, i.e., $X_{i-1} \prec X_i$ for all $1 \leq i \leq |\mathcal{F}(\sigma, d)^*|$ and $X_0 = \emptyset$. Then the sequence $s_{\mathcal{F}(\sigma, d)^*} \in [0, 1]^{|\mathcal{F}(\sigma, d)^*|}$ is

$$s_{\mathcal{F}(\sigma, d)^*} = s[1] \ldots s[|\mathcal{F}(\sigma, d)^*|] = fr(X_1, d) \ldots fr(X_{|\mathcal{F}(\sigma, d)^*|}, d). \tag{2}$$

The sequence $s_{\mathcal{F}(\sigma, d)^*}$ can be decoded to the frequencies of σ-frequent itemsets in d by Algorithm 1. Thus, we have the following result:

Proposition 3. *A minimum frequency threshold σ, a sequence $s_{\mathcal{F}(\sigma, d)^*}$, Algorithm 1, the set $\mathcal{I}$ of items and the ordering $<_{\mathcal{I}}$ form an implicit frequent itemset representation of $fr|_{\mathcal{F}(\sigma, d)}$.*

3.2   Implicit Frequent Free Itemset Representation

It has been recently noticed that some frequencies of frequent itemsets can be deduced from the frequencies of other frequent itemsets [29]. The simplest example of this phenomenon are *free itemsets* [17] (also known as *generators* [16] and *key patterns* [29]).

Definition 2 (Free Itemsets). *An itemset $X \subseteq \mathcal{I}$ is free if $fr(X, d) < fr(Y, d)$ for all $Y \subset X$. The collection of σ-frequent free itemsets in d is denoted by $\mathcal{G}(\sigma, d)$.*

The collections of free itemsets has the desirable property of being downward closed, similarly to the collections of frequent itemsets. That is, all subsets of free itemsets are free itemsets, too.

Algorithm 1

Input: The set $\mathcal{I}$ of items, an ordering $<_\mathcal{I}$ over $\mathcal{I}$, a minimum frequency threshold $\sigma \in [0, 1]$, and a sequence s of frequencies in the range of $fr|_{\mathcal{F}(\sigma,d)^*}$.
Output: The mapping $fr|_{\mathcal{F}(\sigma,d)}$.

1: **function** FREQUENT-ITEMSETS($\mathcal{I}, <_\mathcal{I}, \sigma, s$)
2:     $fr(\emptyset, d) \leftarrow 1$
3:     $\mathcal{F}(\sigma, d) \leftarrow \{\emptyset\}$
4:     $i \leftarrow 1$
5:     $\mathcal{K} \leftarrow \{\{A\} : A \in \mathcal{I}\}$
6:     **while** $\mathcal{K} \neq \emptyset$ and $i < |s|$ **do**
7:         $\mathcal{F} \leftarrow \emptyset$
8:         **for each** $X \in \mathcal{K}$ in ascending order in $\prec$ **do**
9:             **if** $s[i] \geq \sigma$ **then**
10:                $fr(X, d) \leftarrow s[i]$
11:                $\mathcal{F} \leftarrow \mathcal{F} \cup \{X\}$
12:            **end if**
13:            $i \leftarrow i + 1$
14:        **end for**
15:        $\mathcal{F}(\sigma, d) \leftarrow \mathcal{F}(\sigma, d) \cup \mathcal{F}$
16:        $\mathcal{K} \leftarrow \{X \cup Y : X, Y \in \mathcal{F}, |X \cup Y| = |X| + 1, (Z \subset (X \cup Y) \Rightarrow Z \in \mathcal{F}(\sigma, d))\}$
17:    **end while**
18:    **return** $fr|_{\mathcal{F}(\sigma,d)}$
19: **end function**

Although the frequencies of all free itemsets in d determine all frequencies of all itemsets, the frequencies of σ-frequent free itemsets are not always sufficient determine the frequencies of all frequent itemsets correctly: the frequencies computed from the frequencies of the σ-frequent free itemsets are each at least σ. In addition to $\mathcal{G}(\sigma, d)$ also the collection $\mathcal{IG}(\sigma, d)$ of the minimal σ-infrequent free itemsets (i.e., the free itemsets X such that $fr(X, d) < \sigma$ and $Y \in \mathcal{G}(\sigma, d)$ for all $Y \subset X$) is needed.

When enumerating the frequent itemsets implicitly by free itemsets, also the frequencies of those non-free itemsets whose all subsets are frequent free itemsets are needed in the implicit representation. Let us denote the itemsets that are needed in the representation but are not σ-frequent free itemsets by

$$\mathcal{G}(\sigma, d)^- = \{X \subseteq \mathcal{I} : X \notin \mathcal{G}(\sigma, d), Y \in \mathcal{G}(\sigma, d) \forall Y \subset X\}.$$

The collection sufficient for the implicit enumeration based on free itemsets is

$$\mathcal{G}(\sigma, d)^* = \left(\mathcal{G}(\sigma, d) \cup \mathcal{G}(\sigma, d)^-\right) \setminus \{\emptyset\}.$$

Let $X_0, X_1, \ldots, X_{|\mathcal{G}(\sigma,d)^*|}$ be the itemsets in $\mathcal{G}(\sigma, d)^* \cup \{\emptyset\}$ ordered in ascending order with respect to $\prec$, i.e., $X_{i-1} \prec X_i$ for all $1 \leq i \leq |\mathcal{G}(\sigma, d)^*|$ and $X_0 = \emptyset$. Then the sequence $s_{\mathcal{G}(\sigma,d)^*} \in [0, 1]^{|\mathcal{G}(\sigma,d)^*|}$ is

$$s_{\mathcal{G}(\sigma,d)^*} = s[1] \ldots s[|\mathcal{G}(\sigma, d)^*|] = fr(X_1, d) \ldots fr(X_{|\mathcal{G}(\sigma,d)^*|}, d). \tag{3}$$

Algorithm 2

Input: The set $\mathcal{I}$ of items, an ordering $<_\mathcal{I}$ over $\mathcal{I}$, a minimum frequency threshold
   $\sigma \in [0,1]$, and a sequence s of frequencies in the range of $fr|_{\mathcal{G}(\sigma,d)^*}$.
Output: The mapping $fr|_{\mathcal{F}(\sigma,d)}$.

 1: **function** FREQUENT-FREE-ITEMSETS($\mathcal{I}, <_\mathcal{I}, \sigma, s$)
 2:    $fr(\emptyset, d) \leftarrow 1$
 3:    $\mathcal{G}(\sigma, d) \leftarrow \{\emptyset\}$
 4:    $\mathcal{IG}(\sigma, d) \leftarrow \emptyset$
 5:    $i \leftarrow 1$
 6:    $\mathcal{K} \leftarrow \{\{A\} : A \in \mathcal{I}\}$
 7:    **while** $\mathcal{K} \neq \emptyset$ and $i < |s|$ **do**
 8:       $\mathcal{F} \leftarrow \emptyset$
 9:       **for each** $X \in \mathcal{K}$ in ascending order in $\prec$ **do**
10:          **if** $Y \in \mathcal{G}(\sigma, d)$ for all $Y \subset X$ such that $|X| = |Y| + 1$ **then**
11:             **if** $s[i] \geq \sigma$ **then**
12:                $\mathcal{F} \leftarrow \mathcal{F} \cup \{X\}$
13:                $fr(X, d) \leftarrow s[i]$
14:                **if** $s[i] < fr(Y, d)$ for all $Y \subset X$ such that $|X| = |Y| + 1$ **then**
15:                   $\mathcal{G}(\sigma, d) \leftarrow \mathcal{G}(\sigma, d) \cup \{X\}$
16:                **end if**
17:             **else**
18:                $\mathcal{IG}(\sigma, d) \leftarrow \mathcal{IG}(\sigma, d) \cup \{X\}$
19:             **end if**
20:             $i \leftarrow i + 1$
21:          **else**
22:             **if** $\forall Y \subseteq X, |X| = |Y| + 1 : Y \notin \mathcal{IG}(\sigma, d)$ **then**
23:                $\mathcal{F} \leftarrow \mathcal{F} \cup \{X\}$
24:                $fr(X, d) \leftarrow \min \{Y \subset X : |X| = |Y| + 1\}$
25:             **end if**
26:          **end if**
27:       **end for**
28:       $\mathcal{F}(\sigma, d) \leftarrow \mathcal{F}(\sigma, d) \cup \mathcal{F}$
29:       $\mathcal{K} \leftarrow \{X \cup Y : X, Y \in \mathcal{F}, |X \cup Y| = |X| + 1, (Z \subset (X \cup Y) \Rightarrow Z \in \mathcal{F}(\sigma, d))\}$
30:    **end while**
31:    **return** $fr|_{\mathcal{F}(\sigma,d)}$
32: **end function**

The frequencies of σ-frequent itemsets in d can be decoded from the sequence $s_{\mathcal{G}(\sigma,d)^*}$ by Algorithm 2. Thus, we have:

Proposition 4. *A minimum frequency threshold σ, a sequence $s_{\mathcal{G}(\sigma,d)^*}$, Algorithm 2, the set $\mathcal{I}$ of items and the ordering $<_\mathcal{I}$ form an implicit frequent free itemset representation of $fr|_{\mathcal{F}(\sigma,d)}$.*

3.3   Implicit Frequent Closed Itemset Representation

Instead of looking for itemsets that have lower frequencies than any of their subsets, one can look for itemsets whose frequencies are greater than any of their supersets. These itemsets are called the *closed itemsets* [16].

Definition 3 (Closed Itemsets). *An itemset $X \subseteq \mathcal{I}$ is closed if $fr(X, d) > fr(Y, d)$ for all $Y \supset, Y \subseteq \mathcal{I}$. The collection of σ-frequent closed itemsets in d is denoted by $\mathcal{C}(\sigma, d)$.*

The collection $\mathcal{F}(\sigma, d)$ of σ-frequent itemsets and their frequencies can be determined from the collection $\mathcal{C}(\sigma, d)$ of σ-frequent closed itemsets and their frequencies as follows:

$$\mathcal{F}(\sigma, d) = \{X \subseteq \mathcal{I} : X \subseteq Y \in \mathcal{C}(\sigma, d)\}$$

and

$$fr(X, d) = \max \{fr(Y, d) : X \subseteq Y \in \mathcal{C}(\sigma, d)\}.$$

Closed itemsets are a very desirable representation of the frequent itemsets when the itemsets are represented explicitly (e.g., as a list or as a trie) for many reasons. For example, the number of (σ-frequent) closed itemsets is never greater than the number of (σ-frequent) free itemsets. To see this, let us consider the closures of itemsets.

Definition 4 (Closures of Itemsets). *A closure $cl(X, d)$ of an itemset $X \subseteq \mathcal{I}$ with respect to a transaction database d is the intersection of the transactions in d containing X, i.e.,*

$$cl(X, d) = \bigcap_{i \in cover(X, d)} d_i.$$

Each itemset has only one closure. Thus, the number of free itemsets is at least the number of closures of free itemsets. The closures of frequent free itemsets are also frequent itemsets. Furthermore, it is easy to see that there is a free frequent itemset for each closure of frequent itemset. Thus, based on Proposition 5, the number of free frequent itemsets is at least the number of closed frequent itemsets.

Proposition 5. *An itemset $X \subseteq \mathcal{I}$ is closed in d if and only if $cl(X, d) = Y$. Furthermore, $\{cl(X, d) : X \in \mathcal{F}(\sigma, d)\}$ is equal to $\mathcal{C}(\sigma, d)$.*

Proof. If X is closed, then $fr(X, d) > fr(Y, d)$ for all $Y \supset X, Y \subseteq \mathcal{I}$. This implies that there is $i \in cover(X, d)$ such that d_i contains X but not Y.

If X is not closed, then there is $Y \supset X, Y \subseteq \mathcal{I}$ such that $fr(X, d) = fr(Y, d)$, and thus $cover(X, d) = cover(Y, d)$. Thus, $X \subset cl(X, d) = cl(Y, d)$.

Each closed itemset is its own closure. Thus, the collection of the closures of frequent itemsets contains at least each closed frequent itemset.

Assume that there is an itemset $X \in \mathcal{F}(\sigma, d) \setminus \mathcal{C}(\sigma, d)$ that is a closure of some itemset $Y \subset X$. However, $cl(X, d) \supset X$ since X is not closed and thus it is not its own closure. Thus, X cannot be the closure of Y.   □

Proposition 5 explicates perhaps the greatest advantage of closed itemsets, namely their interpretations as intersections of transactions in a transaction database d: each closed itemset is an intersection of certain subset of transactions and each subset of transaction corresponds to some closed itemset.

Another advantage of closed itemsets compared to free itemsets is that the collection σ-frequent closed itemsets is a sufficient representation of frequent itemsets, i.e., no infrequent itemsets are needed in the closed itemset representation of frequent itemsets, whereas σ-frequent free itemsets are not.

Furthermore, the number of frequent closed itemsets can be sometimes even smaller than the number of frequent free itemsets as shown by the following example:

Example 2. Let $d = \{\{A, B\}, \{C\}\}$ and let the minimum frequency threshold σ be $1/2$. Then the σ-frequent closed itemsets are $\emptyset$, $\{A, B\}$ and $\{C\}$ whereas the σ-frequent free itemsets are $\emptyset$, $\{A\}$, $\{B\}$ and $\{C\}$.

A major disadvantage of closed itemsets to be represented implicitly as a list of frequencies became apparent in the previous example: the collection of closed itemsets is not necessarily downward closed. A straightforward solution would be to list also all subsets of closed itemsets that are not closed. In addition to that also some infrequent itemsets would have to be listed. Thus, much of the benefits of closed itemsets would be lost.

Fortunately, it is possible to find a more suitable encoding for the closed itemsets without losing their benefits: Instead of listing just frequencies, the list can consist of pairs for each (σ-frequent) closed itemset. The pair corresponding to closed itemset X consists of its distance from previous closed itemset in the enumeration and the frequency $fr(X, d)$.

Let $X_0, X_1, \ldots, X_{|\mathcal{C}(\sigma, d)|}$ be the itemsets in $\mathcal{C}(\sigma, d) \cup \emptyset$ ordered in ascending order with respect to $\prec$, i.e., $X_{i-1} \prec X_i$ for all $1 \leq i \leq |\mathcal{C}(\sigma, d)|$. Then the sequence $s_{\mathcal{C}(\sigma,d)}$ is consists of pairs

$$s[i] = \langle fr(X_i, d), \delta(X_{i-1}, X_i) \rangle \tag{4}$$

where $\delta(X, Y)$ is the distance of itemsets X and Y in the ordering $\prec$, i.e., $\delta(X, Y) = |\{Z \subseteq \mathcal{I} : X \prec Z \preceq Y\}| + |\{Z \subseteq \mathcal{I} : Y \prec Z \preceq X\}|$. Thus,

$$s_{\mathcal{C}(\sigma,d)} = s[1] \ldots s[|\mathcal{C}(\sigma, d) \setminus \{\emptyset\}|].$$

Since $\delta(X, Y) = |\delta(\emptyset, X) - \delta(\emptyset, Y)|$, it is sufficient to be able to compute the distance of an itemset from the empty itemset. First, we know that there are

$$\sum_{k=0}^{|X|-1} \binom{|\mathcal{I}|}{k}$$

itemsets smaller than X in cardinality. In addition to that we need to know how many itemsets $Y \subseteq \mathcal{I}$ of the same cardinality such that $Y \prec X$ there are. This can be counted by partitioning the set $\{Y \subseteq \mathcal{I} : |Y| = |X|\}$ into groups based on how long prefix they share with X. The length l-prefix of an itemset X is an itemset consisting of its l smallest elements and it is denoted by X_l. Let $\mathcal{I}_{<A} = \{B \in \mathcal{I} : B <_{\mathcal{I}} A\}$. Then the number of itemsets $Y \subseteq \mathcal{I}$ such that $|X| = |Y|$, $Y \prec X$ and sharing l-prefix with X is

$$\sum_{k=1}^{|X \setminus X_l|} \binom{\left|\mathcal{I}_{<\max X \setminus X_l}\right| \setminus X_l}{k} \binom{\left|\mathcal{I} \setminus \mathcal{I}_{<\max X \setminus X_k}\right|}{|X \setminus X_l| - k}$$

Algorithm 3

Input: The set $\mathcal{I}$ of items, an ordering $<_\mathcal{I}$ over $\mathcal{I}$, a minimum frequency threshold $\sigma \in [0, 1]$, and a sequence s of pairs as defined by Equation 4.
Output: The mapping $fr|_{\mathcal{F}(\sigma,d)}$.

```
 1: function FREQUENT-CLOSED-ITEMSETS(𝓘, <𝓘, σ, s)
 2:     𝓒(σ, d) ← ∅
 3:     p ← 0
 4:     for i = 1, ..., |s| do
 5:         ⟨f, j⟩ ← s[i]
 6:         p ← p + j
 7:         k ← 0
 8:         p′ ← p
 9:         while p′ − (|𝓘| choose k) ≥ 0 do
10:             p′ ← p′ − (|𝓘| choose k)
11:             k ← k + 1
12:         end while
13:         X ← ∅
14:         Y ← 𝓘
15:         while k > 0 do
16:             A ← min Y
17:             if p′ − (|Y|−1 choose k−1) ≥ 0 then
18:                 p′ ← p′ − (|Y|−1 choose k−1)
19:                 X ← X ∪ {A}
20:                 k ← k − 1
21:             end if
22:         end while
23:         fr(X, d) ← f
24:         𝓒(σ, d) ← 𝓒(σ, d) ∪ {X}
25:     end for
26:     𝓕(σ, d) ← ∅
27:     𝓕 ← 𝓒(σ, d)
28:     while 𝓕 ≠ ∅ do
29:         𝓕(σ, d) ← 𝓕(σ, d) ∪ 𝓕
30:         𝓚 ← ∅
31:         for each X ∈ 𝓕 do
32:             for each Y ⊆ X such that |Y| = |X| − 1 do
33:                 if Y ∉ 𝓕(σ, d) or fr(Y, d) < fr(X, d) then
34:                     𝓚 ← 𝓚 ∪ {Y}
35:                     fr(Y, d) ← fr(X, d)
36:                 end if
37:             end for
38:         end for
39:         𝓕 ← 𝓚
40:     end while
41:     fr(∅, d) ← 1
42:     return fr|𝓕(σ,d)
43: end function
```

because, by the definition of the ordering (Equation 1) and itemset Y is smaller than X if and only if

$$\min\left(Y \setminus X\right) <_{\mathcal{I}} \min\left(X \setminus Y\right).$$

(These observations are implemented in Algorithm 3.)

The downside of this encoding is that expressing the distance from previous closed itemset might cost even $|\mathcal{I}|$ bits. This is the case e.g. when $\mathcal{I}$ is the only σ-frequent closed itemset, i.e., when $d = \{\mathcal{I}, \dots, \mathcal{I}\}$. Still, this is not very bad compared to listing all frequencies of frequent itemsets, i.e., the (implicit) frequent itemset representation.

The frequencies of the σ-frequent itemsets in d can be decoded from the sequence $s_{\mathcal{C}(\sigma,d)}$ by Algorithm 3 and thus we have the following result:

Proposition 6. *A minimum frequency threshold σ, a sequence $s_{\mathcal{C}(\sigma,d)}$, a sequence $s_{\mathcal{C}(\sigma,d)}$, Algorithm 3, the set $\mathcal{I}$ of items and the ordering $<_{\mathcal{I}}$ form an implicit frequent closed itemset representation of $fr|_{\mathcal{F}(\sigma,d)}$.*

3.4   Implicit Frequent Non-derivable Itemset Representation

The idea of deducing the frequencies of the frequent itemsets from the frequencies of their subsets can be further developed as follows. Based on the inclusion-exclusion principle, the inequality

$$\sum_{Y \subseteq Z \subseteq X} (-1)^{|Z \setminus Y|} fr(Z, d) \geq 0$$

holding for all $Y \subseteq X$ gives a lower bound $\underline{fr}(X, d)$ and an upper bound $\overline{fr}(X, d)$ for the frequency $fr(X, d)$ of each itemset X based on the frequencies of its subsets (see Equation 5 and Equation 6).

$$\overline{fr}(X, d) = \min_{Y \subset X} \left\{ \sum_{Y \subseteq Z \subset X} (-1)^{|X \setminus Z|+1} fr(Z, d) : |X \setminus Y| \text{ is odd} \right\} \qquad (5)$$

$$\underline{fr}(X, d) = \max_{Y \subset X} \left\{ \sum_{Y \subseteq Z \subset X} (-1)^{|X \setminus Z|+1} fr(Z, d) : |X \setminus Y| \text{ is even} \right\} \qquad (6)$$

Note that the anti-monotonicity property is a special case of these bounds. Namely, $fr(X, d) \leq \min_{A \in X} \{fr(X \setminus \{A\}, d)\}$. In general these bounds lead to the concept of *non-derivable itemsets* [21].

Definition 5 (Non-derivable Itemsets). *An itemset $X \subseteq \mathcal{I}$ is non-derivable in d if $\underline{fr}(X, d) < \overline{fr}(X, d)$. The collection of σ-frequent non-derivable itemsets is denoted by $\mathcal{N}(\sigma, d)$.*

Algorithm 4

Input: The set $\mathcal{I}$ of items, an ordering $<_\mathcal{I}$ over $\mathcal{I}$, a minimum frequency threshold
   $\sigma \in [0, 1]$, and a sequence s of frequencies in the range of $fr|_{\mathcal{N}(\sigma,d)^*}$.
Output: The mapping $fr|_{\mathcal{F}(\sigma,d)}$.
1: **function** FREQUENT-NON-DERIVABLE-ITEMSETS($\mathcal{I}, <_\mathcal{I}, \sigma, s$)
2:     $fr(\emptyset, d) \leftarrow 1$
3:     $\mathcal{N}(\sigma, d) \leftarrow \{\emptyset\}$
4:     $i \leftarrow 1$
5:     $\mathcal{K} \leftarrow \{\{A\} : A \in \mathcal{I}\}$
6:     **while** $\mathcal{K} \neq \emptyset$ and $i \leq |s|$ **do**
7:         $\mathcal{F} \leftarrow \emptyset$
8:         **for each** $X \in \mathcal{K}$ in ascending order in $\prec$ **do**
9:             **if** $\overline{fr}(X, d) \geq \sigma$ **then**
10:                 **if** $\underline{fr}(X, d) = \overline{fr}(X, d)$ **then**
11:                     $fr(X, d) \leftarrow \overline{fr}(X, d)$
12:                     $\mathcal{F} \leftarrow \mathcal{F} \cup \{X\}$
13:                 **else**
14:                     **if** $s[i] \geq \sigma$ **then**
15:                         $fr(X, d) \leftarrow s[i]$
16:                         $\mathcal{F} \leftarrow \mathcal{F} \cup \{X\}$
17:                     **end if**
18:                     $i \leftarrow i + 1$
19:                 **end if**
20:             **end if**
21:         **end for**
22:         $\mathcal{F}(\sigma, d) \leftarrow \mathcal{F}(\sigma, d) \cup \mathcal{F}$
23:         $\mathcal{K} \leftarrow \{X \cup Y : X, Y \in \mathcal{F}, |X \cup Y| = |X| + 1, (Z \subset (X \cup Y) \Rightarrow Z \in \mathcal{F}(\sigma, d))\}$
24:     **end while**
25:     **return** $fr|_{\mathcal{F}(\sigma,d)}$
26: **end function**

Unlike in the case of σ-frequent free itemsets, the frequencies of the σ-frequent itemsets can be deduced from the frequencies of the σ-frequent non-derivable itemsets since non-derivable infrequent itemsets can be detected based on the fact that their upper and lower bounds do not agree.

The collection of non-derivable itemsets is known to be downward closed [21]. For the implicit representation, also the collection

$$\mathcal{N}(\sigma, d)^- = \left\{ X \subseteq \mathcal{I} : \underline{fr}(X, d) < \overline{fr}(X, d) \geq \sigma, X \notin \mathcal{N}(\sigma, d) \right\}.$$

is needed. Thus, the collection sufficient for the implicit enumeration based on non-derivable itemsets is

$$\mathcal{N}(\sigma, d)^* = \left(\mathcal{N}(\sigma, d) \cup \mathcal{N}(\sigma, d)^- \right) \setminus \{\emptyset\}.$$

Let $X_0, X_1, \ldots, X_{|\mathcal{N}(\sigma,d)^*|}$ be the itemsets in $\mathcal{N}(\sigma, d)^* \cup \{\emptyset\}$ ordered in ascending order with respect to $\prec$, i.e., $X_{i-1} \prec X_i$ for all $1 \leq i \leq |\mathcal{N}(\sigma, d)^*|$ and $X_0 = \emptyset$. Then the sequence $s_{\mathcal{N}(\sigma,d)^*} \in [0, 1]^{|\mathcal{N}(\sigma,d)^*|}$ is

$$s_{\mathcal{F}(\sigma,d)^*} = s[1] \ldots s[|\mathcal{N}(\sigma, d)^*|] = fr(X_1, d) \ldots fr(X_{|\mathcal{N}(\sigma,d)^*|}, d). \tag{7}$$

Proposition 7. *A minimum frequency threshold σ, a sequence $s_{\mathcal{N}(\sigma,d)^*}$, Algorithm 4, the set $\mathcal{I}$ of items and the ordering $<_\mathcal{I}$ form an* implicit frequent non-derivable itemset representation *of $fr|_{\mathcal{F}(\sigma,d)}$.*

4   Describing the Interestingness Values

In addition to the number of frequencies listed in the enumeration, also the number of bits used to represent the frequencies can make a huge difference in the space consumption of the representation of the frequent itemsets.

4.1   Worst Case Bounds

Clearly, each frequency can be represented by $\log(n+1)$ bits as all possible frequencies in d are $0/n, 1/n, \ldots, n/n$. (Recall that it is not necessary to round the logarithms to integer values since using e.g. arithmetic coding it is possible to represent each value by a fractional number of bits [30].) Moreover, as there is a minimum frequency threshold σ, it is sufficient to be able to represent the values $\lceil \sigma n \rceil /n, \ldots, 1$ to represent the frequencies of the frequent itemsets and one value for infrequent itemsets. Thus,

$$\log\left(\lfloor(1-\sigma)\,n\rfloor + 2\right) \tag{8}$$

bits suffice to represent such values.

The number of bits needed can be further reduced by the frequencies of the previous itemsets in the enumeration. The simplest solution is to prune by the anti-monotonicity of frequencies. This way the frequency of a potentially frequent itemset X can be encoded using

$$\log\left(\lfloor(\min\{fr(X\setminus\{A\},d):A\in X\}-\sigma)\,n\rfloor + 2\right) \tag{9}$$

bits. This can provide considerable reduction to the space consumption of the frequencies since in practice there seems to be many itemsets with frequencies close to the minimum frequency threshold σ.

Also the lower and upper bounds for frequencies can be used to reduce the space consumption: If $\overline{fr}(X,d) < \sigma$ or $\lceil \underline{fr}(X,d)n \rceil = \lfloor \overline{fr}(X,d)n \rfloor$ then no bits are needed to describe the frequency of X. Otherwise the sufficient number of bits is

$$\log\left(\lfloor\overline{fr}(X,d)n\rfloor - \max\{\lceil\sigma n\rceil - 1, \lceil\underline{fr}(X,d)n\rceil\} + 1\right). \tag{10}$$

4.2   Predicting the Interestingness Values

The bounds given in Section 4.1 are tight in the worst case. In practice, however, one can often improve the compression even further by modeling the frequencies more accurately. Although it might be difficult to say for sure what is the frequency of some particular itemset, it is usually possible to assign higher probability to the correct frequency than the average probability in the interval of all possible frequencies.

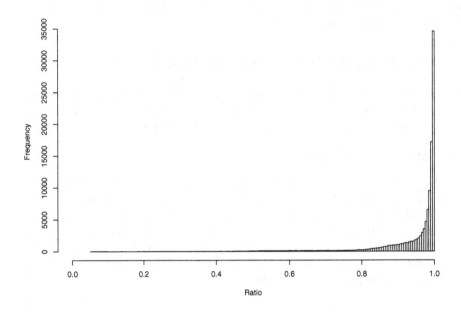

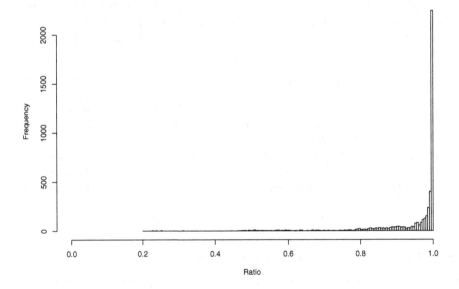

Fig. 1. The histograms of ratios $fr(X,d)/\overline{fr}(X,d)$ for Internet Usage data (top) and IPUMS Census data (bottom)

The simplest solution would be to count how many itemsets X have contain frequency $fr(X, d)$ in d, i.e., to compute the multinomial distribution over the frequencies of the frequent itemsets. There are several difficulties with this approach.

First, the lower bound $\underline{fr}(X, d)$ and the upper bound $\overline{fr}(X, d)$ often restrict the interval of possible values of $fr(X, d)$ considerably. This information is not exploited at all with the straightforward construction of the multinomial distribution. Second, also the distribution has to be described. Although the uniform distribution over the interval $\left[\max\left\{\underline{fr}(X, d), (\lceil \sigma n \rceil - 1)/n\right\}, \overline{fr}(X, d)\right]$ might be quite crude estimate for the best distribution over the frequencies, no parameter is needed to be described. The number of parameters needed with multinomial distribution is equal to the number of different frequencies in the range of $fr|_{\mathcal{F}(\sigma, d)}$. The latter problem with multinomial distribution can be diminished by discretizing the frequencies but still it would be more preferable to have simpler model even with slightly worse compression ratio.

Slightly more sophisticated solution can be derived from the concept of free itemsets. Recall that itemset is not free if it has the same frequency than some of its subsets. Free itemsets (see Definition 2) have shown good condensation performance on real data [17]. Thus, it is natural to consider its relaxations by considering how close the frequencies of the itemsets are to the minimum frequencies of their subsets. The idea can be further improved by considering the ratios between the minimum upper bound $\overline{fr}(X, d)$ and the correct frequency $fr(X, d)$. The histogram of the ratios are shown for two transaction databases (See Section 6) in Figure 1. The ratios are concentrated close to the ratio 1 and hence supporting the intuition behind the encoding of frequencies as the ratios. Furthermore, both histograms could be approximated reasonably well by polynomials with small number of terms since they are quite smooth.

A different approach would be to first determine a good estimate of the frequency $fr(X, d)$ of the itemset $X \subseteq \mathcal{I}$ and then correct it. In practice, the maximum entropy estimate of $fr(X, d)$ computed from the frequencies $fr(Y, d)$ of the subsets Y of the itemset X has been detected to be often a good estimate of the correct frequency [31]. Thus, having a high probability for the maximum entropy estimate of $fr(X, d)$ and its near-by frequencies could result good compression. The probabilities to the possible frequencies could be assigned in this case by maximum-entropy centered Gaussian distributions with the variance estimated from the true distribution of frequencies.

These models are still relatively simple as the dependencies of the frequencies, for example, are not modeled directly. The usability of the models depends on the actual transaction databases. Hence, evaluating the suitability of the different models to the transaction database at hand should be the first step of modeling the frequency distributions. Nevertheless, we believe that modeling of frequencies has much unexplored potential in pattern discovery.

5   Measuring the Surprisingness

In addition to representing the frequencies of the frequent itemsets in small space, the bit encodings can be used also to shed some light to pattern collections. Namely, the number of bits needed reflects the complexity of the frequencies with respect to the model of the frequency structure. The benefit of the binary encodings is (at least) two-fold.

First, if the collection of σ-frequent itemsets does not compress much, then the model of the frequencies might not be good enough. That is, the incompressibility of the pattern collection implies that our hypothesis about the frequency structure of the pattern collection should improved.

Second, the number of bits needed to describe some particular itemset gives a measure how unexpected the itemset is with respect to the known frequencies and our model of the frequency structure. As we know the sizes of the binary representations for the frequencies of the itemsets in the collection, we can also compare the complexities of the itemsets and spot the surprising ones, both the itemsets with very small and very large frequency encodings, regions of surprising itemsets and possible some explanations for the surprising values. Very unexpected itemsets can also reveal the weaknesses of our model of the frequency structure.

Although there are several good candidates (such as maximum entropy centered Gaussian distributions) for modeling the interestingness values, the practical usability of this measure of interestingness (e.g., unexpectedness or surprisingness) depends on how well the frequency structure of the pattern collection is modeled. Fortunately the proposed measure of interestingness supports also exploratory analysis of data by indicating possibly too incorrect models of the frequency structure by a large binary encoding of the frequencies.

6   Experiments

The ideas of implicit enumeration were experimented with two data sets from UCI KDD Repository[1]. The data sets used in the experiments were Internet Usage data set consisting of 10104 transactions and 10674 attributes, and IPUMS Census data set consisting of 88443 transactions and 39954 attributes.

Our goal was to examine how large different implicit enumeration representations are and how they compare to explicit representations. More specifically, we did two series of experiments.

In the first series of experiments we tried to find out how much we lose in terms of the number of represented itemsets when using implicit instead of explicit enumeration of frequent itemsets. The results are shown in Table 1 and Table 2.

The columns of the tables are as follows. Column σ is the minimum frequency threshold, column $|\mathcal{F}(\sigma, d)|$ is the number of σ-frequent itemsets, $|\mathcal{F}(\sigma, d)^-|$ is the

---

[1] http://kdd.ics.uci.edu

Table 1. The number of frequencies that determine frequent itemsets in Internet Usage data using different representations

σ	$\mathcal{F}(\sigma,d)^*$		$\mathcal{G}(\sigma,d)^*$		$\mathcal{N}(\sigma,d)^*$		
	$\|\mathcal{F}(\sigma,d)\|$	$\|\mathcal{F}(\sigma,d)^-\|$	$\|\mathcal{G}(\sigma,d)\|$	$\|\mathcal{G}(\sigma,d)^-\|$	$\|\mathcal{IG}(\sigma,d)\|$	$\|\mathcal{N}(\sigma,d)\|$	$\|\mathcal{N}(\sigma,d)^-\|$
0.20	1857	1618	1857	1618	1618	915	1299
0.19	2229	1937	2229	1937	1937	1112	1523
0.18	2668	2226	2668	2226	2226	1313	1818
0.17	3247	2626	3247	2626	2626	1601	2327
0.16	4014	2987	4014	2987	2987	1985	2808
0.15	4984	3451	4984	3451	3451	2445	3473
0.14	6292	4163	6291	4164	4163	3078	4389
0.13	8001	5051	7999	5052	5051	3882	5551
0.12	10477	6337	10473	6338	6337	5071	7187
0.11	13814	7779	13803	7780	7779	6622	9410
0.10	18616	9915	18595	9917	9915	8822	12407
0.09	25730	13265	25687	13270	13265	12073	16720
0.08	36813	18057	36715	18075	18057	16925	23212
0.07	54794	25286	54551	25323	25286	24640	33396
0.06	85493	35958	84874	36041	35958	37449	50142

Table 2. The number of frequencies that determine frequent itemsets in IPUMS Census data using different representations

σ	$\mathcal{F}(\sigma,d)^*$		$\mathcal{G}(\sigma,d)^*$		$\mathcal{N}(\sigma,d)^*$		
	$\|\mathcal{F}(\sigma,d)\|$	$\|\mathcal{F}(\sigma,d)^-\|$	$\|\mathcal{G}(\sigma,d)\|$	$\|\mathcal{G}(\sigma,d)^-\|$	$\|\mathcal{IG}(\sigma,d)\|$	$\|\mathcal{N}(\sigma,d)\|$	$\|\mathcal{N}(\sigma,d)^-\|$
0.40	1518	301	461	313	301	144	275
0.39	1828	340	536	354	340	169	322
0.38	2112	357	608	371	357	188	363
0.37	2500	373	708	387	373	218	409
0.36	2796	396	782	411	396	235	443
0.35	3308	420	902	436	420	259	480
0.34	3976	425	1032	441	425	287	511
0.33	4752	507	1216	525	507	334	598
0.32	5362	533	1348	551	533	367	677
0.31	6648	705	1586	731	705	428	783
0.30	8206	745	1855	771	745	477	933
0.29	9642	804	2118	830	804	531	1084
0.28	11444	899	2401	925	899	587	1243
0.27	13844	916	2771	942	916	642	1378
0.26	17504	1060	3291	1087	1060	741	1615
0.25	20024	1267	3723	1298	1267	840	1783
0.24	23904	1552	4365	1584	1552	975	2090
0.23	31792	1914	5326	1955	1914	1200	2503

number of σ-infrequent itemsets whose allsubsets are σ-frequent, column $|\mathcal{G}(\sigma,d)|$ is the number of σ-frequent free itemsets, column $|\mathcal{G}(\sigma,d)^-|$ is the number of itemsets that are not σ-frequent free itemsets but whose all subsets are, column

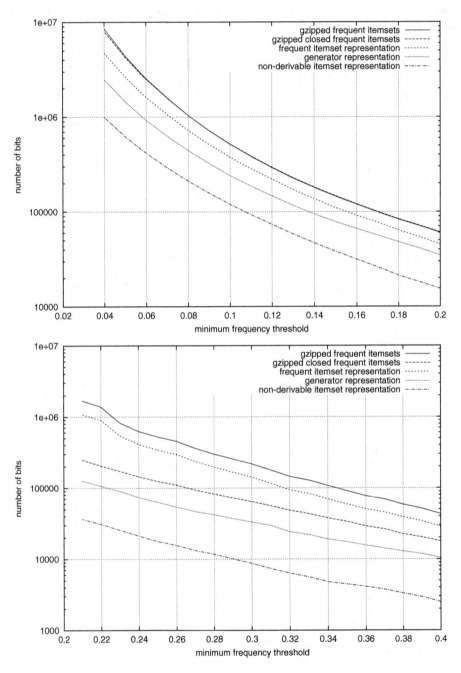

Fig. 2. The number of bits used in different implicit representations and **gzip**-compressed explicit representations of frequent itemsets in Internet Usage data (top) and IPUMS Census data (bottom)

$|\mathcal{IG}(\sigma, d)|$ is the number of minimal σ-infrequent free itemsets, column $|\mathcal{N}(\sigma, d)|$ is the number of σ-frequent non-derivable itemsets and column $|\mathcal{N}(\sigma, d)^-|$ is the number of σ-infrequent non-derivable itemsets with least upper bounds at least the minimum frequency threshold and whose all subsets are σ-frequent non-derivable itemsets. Recall that the number of itemsets in the explicit representations (i.e., listing the itemsets and their frequencies) are $|\mathcal{F}(\sigma, d)|$, $|\mathcal{G}(\sigma, d)| + |\mathcal{IG}(\sigma, d)|$ and $|\mathcal{N}(\sigma, d)|$. The number of itemsets in the implicit representations are $|\mathcal{F}(\sigma, d)| + |\mathcal{F}(\sigma, d)^-|$, $|\mathcal{G}(\sigma, d)| + |\mathcal{G}(\sigma, d)^-|$ and $|\mathcal{N}(\sigma, d)| + |\mathcal{N}(\sigma, d)^-|$, for implicit frequent itemset representations, implicit frequent free itemset representations and implicit frequent non-derivable itemset representations, respectively.

The number of itemsets needed in the implicit representations seems to differ from the number of itemsets needed in the explicit representations reasonably little. As the implicit representations need list only the frequencies and not the actual patterns in contrary to the explicit representations, this small increase in the number of patterns needed is even more acceptable.

Second, we wanted to find out how different pruning strategies affect to the actual sizes of the representations. The number of bits used to represent the frequencies of the frequent itemsets are determined by Equation 8, Equation 9 and Equation 10 in the implicit frequent itemset representations, in the frequent free representation and the frequent non-derivable itemset representation, respectively. As baselines we used `gzip`-compressed frequent itemsets and `gzip`-compressed closed frequent itemsets.

The results for both data sets are shown in Figure 2. Thus, the pruning techniques decrease considerably also the sizes of the binary encodings of the implicit frequent itemset representations and the implicit representations are competitive with the explicit representations.

7   Conclusions

In this paper we have described how pattern collections can be represented by listing the interestingness values of the patterns in some suitable order and showed how this implicit representation can be constructed in the case of frequent itemsets using the order of increasing itemset cardinality.

This approach seems to be quite competitive compared to other representation techniques in terms of space consumption, as shown in Section 6. Also, implicit enumerations offer a complementary viewpoint to pattern collections.

As a side product of this viewpoint we get a natural measure of surprisingness based on how well each interestingness value can be predicted from the interestingness values of previous patterns in the enumeration. This measure of surprisingness can be applied to individual patterns and whole pattern collections: for the individual patterns it expressed how unexpected the pattern is compared to other patterns and for the pattern collection it can be used to evaluate the fitness of our understanding about the relationships between the patterns.

Furthermore, describing a list of interestingness values of one pattern collection based on the interestingness values of another pattern collection seems to have some potential to compare pattern collections, e.g., to detect the changes in evolving transaction databases.

Although the implicit enumeration of patterns seems to be a promising approach to represent patterns, there are some interesting open problems:

- How to make use of the proposed measure of surprisingness in concrete cases? What kind of models on interestingness values would be useful in practice to gain more insight to pattern collections?
- How the patterns should be ordered in terms of understandability, efficient queries and the size of the representation when implicitly enumerating them?
- How the implicit and the explicit enumerations should be combined? How one could move from implicit to explicit representation and vice versa?

Acknowledgments. I wish to thank the anonymous reviewers for their constructive comments and illuminating insights.

References

1. Agrawal, R., Imielinski, T., Swami, A.N.: Mining association rules between sets of items in large databases. In Buneman, P., Jajodia, S., eds.: Proceedings of the 1993 ACM SIGMOD International Conference on Management of Data, Washington, D.C., May 26-28, 1993. ACM Press (1993) 207–216
2. Goethals, B., Zaki, M.J., eds.: Proceedings of the Workshop on Frequent Itemset Mining Implementations (FIMI-03), Melbourne Florida, USA, November 19, 2003. Volume 90 of CEUR Workshop Proceedings. (2003) http://CEUR-WS.org/Vol-90/.
3. Inokuchi, A., Washio, T., Motoda, H.: Complete mining of frequent patterns from graphs: Mining graph data. Machine Learning **50** (2003) 321–354
4. Kurakochi, M., Karypis, G.: Discovering frequent geometric subgraphs. [32] 258–265
5. Wang, X., Wang, J.T., Shasha, D., Shapiro, B.A., Rigoutsos, I., Zhang, K.: Finding patterns in three-dimensional graphs: Algorithms and applications to scientific data mining. IEEE Transactions on Knowledge and Data Engineering **14** (2002) 731–749
6. Yan, X., Han, J.: CloseGraph: mining closed frequent graph patterns. In Getoor, L., Senator, T.E., Domingos, P., Faloutsos, C., eds.: Proceedings of the Ninth ACM SIGKDD International Conference on Knowledge Discovery and Data Mining, Washington, DC, USA, August 24 - 27, 2003. ACM (2003) 286–295
7. Garofalakis, M., Rastogi, R., Shim, K.: Mining sequential patterns with regular expression constraints. IEEE Transactions on Knowledge and Data Engineering **14** (2002) 530–552
8. Mannila, H., Toivonen, H., Verkamo, A.I.: Discovery of frequent episodes in event sequences. Data Mining and Knowledge Discovery **1** (1997) 259–289
9. Zaki, M.J.: SPADE: An efficient algoritm for mining frequent sequences. Machine Learning **42** (2001) 31–60

10. Tan, P.N., Kumar, V., Srivastava, J.: Selecting the right interestingness measure for association patterns. In Hand, D., Keim, D., Ng, R., eds.: Proceedings of the Eighth ACM SIGKDD International Conference on Knowledge Discovery and Data Mining, July 23-26, 2002, Edmonton, Alberta, Canada. ACM (2002)

11. Mannila, H., Toivonen, H.: Multiple uses of frequent sets and condensed representations. In Simoudis, E., Han, J., Fayyad, U.M., eds.: Proceedings of the Second International Conference on Knowledge Discovery and Data Mining (KDD-96). AAAI Press (1996) 189–194

12. De Raedt, L.: A perspective on inductive databases. SIGKDD Explorations **4** (2003) 69–77

13. Imielinski, T., Mannila, H.: A database perspective on knowledge discovery. Communications of The ACM **39** (1996) 58–64

14. Mannila, H.: Inductive databases and condensed representations for data mining. In Maluszynski, J., ed.: Logic Programming, Proceedngs of the 1997 International Symposium, Port Jefferson, Long Island, N.Y., October 13-16, 1997. MIT Press (1997) 21–30

15. Gunopulos, D., Khardon, R., Mannila, H., Saluja, S., Toivonen, H., Sharma, R.S.: Discovering all most specific sentences. ACM Transactions on Database Systems **28** (2003) 140–174

16. Pasquier, N., Bastide, Y., Taouil, R., Lakhal, L.: Discovering frequent closed itemsets for association rules. In Beeri, C., Buneman, P., eds.: Database Theory - ICDT '99, 7th International Conference, Jerusalem, Israel, January 10-12, 1999, Proceedings. Volume 1540 of Lecture Notes in Computer Science. Springer (1999) 398–416

17. Boulicaut, J.F., Bykowski, A., Rigotti, C.: Free-sets: a condensed representation of Boolean data for the approximation of frequency queries. Data Mining and Knowledge Discovery **7** (2003) 5–22

18. Bykowski, A., Rigotti, C.: A condensed representation to find frequent patterns. In: Proceedings of the Twentieth ACM SIGACT-SIGMOD-SIGART Symposium on Principles of Database Systems, May 21-23, 2001, Santa Barbara, California, USA. ACM (2001)

19. Kryszkiewicz, M.: Concise representation of frequent patterns based on disjunction-free generators. In Cercone, N., Lin, T.Y., Wu, X., eds.: Proceedings of the 2001 IEEE International Conference on Data Mining, 29 November - 2 December 2001, San Jose, California, USA. IEEE Computer Society (2001) 305–312

20. Calders, T., Goethals, B.: Minimal k-free representations of frequent sets. [33] 71–82

21. Calders, T., Goethals, B.: Mining all non-derivable frequent itemsets. In Elomaa, T., Mannila, H., Toivonen, H., eds.: Principles of Data Mining and Knowledge Discovery, 6th European Conference, PKDD 2002, Helsinki, Finland, August 19-23, 2002, Proceedings. Volume 2431 of Lecture Notes in Artificial Intelligence. Springer (2002) 74–865

22. Pei, J., Dong, G., Zou, W., Han, J.: On computing condensed pattern bases. [32] 378–385

23. Mielikäinen, T., Mannila, H.: The pattern ordering problem. [33] 327–338

24. Mielikäinen, T.: Chaining patterns. In Grieser, G., Tanaka, Y., Yamamoto, A., eds.: Discovery Science, 6th International Conference, DS 2003, Sapporo, Japan, October 17–19, 2003, Proceedings. Volume 2843 of Lecture Notes in Computer Science. Springer (2003) 232–243

25. Agrawal, R., Mannila, H., Srikant, R., Toivonen, H., Verkamo, A.I.: Fast discovery of association rules. In Fayyad, U.M., Piatetsky-Shapiro, G., Smyth, P., Uthurusamy, R., eds.: Advances in Knowledge Discovery and Data Mining. AAAI/MIT Press (1996) 307–328

26. Hafez, A., Deogun, J., Raghavan, V.V.: The item-set tree: A data structure for data mining. In Mohania, M.K., Tjoa, A.M., eds.: Data Warehousing and Knowledge Discovery, First International Conference, DaWaK '99, Florence, Italy, August 30 - September 1, 1999, Proceedings. Volume 1676 of Lecture Notes in Artificial Intelligence. Springer (1999) 183–192

27. Mielikäinen, T.: An automata approach to pattern collections. In Goethals, B., Siebes, A., eds.: Knowledge Discovery in Inductive Databases, 3rd International Workshop, KDID 2004, Pisa, Italy, September 20, 2004, Revised Papers. Volume 3377 of Lecture Notes in Computer Science. Springer (2005)

28. Mielikäinen, T.: Separating structure from interestingness. In Dai, H., Srikant, R., Zhang, C., eds.: Advances in Knowledge Discovery and Data Mining, 8th Pacific-Asia Conference, PAKDD 2004, Sydney, Australia, May 26-28, 2004, Proceedings. Volume 3056 of Lecture Notes in Artificial Intelligence. Springer (2004) 476–485

29. Bastide, Y., Taouil, R., Pasquier, N., Stumme, G., Lakhai, L.: Mining frequent patterns with counting inference. SIGKDD Explorations **2** (2000) 66–75

30. Moffat, A., Neal, R.M., Witten, I.H.: Arithmetic coding revisited. ACM Transactions on Information Systems **16** (1998) 256–294

31. Pavlov, D., Mannila, H., Smyth, P.: Beyond independence: probabilistic methods for query approximation on binary transaction data. IEEE Transactions on Data and Knowledge Engineering **15** (2003) 1409–1421

32. Kumar, V., Tsumoto, S., eds.: Proceedings of the 2002 IEEE International Conference on Data Mining (ICDM 2002), 9-12 December 2002, Maebashi City, Japan. IEEE Computer Society (2002)

33. Lavrac, N., Gamberger, D., Blockeel, H., Todorovski, L., eds.: Knowledge Discovery in Databases: PKDD 2003, 7th European Conference on Principles and Practice of Knowledge Discovery in Databases, Cavtat-Dubrovnik, Croatia, September 22-26, 2003, Proceedings. Volume 2838 of Lecture Notes in Artificial Intelligence. Springer (2003)

Condensed Representation of EPs and Patterns Quantified by Frequency-Based Measures

Arnaud Soulet, Bruno Crémilleux, and François Rioult

GREYC, CNRS - UMR 6072, Université de Caen,
Campus Côte de Nacre,
F-14032 Caen Cédex France
{Forename.Surname}@info.unicaen.fr

Abstract. Emerging patterns (EPs) are associations of features whose frequencies increase significantly from one class to another. They have been proven useful to build powerful classifiers and to help establishing diagnosis. Because of the huge search space, mining and representing EPs is a hard and complex task for large datasets. Thanks to the use of recent results on condensed representations of frequent closed patterns, we propose here an *exact* condensed representation of EPs (i.e., all EPs and their growth rates). From this condensed representation, we give a method to provide interesting EPs, in fact those with the highest growth rates. We call strong emerging patterns (SEPs) these EPs. We also highlight a property characterizing the jumping emerging patterns. Experiments quantify the interests of SEPs (smaller number, ability to extract longer and less frequent patterns) and show their usefulness (in collaboration with the Philips company, SEPs successfully enabled to identify the failures of a production chain of silicon plates). These concepts of condensed representation and "strong patterns" with respect to a measure are generalized to other interestingness measures based on frequencies.

Keywords: Emerging patterns, condensed representations, closed patterns, characterization of classes, frequency-based measures.

1   Introduction

The characterization of classes and classification are significant fields of research in data mining and machine learning. Initially introduced in [13], emerging patterns (EPs) are patterns whose frequency strongly varies between two datasets (i.e., two classes). EPs characterize the classes in a quantitative and qualitative way. Thanks to their capacity to emphasize the distinctions between classes, EPs enable to build classifiers or to propose a help for diagnosis. They are at the origin of varied works and they are also used in the realization of powerful classifiers [14, 16]. From an applicative point of view, we can quote various works on the characterization of biochemical properties or medical data [18].

B. Goethals and A. Siebes (Eds.): KDID 2004, LNCS 3377, pp. 173–189, 2005.
© Springer-Verlag Berlin Heidelberg 2005

Nevertheless, mining EPs in large datasets remains a challenge because of the very high number of candidate patterns. The pruning property used by the level-wise algorithms [20] and often used in data mining cannot be directly applied. Usual methods use handlings of borders [13] in order to find version spaces.

In this paper, we are interested in the extraction of emerging patterns and the definition and characterization of useful kinds of emerging patterns. One originality of our approach is to take advantage of recent progress on the condensed representations of patterns and more precisely on closed patterns [22, 5]. By synthesizing sets of patterns and making easier a process in which users can query data and patterns, condensed representations are an important concept in inductive databases. A brief overview of the condensed representation based on closed pattern is given in Section 2.3.

This paper mainly proposes four contributions. Firstly, we define an exact condensed representation of the emerging patterns for a dataset. Contrary to the borders approach (Section 2.2) which provides the emerging patterns with a lower bound of their growth rate, this condensed representation easily enables to know the *exact* growth rate for each emerging pattern. Moreover, there are efficient algorithms to extract this condensed representation. Secondly, we highlight a new property characterizing a particular kind of emerging patterns, the jumping emerging patterns which make up an active research topic. Thirdly, we propose a new kind of emerging patterns, we call them " strong emerging patterns " (SEPs): these EPs have the best growth rates and we think that they are of a great interest. Furthermore, we show that SEPs are easily obtained from the exact condensed representation of the emerging patterns. This work is also justified by requests from providers of data. Experiments quantify the interests of SEPs (smaller number, ability to extract longer and less frequent patterns). We also give the results achieved by the use of the strong emerging patterns for characterizing patients with respect to atherosclerosis and for successfully identifying the failures of a production chain of silicon plates in collaboration with the Philips company. Lastly, we show that these concepts of condensed representation and "strong patterns" with respect to a measure can be generalized to other interestingness measures based on frequencies.

This paper is an extension of a preliminary work presented in [29]: new contributions are a property characterizing the jumping emerging patterns, the ability to easily obtain the *exact* growth rate for each emerging pattern, the proofs of the properties, in-depth experiments (qualitative results coming from our collaboration with the Philips company, atherosclerosis dataset, influences of the minimal frequency threshold) and the generalization to other interestingness measures based on frequencies.

The paper is organized in the following way. Section 2 introduces the context, the required notations and the works related to this field. Section 3 proposes a new characterization of the jumping emerging patterns. It defines an exact condensed representation of the emerging patterns and also the strong emerging patterns, which are easily achieved from this condensed representation. Section 4 presents the experimental evaluations which quantify the interests of SEPs and their successful use within a collaboration with the Philips company. Finally, Section 5 extends results highlighted in the case of EPs to other measures based on frequencies.

2   Context and Related Works

2.1   Notations and Definitions

Let $\mathcal{D}$ be a dataset (Table 1), which is an excerpt of the data used for the search for failures in a production chain (cf. Section 4). This table (which is a simplification of the real problem) is used as an elementary example to present the concepts throughout this paper.

Each line (or *transaction*) of Table 1 represents a batch (noted $B_1, \ldots, B_8$) described by features (or *items*) : $A, \ldots, E$ denote the advance of the batch within the production chain and C_1, C_2 the class values. $\mathcal{D}$ is partitioned here into two datasets $\mathcal{D}_1$ (the right batches) and $\mathcal{D}_2$ (the defective batches). The transactions having item C_1 (resp. C_2) belong to $\mathcal{D}_1$ (resp. $\mathcal{D}_2$). A *pattern* is a set of items (e.g., $\{A, B, C\}$) noted by the string ABC. A transaction t contains the pattern X if and only if $X \subseteq t$. Lastly, $|\mathcal{D}|$ (as usual $|.|$ denotes the cardinality of a set) is the number of transactions of $\mathcal{D}$.

The concept of emerging patterns is related to the notion of frequency. The frequency of a pattern X in a dataset $\mathcal{D}$ (noted $\mathcal{F}(X, \mathcal{D})$) is the number of transactions of $\mathcal{D}$ which contain X (for example, $\mathcal{F}(ABC, \mathcal{D}) = 4$). X is *frequent* if its frequency is at least the frequency threshold fixed by the user. From the absolute frequency, we can compute the relative frequency which is $\mathcal{F}(X, \mathcal{D})/|\mathcal{D}|$. Unless otherwise indicated, we use in this paper the absolute frequency. Let us note that by the definition of the partial sets $\mathcal{D}_i$ associated to the class identifiers C_i, we have the relation $\mathcal{F}(X, \mathcal{D}_i) = \mathcal{F}(XC_i, \mathcal{D})$.

Intuitively, an emerging pattern is a pattern whose frequency increases significantly from one class to another. The capture of contrast between classes brought by a pattern is measured by its growth rate. The *growth rate* of a pattern X from $\mathcal{D}_2$ to $\mathcal{D}_1$, noted $GR_1(X)$, is defined as :

Table 1. Example of a transactional dataset

$$\mathcal{D}$$

Batch	Items
B_1	C_1 $A\ B\ C\ D$
B_2	C_1 $A\ B\ C\ D$
B_3	C_1 $A\ B\ C$
B_4	C_1 $A\quad\quad D\ E$
B_5	$C_2\ A\ B\ C$
B_6	$C_2\quad B\ C\ D\ E$
B_7	$C_2\quad B\ C\quad E$
B_8	$C_2\quad B\quad\quad E$

$$\begin{cases} 0, & \text{if } \mathcal{F}(X, \mathcal{D}_1) = 0 \text{ and } \mathcal{F}(X, \mathcal{D}_2) = 0 \\ \infty, & \text{if } \mathcal{F}(X, \mathcal{D}_1) \neq 0 \text{ and } \mathcal{F}(X, \mathcal{D}_2) = 0 \\ \frac{|\mathcal{D}_2| \times \mathcal{F}(X, \mathcal{D}_1)}{|\mathcal{D}_1| \times \mathcal{F}(X, \mathcal{D}_2)}, & \text{otherwise} \end{cases}$$

Thus, the definition of an emerging pattern (EP in summary) is given by :

Definition 1 (Emerging Pattern). *Given a threshold $\rho > 1$, a pattern X is said to be an* emerging pattern *from $\mathcal{D}_2$ to $\mathcal{D}_1$ if $GR_1(X) \geq \rho$.*

Let us give some examples from Table 1. With $\rho = 3$, A, ABC, and $ABCD$ are EPs from $\mathcal{D}_2$ to $\mathcal{D}_1$. Indeed, $GR_1(A) = 4/1 = 4$, $GR_1(ABC) = 3/1 = 3$ and $GR_1(ABCD) = 2/0 = \infty$. Conversely, BCD is not an EP: $GR_1(BCD) = 2/1 = 2$ ($< \rho$). When the pattern X is not present in $\mathcal{D}_2$ (i.e. $\mathcal{F}(X, \mathcal{D}_2) = 0$), we get $GR_1(X) = \infty$ and such a pattern is called *jumping emerging pattern* (JEP). For instance, $ABCD$ is a JEP for $\mathcal{D}_1$ and $BCDE$ is a JEP for $\mathcal{D}_2$. Unless otherwise indicated, we consider that the growth rate of a pattern X must be higher than 1 in order that X is an EP.

2.2   Related Works

Efficient computation of all EPs in high dimensional datasets remains a challenge because the number of candidate patterns is exponential according to the number of items. The naive enumeration of all patterns with their frequencies fails quickly. In addition, the definition of EPs does not provide anti-monotonous (e.g., BCD is an EP for $\mathcal{D}_1$, not BC) constraints to apply a powerful pruning of the search space for methods stemming from the framework of level-wise algorithms [20]. Thus, various authors proposed other ways.

The approach of handling borders, introduced by Dong and al. [13], mines multiple couples of maximal and minimal borders from the datasets. The interval described by these two borders corresponds to EPs. Each couple provides an interval giving a concise description of emerging patterns. Unfortunately, the computation of the intervals must be repeated very often and for all the $\mathcal{D}_i$ and this process does not provide for each EP its growth rate. This technique is particularly effective for the search of JEPs due to the convexity of their search space [17]. Nevertheless, Bailey and al. [2] propose a new tree-based data structure for storing the dataset. Their approach is 2-10 times faster than the technique of handling borders.

Other approaches exist. Zhang et al. [32] introduce an anti-monotonous constraint to be able to apply a level-wise algorithm. But this one eliminates many EPs and loses the completeness of the search. In a more general way, this problem can be seen as the search for the patterns checking the conjunction of an anti-monotonous constraint and a monotonous constraint [12, 11], this work drawing its origins from version spaces [21].

2.3   Condensed Representation Based on Closed Patterns

As indicated in the introduction, this paper revisits the search and the characterization of EPs by taking advantage of recent progress on the condensed representations of patterns. We briefly point out below the main concepts required to understand the rest of this paper.

A condensed representation of patterns provides a synthesis of large data sets highlighting the correlations embedded in the data. There is a twofold advantage to use condensed representations. First, such an approach enables powerful pruning criteria during the extraction which greatly improve the efficiency of algorithms [5, 22]. Second, the synthesis of the data provided by a condensed representation is at the core of relevant and multiple uses of patterns (e.g., redundant or informative rules [31], rules with minimal body [9], clustering [15], classification,...), which are key points in many practical applications. There are several kinds of condensed representations of patterns [22, 5]. The most current ones are based on closed patterns, free (or key) patterns or δ-free. A general framework is presented in [7].

For the rest of the paper, we focus on the condensed representation based on closed patterns. A *closed* pattern in $\mathcal{D}$ is a maximal set of items (with respect to the set inclusion) shared by a set of transactions. This concept is related to the lattice theory [3] and the Galois connection. In Table 1, ABC is a closed pattern because B_1, B_2, B_3 and B_5 do not share another item. The notion of *closure* is linked to the one of closed pattern.

Definition 2 (Closure). *The* closure *of a pattern X in $\mathcal{D}$ is $h(X, \mathcal{D}) = \bigcap\{tran-saction\ t\ in\ \mathcal{D} | X \subseteq t\}$.*

An important property on the frequency stems from this definition. An item A belongs to the closure of X in $\mathcal{D}$ if and only if $\mathcal{F}(XA, \mathcal{D}) = \mathcal{F}(X, \mathcal{D})$. The closure of X is a closed pattern and $\mathcal{F}(X, \mathcal{D}) = \mathcal{F}(h(X, \mathcal{D}), \mathcal{D})$. In our example, $h(AB, \mathcal{D}) = ABC$ and $\mathcal{F}(AB, \mathcal{D}) = \mathcal{F}(ABC, \mathcal{D})$. Thus, the set of the closed patterns is a condensed representation of all patterns because the frequency of any pattern can be inferred from its closure.

3   Condensed Representation and Strong Emerging Patterns

This section highlights a new property to characterize jumping emerging patterns and defines an exact condensed representation of the emerging patterns. Lastly, it proposes the strong emerging patterns.

3.1   Characterization of JEPs

Let us start by generalizing the definition of EPs to data having more than two classes. In Section 2.1, we have $\mathcal{D}_2 = \mathcal{D} \backslash \mathcal{D}_1$. So, $\mathcal{F}(X, \mathcal{D}_2) = \mathcal{F}(X, \mathcal{D}) - \mathcal{F}(X, \mathcal{D}_1)$ (and, similarly, $|\mathcal{D}_2| = |\mathcal{D}| - |\mathcal{D}_1|$). So, the generalization of the growth rate (see its definition in Section 2.1) and thus the definition of EPs, are straightforward.

Let $\mathcal{D}$ be a dataset partitioned into k parts denoted $\mathcal{D}_1, \ldots, \mathcal{D}_k$ ($\mathcal{D} = \bigcup_i \mathcal{D}_i$). The items $C_1, \ldots, C_k$ respectively indicate the membership of a transaction to a dataset $\mathcal{D}_1, \ldots, \mathcal{D}_k$. $\forall i \in \{1, \ldots, k\}$, the growth rate of $\mathcal{D} \backslash \mathcal{D}_i$ in $\mathcal{D}_i$ is:

$$GR_i(X) = \underbrace{\frac{|\mathcal{D}| - |\mathcal{D}_i|}{|\mathcal{D}_i|}}_{noted\ \alpha_i} \times \frac{\mathcal{F}(X, \mathcal{D}_i)}{\mathcal{F}(X, \mathcal{D}) - \mathcal{F}(X, \mathcal{D}_i)} \tag{1}$$

We are now able to provide a new characterization of JEPs for data having any number of classes. An item A belongs to the closure of X in $\mathcal{D}$ if and only if $\mathcal{F}(XA, \mathcal{D}) - \mathcal{F}(X, \mathcal{D}) = 0$ (Definition 2). Then, Property 1 shows how to characterize JEPs:

Property 1 (Characterization of JEPs Based on Closed Patterns).

$$X \text{ is a JEP of } \mathcal{D}_i \iff C_i \in h(X, \mathcal{D})$$

Proof. $C_i \in h(X, \mathcal{D}) \iff \mathcal{F}(XC_i, \mathcal{D}) = \mathcal{F}(X, \mathcal{D})$. By definition of $\mathcal{D}_i$, $\mathcal{F}(X, \mathcal{D}_i) = \mathcal{F}(XC_i, \mathcal{D})$. Then $\mathcal{F}(X, \mathcal{D}) = \mathcal{F}(X, \mathcal{D}_i)$ and the denominator of $GR_i(X)$ is null (cf. Equation 1) and X is a JEP.

This property is helpful: it enables to easily obtain JEPs from the closures. Indeed, for each closed pattern XC_i, it is enough to check if X is contained in the condensed representation. If X does not belong to the condensed representation, it means that its closure is XC_i (because XC_i is a closed pattern) and X is a jumping emerging pattern of $\mathcal{D}_i$.

3.2   Exact Condensed Representation of Emerging Patterns

Let us move now how to get the growth rate of any pattern X. Equation 1 shows that it is enough to compute $\mathcal{F}(X, \mathcal{D})$ and $\mathcal{F}(X, \mathcal{D}_i)$. These frequencies can be obtained from the condensed representation of frequent closed patterns. Indeed, $\mathcal{F}(X, \mathcal{D}) = \mathcal{F}(h(X, \mathcal{D}), \mathcal{D})$ (closure property) and by definition of the partial bases $\mathcal{D}_i$, $\mathcal{F}(X, \mathcal{D}_i) = \mathcal{F}(XC_i, \mathcal{D}) = \mathcal{F}(h(XC_i, \mathcal{D}), \mathcal{D})$. Unfortunately, these relations require the computation of two closures ($h(X, \mathcal{D})$ and $h(XC_i, \mathcal{D})$), which it is not efficient. The following properties solve this disadvantage:

Property 2. *Let X be a pattern and $\mathcal{D}_i$ a dataset, $\mathcal{F}(X, \mathcal{D}_i) = \mathcal{F}(h(X, \mathcal{D}), \mathcal{D}_i)$.*

Proof. The properties of the closure operator ensure that for any transaction t, $X \subseteq t \iff h(X, \mathcal{D}) \subseteq t$. In particular, the transactions of $\mathcal{D}_i$ containing X are identical to those containing $h(X, \mathcal{D})$ and we have the equality of the frequencies.

It is now simple to show that the growth rate of every pattern X is obtained thanks to the only knowledge of the growth rate of $h(X, \mathcal{D})$:

Property 3. *Let X be a pattern, we have $GR_i(X) = GR_i(h(X, \mathcal{D}))$.*

Proof. Let X be a pattern. By replacing $\mathcal{F}(X, \mathcal{D})$ with $\mathcal{F}(h(X, \mathcal{D}), \mathcal{D})$ and $\mathcal{F}(X, \mathcal{D}_i)$ with $\mathcal{F}(h(X, \mathcal{D}), \mathcal{D}_i)$ in Equation 1, we immediately recognize the growth rate of $h(X, \mathcal{D})$.

For instance, $h(AB, \mathcal{D}) = ABC$ and $GR_1(AB) = GR_1(ABC) = 3$. The closed patterns with their growth rates are enough to synthesize the whole set of EPs with their growth rates. So, we obtain an *exact* condensed representation of the EPs (i.e. the growth rate of each emerging pattern is exactly known). Let us recall that the borders technique (cf. Section 2.2) only gives a lower bound of the growth rate. This property is significant because the number of closed patterns is lower (and, in general, much lower) than that of all patterns [6]. In practice, $h(X, \mathcal{D})$ is directly obtained by the minimal (with respect to the set inclusion) closed pattern containing X of the condensed representation.

3.3   Strong Emerging Patterns

The number of emerging patterns of a dataset can be crippling for their use. In practice, it is judicious to keep only the most frequent EPs having the best growth rates. But thoughtlessly raising these two thresholds may be problematic. On the one hand, if the minimal growth rate threshold is too high, the EPs found tend to be too specific (i.e. too long). On the other hand, if the minimal frequency threshold is too high, EPs have a too low growth rate.

We define here the strong emerging patterns which are the patterns having the best possible growth rates. They are a trade-off between the frequency and the growth rate.

Definition 3 (Strong Emerging Pattern). *A strong emerging pattern X (SEP in summary) for $\mathcal{D}_i$ is an emerging pattern such that XC_i is a closed pattern in $\mathcal{D}_i$.*

A great interest of SEPs concerns their growth rate: the following property indicates that the SEPs have the best possible growth rates.

Property 4 (SEPs: EPs with Maximum Growth Rate). *Let X be a pattern not containing the item C_i. Then the SEP coming from $h(X, \mathcal{D}_i)$ has a better growth rate than X, i.e. one has $GR_i(X) \leq GR_i(h(X, \mathcal{D}_i) \backslash \{C_i\})$.*

Proof. Let $Y = h(X, \mathcal{D}_i) \backslash \{C_i\}$. Thanks to the closure property, $\mathcal{F}(X, \mathcal{D}_i) = \mathcal{F}(Y, \mathcal{D}_i)$. We can then write (Equation 1) $GR_i(Y) = \alpha_i \times \frac{\mathcal{F}(X, \mathcal{D}_i)}{\mathcal{F}(Y, \mathcal{D}) - \mathcal{F}(X, \mathcal{D}_i)}$. The extensivity of the closure operator makes it possible to write $X \subseteq h(X, \mathcal{D}_i)$ and $C_i \notin X$ thus $X \subseteq Y$ and $\mathcal{F}(X, \mathcal{D}) \geq \mathcal{F}(Y, \mathcal{D})$ due to the property of frequency, which shows that $GR_i(X) \leq GR_i(Y)$.

Let us illustrate Property 4 on the elementary example. The pattern BC is not a SEP for class 1 (because $h(BC, \mathcal{D}_1) \backslash \{C_1\} = ABC$), its growth rate is 1, one has $GR_1(BC) \leq GR_1(ABC) = 3$ and we notice that $\mathcal{F}(BC, \mathcal{D}_1) = \mathcal{F}(ABC, \mathcal{D}_1)$. Let us note that Property 4 enables to highlight an alternative definition of SEPs: an emerging pattern X is said to be a SEP in $\mathcal{D}_i$ when

$GR_i(X) > GR_i(Y)$ for all supersets Y of X such that $\mathcal{F}(X, \mathcal{D}_i) = \mathcal{F}(Y, \mathcal{D}_i)$. This new definition is based on two key points. First, the condition on frequency (i.e. $\mathcal{F}(X, \mathcal{D}_i) = \mathcal{F}(Y, \mathcal{D}_i)$) indicates that we choose a particular pattern for each equivalence class of frequency. Second, this pattern must maximize the growth rate in this equivalence class and Property 4 shows that this pattern corresponds to the closed one.

As for EPs, the property of "being a SEP" is neither monotonous (e.g., B is a SEP for $\mathcal{D}_2$, not BC), nor convertible [23] because no ordering relation over items allows to get a pruning criterion for prefixes. Nevertheless, SEPs are efficiently mined thanks to the properties of the condensed representations (see Section 2.3) and the simple post-processing step to get them. The second advantage of the strong emerging patterns is that their growth rates are immediately known (cf. Property 5). We start by giving Lemma 1 which facilitates the understanding of this property.

Lemma 1. *If XC_i is closed in $\mathcal{D}_i$, then XC_i is closed in $\mathcal{D}$.*

Proof. No transaction of $\mathcal{D}\backslash\mathcal{D}_i$ contains item C_i. If XC_i is closed in $\mathcal{D}_i$, the only transactions of $\mathcal{D}$ containing XC_i are in $\mathcal{D}_i$ and $h(XC_i, \mathcal{D}) = XC_i$, therefore XC_i is closed in $\mathcal{D}$.

Property 5 indicates that the growth rate of SEPs is immediately obtained.

Property 5 (SEPs: Computing Their Growth Rate). *If X is a strong emerging pattern for $\mathcal{D}_i$, then $GR_i(X)$ can be obtained directly with the frequencies of the condensed representation based on the frequent closed patterns of $\mathcal{D}$.*

Proof. Let X be a SEP, therefore XC_i is closed in $\mathcal{D}_i$ (Definition 3). To calculate $GR_i(X)$, it is necessary to calculate $\mathcal{F}(X, \mathcal{D}_i)$ and $\mathcal{F}(X, \mathcal{D})$. By definition of $\mathcal{D}_i$, $\mathcal{F}(X, \mathcal{D}_i) = \mathcal{F}(XC_i, \mathcal{D})$ and Lemma 1 ensures that XC_i is closed in $\mathcal{D}$, thus, its frequency is provided by the condensed representation of the closed patterns of $\mathcal{D}$. To calculate $\mathcal{F}(X, \mathcal{D})$, two cases arise: if X is closed in $\mathcal{D}$, its frequency is directly available. If not, XC_i being closed in $\mathcal{D}$, Property 1 indicates that X is a JEP: its growth rate is infinite.

SEPs are computed thanks to the condensed representation of closed patterns in $\mathcal{D}$ by filtering the closed patterns containing a class value C_i. For each of them, we simply deduce $GR_i(X)$ by considering the pattern X as indicated in the proof above.

Compared to EPs, Properties 4 and 5 show two meaningful advantages of SEPs: on the one hand, they have the best possible growth rates, on the other hand, they are easy to discover from the condensed representation of frequent closed patterns of $\mathcal{D}$ (Lemma 1 ensures that we only have to filter frequent closed patterns containing C_i). Let us note that the EPs based on X and $h(X, \mathcal{D}_i)$ have the same frequency, thus they have the same quality according to this criterion. However, the SEP coming from $h(X, \mathcal{D}_i)$ has a stronger (i.e. higher) growth rate and thus offers a better compromise between frequency and growth rate.

4   Experiments

Experiments provide both quantitative and qualitative results. Quantitative results address the number of SEPs with regard to other kinds of EPs, according to the frequency threshold, etc. and qualitative results deal with the successful use of SEPs to identify the failures of a production chain of silicon plates within a collaboration with the Philips company. Even if some overall results are expected (for instance, the number of SEPs can be only smaller than the number of EPs), we think that it is interesting to quantify them (following our example on the number of SEPs versus those of EPs, is it a drastic reduction or not?).

We use the MVMINER prototype [26] to produce the condensed representation of frequent closed patterns which enables to provide SEPs (see the previous section). In order to compare quantitative results achieved by SEPs with regard to EPs, it is necessary to obtain EPs. For that, we used an APRIORI-like prototype, which computes frequent patterns and selects those having a growth rate greater than a threshold (let us recall that the use of borders does not allow to get the exact growth rate of each pattern [13], so we cannot compare straightforwardly this approach with results stemming from the exact condensed representation of EPs). We did not perform run-time experiments about the efficiency of the extraction of the condensed representation of closed patterns because this efficiency has been shown by several authors [5, 22, 24].

4.1   Data Overview

Experiments were carried out on two real datasets. This first dataset $\mathcal{D}_{athero}$ comes from the STULONG project[1]. These data address a twenty-year longitudinal study of the risk factors of atherosclerosis in a population of 1417 men in former Czechoslovakia. We are interested in characterizing patients according to whether they die or not due to atherosclerosis. From this available data base, we prepare a dataset constituted of 748 rows (divided into 2 classes) described by 119 items (details are in [10]).

The second dataset $\mathcal{D}_{Philips}$ comes from a collaboration with the Philips company. The industrial aim is to identify mistaken tools in a silicon plate production chain. Data are composed of batches, a batch gathers several silicon plates. Briefly speaking, a batch is described by the equipment used at each stage of the flow-chart which is followed during the production. The quality test leads to three quasi-homogeneous classes corresponding to three quality levels. Finally, the characterization is performed on a dataset made up of 44 items (i.e. stage/equipment) and comprising 84 lines (i.e. 84 batches).

4.2   Quantitative Results About SEPs Versus Other Kinds of EPs

Numbers of EPs, Closed EPs and SEPs. We compare here the numbers of EPs, closed EPs (which stemmed from closed patterns) and SEPs. The number of closed EPs is a measure of the size of the condensed representation. Figure 1

---

[1] Euromise data, http://lisp.vse.cz/challenge/ecmlpkdd2003/

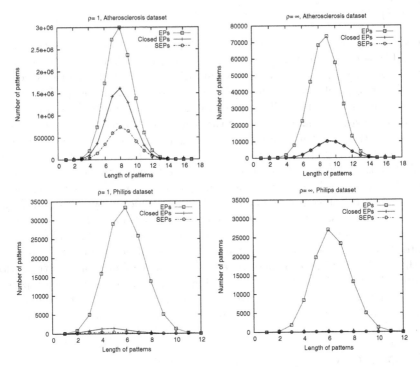

Fig. 1. Comparison between the different kinds of emerging patterns

depicts the distributions of EPs according to the length of patterns for a minimal frequency threshold of 4.0% in $\mathcal{D}_{athero}$ and 1.2% in $\mathcal{D}_{Philips}$. Two threshold values of the minimal growth rate (1 and ∞) are used. This figure shows that the number of EPs is very high compared to the number of closed EPs or SEPs. In $\mathcal{D}_{Philips}$, this disproportion does not decrease in spite of the rise of the minimal growth rate. These too large numbers of EPs cannot be presented to an expert for his analysis task.

Influences of the Minimal Frequency Threshold. Let us see now the role of the minimal frequency threshold. Figure 2 compares the number of EPs with a minimal growth rate of 1 according to the minimal frequency thresholds. We see that the numbers of closed EPs and SEPs increase less quickly than the number of EPs when the frequency decreases. It means that the search for SEPs can be carried out with a smaller minimum frequency. In other words, as the number of SEPs and the size of the exact condensed representation are small compared to the number of EPs, it is possible to examine longer and less frequent patterns.

Figure 3 indicates the variations of the number of EPs, closed EPs and SEPs according to the length of patterns on $\mathcal{D}_{athero}$ (the minimal frequency threshold is 2.3%). We note that the number of SEPs and the size of the exact condensed representation of the EPs increase less quickly when the minimal frequency decreases. For searching long emerging patterns, the combinatory explosion is con-

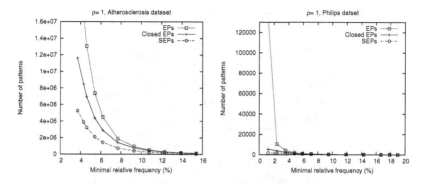

Fig. 2. Number of patterns according to the frequency threshold

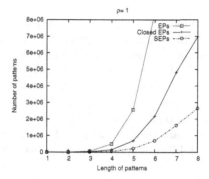

Fig. 3. Number of patterns according to their length ($\mathcal{D}_{athero}$)

trolled in the case of the exact condensed representation of the EPs and the SEPs, but the extraction of EPs fails for patterns longer than 6 items. Again, it allows to mine less frequent and longer patterns.

4.3   Results on Applications

Let us say a few words on the applicative results brought by these experiments. On $\mathcal{D}_{athero}$, we have proposed SEPs to distinguish the patients who die or not due to atherosclerosis. Experiments highlighted SEPs with a quite high growth rate and frequency, and physicians are interested in continuing this work. Furthermore, experts have a strong interest in the quantification of the results (growth rate, frequency).

In our collaboration with Philips (dataset $\mathcal{D}_{Philips}$), experts were the most interested by the confrontation of SEPs having the strongest growth rates and a length equals 1 or 2. Table 2 indicates the most useful SEPs. There is no reliable characteristic SEP of length 1. For instance, the pattern E=727 has a growth rate close to 1 and it is present both in Low and High. On the contrary, SEPs of length 2 appeared relevant. The contrast between the pattern E=727 A=284

Table 2. Examples of strong emerging patterns

SEPs with a length of 1			
Class	Pattern	GR	Frequency
Low	E=727	1.01	100% (45)
Medium	F=232	1.03	100% (37)
High	E=727	1.01	100% (45)

SEPs with a length of 2 and $GR > 1.5$			
Class	Pattern	GR	Frequency
Low	E=727 A=284	3.64	75.6 % (34)
Medium	I=504 F=232	1.84	91.9 % (34)
Medium	L=490 F=232	1.62	54.0 % (20)
High	E=727 B=288	2.92	71.1 % (32)
High	E=727 A=222	2.33	91.1 % (41)

(for Low) and the pattern E=727 A=222 (for High) enabled to suspect a problem on the stage A (since E=727 is not a discriminant item). Moreover, the stage A comprises only two kinds of equipment (the 222 and the 284). This result tends to show the need for modifying the adjustments of equipment 284 in order that they are similar to those of the equipment 222. After talks with the experts, they have confirmed that the stage suspected by the SEPs was the real cause of the failures (an equipment was badly tuned). This experiment shows the practical contribution of SEPs on real-world data. In other contexts [10], longer SEPs were proved useful to establish diagnostic and the brute force did not allow to obtain these patterns.

Let us recall that SEPs have the advantage of giving a precise growth rate contrary to EPs which would be found by handlings of borders. This quantification is useful at the same time for the selection of EPs and the judgment of the experts. Lastly, thanks to their fewer number, they provide a more understanding characterization of the data than ordinary EPs.

5 Generalization to Frequency-Based Measures

In this section, we generalize the concepts of exact condensed representations and "strong patterns" with respect to other usual interestingness measures based on frequencies. As for the growth rate, which can be seen as a particular measure, the closure operator provides good properties to extend these concepts.

5.1 Exact Condensed Representation of a Frequency-Based Measure

We consider various interestingness measures based on frequencies proposed in statistics, machine learning and data mining. Metrics such as support, confidence, lift, correlation and collective strength are useful to evaluate the quality of classification rules $X \rightarrow C_i$ [27, 8, 28, 1, 19].

Let us define a frequency-based measure M_i which enables to estimate the quality of the premise of the rule $X \rightarrow C_i$ to characterize the class i. For instance, such a measure can be the growth rate. More formally:

Definition 4 (Frequency-Based Measure). *Let $\mathcal{D}$ be a dataset partitioned into k parts denoted $\mathcal{D}_1, \dots, \mathcal{D}_k$, a frequency-based measure M_i to characterize $\mathcal{D}_i$ is a function of frequencies $\mathcal{F}(X, \mathcal{D}_1), \dots, \mathcal{F}(X, \mathcal{D}_k)$ i.e. $M_i(X) = F(\mathcal{F}(X, \mathcal{D}_1), \dots, \mathcal{F}(X, \mathcal{D}_k))$.*

A frequency-based measure is limited to a combination of frequencies of $\mathcal{D}_i$. In particular, such a measure cannot contain other parameters (e.g., the length of a pattern). Some frequency-based measures are indicated in Table 3. Notice that all these measures are expressed in term of frequencies while the literature about interestingness measures often writes these measures by using probabilities (e.g., $P(A|C_i)$ corresponding to $\mathcal{F}(X, \mathcal{D}_i)/|\mathcal{D}_i|$). Some measures (e.g., lift, J-Measure) use frequencies non restricted to datasets $\mathcal{D}_1, \dots, \mathcal{D}_k$ but these frequencies can be computed from $\mathcal{F}(X, \mathcal{D}_1), \dots, \mathcal{F}(X, \mathcal{D}_k)$. For example, the frequency $\mathcal{F}(X, \mathcal{D})$ corresponds to $\sum_{j=1}^{k} \mathcal{F}(X, \mathcal{D}_j)$. Thus, these measures respect Definition 4.

As for the emerging patterns, we can know the value of a frequency-based measure on any pattern X from its closure in $\mathcal{D}$:

Theorem 1. *Let X be a pattern, we have $M_i(X) = M_i(h(X, \mathcal{D}))$.*

Proof. Let X be a pattern. For each i, Property 2 allows to replace $\mathcal{F}(X, \mathcal{D}_i)$ by $\mathcal{F}(h(X, \mathcal{D}), \mathcal{D}_i)$. $M_i(X) = F(\mathcal{F}(X, \mathcal{D}_1), \dots, \mathcal{F}(X, \mathcal{D}_k)) = F(\mathcal{F}(h(X, \mathcal{D}), \mathcal{D}_1), \dots, \mathcal{F}(h(X, \mathcal{D}), \mathcal{D}_k)) = M_i(h(X, \mathcal{D}))$.

For instance, the closure of AB in $\mathcal{D}$ is ABC and we have $lift_1(AB) = lift_1(ABC) = 3/2$. In the same way, $h(CDE, \mathcal{D}) = BCDE$ and $L_2(CDE) = L_2(BCDE) = 0.529$ with $k = 2$.

The closed patterns with their measure M_i are enough to synthesize the whole set of patterns according to M_i. In practice, the number of closed patterns is lower (and often, much lower) than that of all patterns [4]. Thus, the closed patterns with their measure M_i are an *exact* condensed representation of the measure M_i.

5.2   Strong Frequency-Based Measure

In large datasets, the number of a priori interestingness patterns satisfying a given threshold for a measure M_i can be too huge for their use. As for the SEPs, the notion of strength can be extended to select the patterns which maximalize a measure M_i.

Definition 5 (Strong Frequency-Based Measure). *A frequency-based measure M_i which decreases with $\mathcal{F}(X, \mathcal{D})$, when $\mathcal{F}(X, \mathcal{D}_i)$ remains unchanged, is a strong frequency-based measure.*

For instance, the lift is $\frac{|\mathcal{D}| \times \mathcal{F}(X, \mathcal{D}_i)}{|\mathcal{D}_i| \times \mathcal{F}(X, \mathcal{D})}$. When $\mathcal{F}(X, \mathcal{D}_i)$ remains unchanged and $\mathcal{F}(X, \mathcal{D})$ increases, the lift decreases because the denominator increases. Thus,

Table 3. Examples of frequency-based measures to characterize $\mathcal{D}_i$

Frequency-based measure	Formula	Strong	P_3
J-Measure (J) [28]	$\frac{\mathcal{F}(X,\mathcal{D}_i)}{|\mathcal{D}|} \times log(\frac{\mathcal{F}(X,\mathcal{D}_i) \times \mathcal{D}}{|\mathcal{D}_i| \times \mathcal{F}(X,\mathcal{D})})$ $+ \frac{\mathcal{F}(X,\mathcal{D}\backslash\mathcal{D}_i)}{|\mathcal{D}|} \times log(\frac{\mathcal{F}(X,\mathcal{D}\backslash\mathcal{D}_i) \times \mathcal{D}}{\mathcal{F}(X,\mathcal{D}) \times |\mathcal{D}\backslash\mathcal{D}_i|})$	no	no
Support [1]	$\mathcal{F}(X,\mathcal{D}_i)/|\mathcal{D}|$	yes	no
Confidence [1]	$\mathcal{F}(X,\mathcal{D}_i)/\mathcal{F}(X,\mathcal{D})$	yes	no
Sensitivity	$\mathcal{F}(X,\mathcal{D}_i)/|\mathcal{D}_i|$	yes	no
Success rate	$\frac{\mathcal{F}(X,\mathcal{D}_i)}{|\mathcal{D}|} + \frac{|\mathcal{D}\backslash\mathcal{D}_i| - \mathcal{F}(X,\mathcal{D}\backslash\mathcal{D}_i)}{|\mathcal{D}|}$	yes	yes
Specificity	$\frac{|\mathcal{D}\backslash\mathcal{D}_i| - \mathcal{F}(X,\mathcal{D}\backslash\mathcal{D}_i)}{|\mathcal{D}|}$	yes	yes
Piatetsky-Shapiro's (PS) [25]	$\frac{\mathcal{F}(X,\mathcal{D}_i)}{|\mathcal{D}|} - \frac{\mathcal{F}(X,\mathcal{D})}{|\mathcal{D}|} \times \frac{|\mathcal{D}_i|}{|\mathcal{D}|}$	yes	yes
Lift [19]	$\frac{|\mathcal{D}| \times \mathcal{F}(X,\mathcal{D}_i)}{|\mathcal{D}_i| \times \mathcal{F}(X,\mathcal{D})}$	yes	yes
Odds ratio (α)	$\frac{\mathcal{F}(X,\mathcal{D}_i) \times (|\mathcal{D}\backslash\mathcal{D}_i| - \mathcal{F}(X,\mathcal{D}\backslash\mathcal{D}_i))}{(\mathcal{F}(X,\mathcal{D}) - \mathcal{F}(X,\mathcal{D}_i)) \times (|\mathcal{D}_i| - \mathcal{F}(X,\mathcal{D}_i))}$	yes	yes
Laplace (L) [8]	$\frac{\mathcal{F}(X,\mathcal{D}_i)/|\mathcal{D}|+1}{\mathcal{F}(X,\mathcal{D})/|\mathcal{D}|+k}$ with $k > 1$	yes	yes
Growth rate (GR) [27]	$\frac{|\mathcal{D}|-|\mathcal{D}_i|}{|\mathcal{D}_i|} \times \frac{\mathcal{F}(X,\mathcal{D}_i)}{\mathcal{F}(X,\mathcal{D})-\mathcal{F}(X,\mathcal{D}_i)}$	yes	yes

the lift is a strong frequency-based measure. In the same way, for the growth rate (Equation 1), when $\mathcal{F}(X,\mathcal{D})$ increases and $\mathcal{F}(X,\mathcal{D}_i)$ is unchanged, the numerator is constant and the denominator increases. So, the growth rate decreases and it is also a strong frequency-based measure.

We link now Definition 5 and the framework defining a good measure given by Piatetsky-Shapiro [25]. The latter has proposed three key properties which have to be satisfied to get a good measure. On a formal point of view, Definition 5 is almost similar to the third property P_3 given by Piatetsky-Shapiro: M_i mono-tonically decreases with $P(X)$ when the rest of the parameters (i.e. $P(X, C_i)$ and $P(C_i)$) remain unchanged. Indeed, we can observe that $P(X) = \mathcal{F}(X,\mathcal{D})/|\mathcal{D}|$, $P(X, C_i) = \mathcal{F}(X,\mathcal{D}_i)/|\mathcal{D}|$ and $P(C_i) = |\mathcal{D}_i|/|\mathcal{D}|$. In comparison with Definition 5, the only slight difference is that M_i must strictly decrease when $\mathcal{F}(X,\mathcal{D})$ in-creases whereas, in our definition, M_i may remain unchanged. In practice, most of usual measures are strong frequency-based measure because most of them check the property P_3. A survey [30] is carried out on the property P_3 about twenty one interestingness measures. Table 3 gives, for several measures, these ones satisfying or not Definition 5 and property P_3.

Theorem 2. *Let M_i be a strong frequency-based measure and X be a pattern, we have $M_i(X) \leq M_i(h(X, \mathcal{D}_i)\backslash\{C_i\})$. $h(X, \mathcal{D}_i)\backslash\{C_i\}$ is called a strong pattern in class i.*

Proof. Let M_i be a strong measure of frequencies and X be a pattern. If we note $Y = h(X, \mathcal{D}_i)\backslash\{C_i\}$, X and Y have the same frequency in dataset $\mathcal{D}_i$ (property of the closure operator) i.e. $\mathcal{F}(X, \mathcal{D}_i) = \mathcal{F}(Y, \mathcal{D}_i)$. As $X \subseteq Y$, we obtain that $\mathcal{F}(X, \mathcal{D}) \geq \mathcal{F}(Y, \mathcal{D})$. Thus, Definition 5 allows to conclude that $M_i(X) \leq M_i(Y)$.

Let us illustrate Theorem 2 on the running example. The pattern CD is not a strong pattern for class 1 (because $h(CD, \mathcal{D}_1)\backslash\{C_1\} = ABCD$), its Piatetsky-Shapiro's measure is 0.0625 and one has $PS_1(CD) \leq PS_1(ABCD) = 0.125$ as well.

The pattern X and its corresponding strong pattern $h(X, \mathcal{D}_i)\backslash\{C_i\}$ have the same frequency in dataset $\mathcal{D}_i$ and the strong pattern coming from X has an higher value of the measure. Thus, the strong patterns are a good choice to reduce the number of patterns and preserve the best patterns with respect to the measure.

Let us note that as for the SEPs, only $\mathcal{F}(X, \mathcal{D}_i)$ and $\mathcal{F}(X, \mathcal{D})$ are necessary to compute any measure M_i. The same filtering proposed in Section 3.3 can be applied to efficiently mine strong patterns with respect to M_i thanks to the condensed representation of frequent closed patterns.

6   Conclusion

Based on recent results in condensed representations, we have revisited the field of emerging patterns. We have defined an exact condensed representation of the emerging patterns and a new characterization of the jumping emerging patterns. We have proposed a new kind of emerging patterns, the strong emerging patterns which are the EPs with the highest growth rates. We have provided an efficient method to extract SEPs from the exact condensed representation of EPs.

In addition to the simplicity of their extraction, this approach produces only few SEPs which are particularly useful for helping to diagnosis. So, it is easier to use SEPs than search relevant EPs among a large number of EPs. Dealing with our collaboration with the Philips company, SEPs enabled to successfully identify the failures of a production chain of silicon plates. These promising results encourage the use of SEPs in many practical domains.

Finally, we have extended the main ideas to frequency-based measures. We have proven that any frequency-based measure can be exactly and concisely represented in the condensed representation of the closed patterns. This result stems from the properties of the closure operator. As for the SEPs, the concept of strength allows to select less patterns, called strong patterns, which maximalize most of the interestingness measures. Further work is the use of the exact condensed representation and strong patterns for classification tasks.

Acknowledgements. The authors wish to thank the Philips company and in particular, G. Ferru for having provided data and many valuable comments. F. Rioult is supported by the IRM department (University Hospital of Caen France) and the "Comité de la Ligue contre le Cancer de la Manche" and the "Conseil Régional de Basse-Normandie". This work has been partially funded by the AS "Discovery Challenge" supported by the French research organism (CNRS).

References

[1] R. Agrawal, T. Imielinsky, and A Swami. Mining associations rules between sets of items in large databases. In *In Proceedings of the ACM SIGMOD'93*, pages 207–216, 1993.

[2] J. Bailey, T. Manoukian, and K. Ramamohanarao. Fast algorithms for mining emerging patterns. In *Sixth European Conference on Principles Data Mining and Knowledge Discovery, PKDD'02*, pages 39–50, Helsinki, Finland, 2002. Springer.

[3] G. Birkhoff. Lattices theory. *American Mathematical Society, vol. 25*, 1967.

[4] E. Boros, V.r Gurvich, L. Khachiyan, and K. Makino. On the complexity of generating maximal frequent and minimal infrequent sets. In *Symposium on Theoretical Aspects of Computer Science*, pages 133–141, 2002.

[5] J. F. Boulicaut, A. Bykowski, and C. Rigotti. Free-sets: a condensed representation of boolean data for the approximation of frequency queries. *Data Mining and Knowledge Discovery journal*, 7(1):5–22, 2003. Kluwer Academics Publishers.

[6] T. Calders and B. Goethals. Mining all non-derivable frequent itemsets. In T. Elomaa, H. Mannila, and H. Toivonen, editors, *proceedings of the 6th European Conference on Principles of Data Mining and Knowledge Discovery (PKDD'02)*, pages 74–85. Springer, 2002.

[7] T. Calders and B. Goethals. Minimal k-free representations of frequent sets. In *In proceedings of the 7th European Conference on Principles and Practice of Knowledge Discovery in Databases (PKDD'03)*, pages 71–82. Springer, 2003.

[8] P. Clark and R. Boswell. Rule induction with CN2: Some recent improvements. In *Proc. Fifth European Working Session on Learning*, pages 151–163, Berlin, 1991. Springer.

[9] B. Crémilleux and J. F. Boulicaut. Simplest rules characterizing classes generated by delta-free sets. In *22nd Int. Conf. on Knowledge Based Systems and Applied Artificial Intelligence*, pages 33–46, Cambridge, UK, December 2002.

[10] B. Crémilleux, A. Soulet, and F. Rioult. Mining the strongest emerging patterns characterizing patients affected by diseases due to atherosclerosis. In *proceedings of the workshop Discovery Challenge, PKDD'03*, pages 59–70, 2003.

[11] L. De Raedt, M. Jäger, S. D. Lee, and H. Mannila. A theory of inductive query answering. In *proceedings of the IEEE Conference on Data Mining*, pages 123–130, Maebashi, Japan.

[12] L. De Raedt and S. Kramer. The levelwise version space algorithm and its application to molecular fragment finding. In *IJCAI*, pages 853–862, 2001.

[13] G. Dong and J. Li. Efficient mining of emerging patterns: Discovering trends and differences. In *Knowledge Discovery and Data Mining*, pages 43–52, 1999.

[14] G. Dong, X. Zhang, W. Wong, and J. Li. CAEP: Classification by aggregating emerging patterns. In *Discovery Science*, pages 30–42, 1999.

[15] E-H. Han, G. Karypis, V. Kumar, and B. Mobasher. Clustering based on association rule hypergraphs. In *proceedings of the workshop on Research Issues on Data Mining And Knowledge Discovery, SIGMOD 97*, 1997.

[16] J. Li, G. Dong, and K. Ramamohanarao. Making use of the most expressive jumping emerging patterns for classification. In *Pacific-Asia Conference on Knowledge Discovery and Data Mining*, pages 220–232. Morgan Kaufmann, San Francisco, CA, 2000.

[17] J. Li and K. Ramamohanarao. The space of jumping emerging patterns and its incremental maintenance algorithms. In *Proc. 17th International Conf. on Machine Learning*, pages 551–558. Morgan Kaufmann, San Francisco, 2000.

[18] J. Li and L. Wong. Emerging patterns and gene expression data. In *Genome Informatics 12*, pages 3–13, 2001.

[19] International Business Machines. IBM intelligent miner, user's guide, version 1, release 1, 1996.

[20] H. Mannila and H. Toivonen. Levelwise search and borders of theories in knowledge discovery. *Data Mining and Knowledge Discovery*, 1(3):241–258, 1997.

[21] T. Mitchell. Generalization as search. *Artificial Intelligence, vol. 18*, pages 203–226, 1980.

[22] N. Pasquier, Y. Bastide, T. Taouil, and L. Lakhal. Discovering frequent closed itemsets for association rules. *Lecture Notes in Computer Science*, 1540:398–416, 1999.

[23] J. Pei, J. Han, and L. V. S. Lakshmanan. Mining frequent item sets with convertible constraints. In *ICDE*, pages 433–442, 2001.

[24] J. Pei, J. Han, and Mao R. CLOSET: An efficient algorithm for mining frequent closed itemsets. In *ACM SIGMOD Workshop on Research Issues in Data Mining and Knowledge Discovery*, pages 21–30, 2000.

[25] G. Piatetsky-Shapiro. Discovery, analysis and presentation of strong rules. In G. Piatetsky-Shapiro and W. Frawley, editors, *Knowledge Discovery in Databases*, pages 229–248, Cambridge, MA, 1991. AAAI/MIT Press.

[26] F. Rioult and B. Crémilleux. Condensed representations in presence of missing values. In *5th International Conference on Intelligent Data Analysis (IDA'03)*, 2003.

[27] M. Sebag and M Schoenauer. Generation of rules with certainty and confidence factors from incomplete and incoherent learning bases. In G. Piatetsky-Shapiro and W. Frawley, editors, *in proceedings pf the European Knowledge Acquisition Workshop, EKAW'88*, 1988.

[28] P. Smyth and R. M. Goodman. Rule induction using information theory. In G. Piatetsky-Shapiro and W. Frawley, editors, *Knowledge Discovery in Databases*, pages 159–176, Cambridge, MA, 1991. AAAI/MIT Press.

[29] A. Soulet, B. Crémilleux, and F. Rioult. Condensed representation of emerging patterns. In *8th Pacific-Asia Conference on Knowledge Discovery and Data Mining*, Lecture Notes in Computer Science, pages 127–132, Sydney, 2004.

[30] P. Tan, V. Kumar, and J. Srivastava. Selecting the right interestingness measure for association patterns. In *In proceedings The Eighth ACM Special Interest Group on Knowledge Discovery in Data and Data Mining (SIGKDD'02)*, Edmonton, Alberta, Canada, 2002.

[31] M. Zaki. Generating non-redundant association rules. In *In proceedings The 6th ACM Special Interest Group on Knowledge Discovery in Data and Data Mining (SIGKDD'00)*, pages 34–43, 2000.

[32] X. Zhang, G. Dong, and K. Ramamohanarao. Exploring constraints to efficiently mine emerging patterns from large high-dimensional datasets. In *Knowledge Discovery and Data Mining*, pages 310–314, 2000.

Author Index

Antunes, Cláudia   11

Besson, Jérémy   33
Boulicaut, Jean-François   33

Calders, Toon   46
Crémilleux, Bruno   173

Dexters, Nele   46
De Raedt, Luc   108
Dillon, Tharam   66

Feng, Ling   66

Jeudy, Baptiste   89

Lee, Sau Dan   108

Mielikäinen, Taneli   130, 150

Oliveira, Arlindo L.   11

Rioult, François   89, 173
Robardet, Céline   33

Sarawagi, Sunita   1
Soulet, Arnaud   173

Lecture Notes in Computer Science

For information about Vols. 1–3311

please contact your bookseller or Springer

Vol. 3418: U. Brandes, T. Erlebach (Eds.), Network Analysis. XII, 471 pages. 2005.

Vol. 3416: M. Böhlen, J. Gamper, W. Polasek, M.A. Wimmer (Eds.), E-Government: Towards Electronic Democracy. XIII, 311 pages. 2005. (Subseries LNAI).

Vol. 3412: X. Franch, D. Port (Eds.), COTS-Based Software Systems. XVI, 312 pages. 2005.

Vol. 3411: S.H. Myaeng, M. Zhou, K.-F. Wong, H.-J. Zhang (Eds.), Information Retrieval Technology. XIII, 337 pages. 2005.

Vol. 3410: C.A. Coello Coello, A. Hernández Aguirre, E. Zitzler (Eds.), Evolutionary Multi-Criterion Optimization. XVI, 912 pages. 2005.

Vol. 3409: N. Guelfi, G. Reggio, A. Romanovsky (Eds.), Scientific Engineering of Distributed Java Applications. X, 127 pages. 2005.

Vol. 3406: A. Gelbukh (Ed.), Computational Linguistics and Intelligent Text Processing. XVII, 829 pages. 2005.

Vol. 3404: V. Diekert, B. Durand (Eds.), STACS 2005. XVI, 706 pages. 2005.

Vol. 3403: B. Ganter, R. Godin (Eds.), Formal Concept Analysis. XI, 419 pages. 2005. (Subseries LNAI).

Vol. 3401: Z. Li, L. Vulkov, J. Waśniewski (Eds.), Numerical Analysis and Its Applications. XIII, 630 pages. 2005.

Vol. 3398: D.-K. Baik (Ed.), Systems Modeling and Simulation: Theory and Applications. XIV, 733 pages. 2005. (Subseries LNAI).

Vol. 3397: T.G. Kim (Ed.), Artificial Intelligence and Simulation. XV, 711 pages. 2005. (Subseries LNAI).

Vol. 3396: R.M. van Eijk, M.-P. Huget, F. Dignum (Eds.), Advances in Agent Communication. X, 261 pages. 2005. (Subseries LNAI).

Vol. 3393: H.-J. Kreowski, U. Montanari, F. Orejas, G. Rozenberg, G. Taentzer (Eds.), Formal Methods in Software and Systems Modeling. XXVII, 413 pages. 2005.

Vol. 3391: C. Kim (Ed.), Information Networking. XVII, 936 pages. 2005.

Vol. 3388: J. Lagergren (Ed.), Comparative Genomics. VIII, 133 pages. 2005. (Subseries LNBI).

Vol. 3387: J. Cardoso, A. Sheth (Eds.), Semantic Web Services and Web Process Composition. VIII, 147 pages. 2005.

Vol. 3386: S. Vaudenay (Ed.), Public Key Cryptography - PKC 2005. IX, 436 pages. 2005.

Vol. 3385: R. Cousot (Ed.), Verification, Model Checking, and Abstract Interpretation. XII, 483 pages. 2005.

Vol. 3383: J. Pach (Ed.), Graph Drawing. XII, 536 pages. 2005.

Vol. 3382: J. Odell, P. Giorgini, J.P. Müller (Eds.), Agent-Oriented Software Engineering V. X, 239 pages. 2005.

Vol. 3381: P. Vojtáš, M. Bieliková, B. Charron-Bost, O. Sýkora (Eds.), SOFSEM 2005: Theory and Practice of Computer Science. XV, 448 pages. 2005.

Vol. 3379: M. Hemmje, C. Niederee, T. Risse (Eds.), From Integrated Publication and Information Systems to Information and Knowledge Environments. XXIV, 321 pages. 2005.

Vol. 3378: J. Kilian (Ed.), Theory of Cryptography. XII, 621 pages. 2005.

Vol. 3377: B. Goethals, A. Siebes (Eds.), Knowledge Discovery in Inductive Databases. VII, 191 pages. 2005.

Vol. 3376: A. Menezes (Ed.), Topics in Cryptology – CT-RSA 2005. X, 385 pages. 2004.

Vol. 3375: M.A. Marsan, G. Bianchi, M. Listanti, M. Meo (Eds.), Quality of Service in Multiservice IP Networks. XIII, 656 pages. 2005.

Vol. 3374: D. Weyns, H.V.D. Parunak, F. Michel (Eds.), Environments for Multi-Agent Systems. X, 279 pages. 2005. (Subseries LNAI).

Vol. 3372: C. Bussler, V. Tannen, I. Fundulaki (Eds.), Semantic Web and Databases. X, 227 pages. 2005.

Vol. 3369: V.R. Benjamins, P. Casanovas, J. Breuker, A. Gangemi (Eds.), Law and the Semantic Web. XII, 249 pages. 2005. (Subseries LNAI).

Vol. 3368: L. Paletta, J.K. Tsotsos, E. Rome, G.W. Humphreys (Eds.), Attention and Performance in Computational Vision. VIII, 231 pages. 2005.

Vol. 3366: I. Rahwan, P. Moraitis, C. Reed (Eds.), Argumentation in Multi-Agent Systems. XII, 263 pages. 2005. (Subseries LNAI).

Vol. 3365: G. Mauri, G. Păun, M.J. Pérez-Jiménez, G. Rozenberg, A. Salomaa (Eds.), Membrane Computing. IX, 415 pages. 2005.

Vol. 3363: T. Eiter, L. Libkin (Eds.), Database Theory - ICDT 2005. XI, 413 pages. 2004.

Vol. 3362: G. Barthe, L. Burdy, M. Huisman, J.-L. Lanet, T. Muntean (Eds.), Construction and Analysis of Safe, Secure, and Interoperable Smart Devices. IX, 257 pages. 2005.

Vol. 3361: S. Bengio, H. Bourlard (Eds.), Machine Learning for Multimodal Interaction. XII, 362 pages. 2005.

Vol. 3360: S. Spaccapietra, E. Bertino, S. Jajodia, R. King, D. McLeod, M.E. Orlowska, L. Strous (Eds.), Journal on Data Semantics II. XI, 223 pages. 2005.

Vol. 3359: G. Grieser, Y. Tanaka (Eds.), Intuitive Human Interfaces for Organizing and Accessing Intellectual Assets. XIV, 257 pages. 2005. (Subseries LNAI).

Vol. 3358: J. Cao, L.T. Yang, M. Guo, F. Lau (Eds.), Parallel and Distributed Processing and Applications. XXIV, 1058 pages. 2004.

Vol. 3357: H. Handschuh, M.A. Hasan (Eds.), Selected Areas in Cryptography. XI, 354 pages. 2004.

Vol. 3356: G. Das, V.P. Gulati (Eds.), Intelligent Information Technology. XII, 428 pages. 2004.

Vol. 3355: R. Murray-Smith, R. Shorten (Eds.), Switching and Learning in Feedback Systems. X, 343 pages. 2005.

Vol. 3353: J. Hromkovič, M. Nagl, B. Westfechtel (Eds.), Graph-Theoretic Concepts in Computer Science. XI, 404 pages. 2004.

Vol. 3352: C. Blundo, S. Cimato (Eds.), Security in Communication Networks. XI, 381 pages. 2005.

Vol. 3351: G. Persiano, R. Solis-Oba (Eds.), Approximation and Online Algorithms. VIII, 295 pages. 2005.

Vol. 3350: M. Hermenegildo, D. Cabeza (Eds.), Practical Aspects of Declarative Languages. VIII, 269 pages. 2005.

Vol. 3349: B.M. Chapman (Ed.), Shared Memory Parallel Programming with Open MP. X, 149 pages. 2005.

Vol. 3348: A. Canteaut, K. Viswanathan (Eds.), Progress in Cryptology - INDOCRYPT 2004. XIV, 431 pages. 2004.

Vol. 3347: R.K. Ghosh, H. Mohanty (Eds.), Distributed Computing and Internet Technology. XX, 472 pages. 2004.

Vol. 3346: R.H. Bordini, M. Dastani, J. Dix, A.E.F. Seghrouchni (Eds.), Programming Multi-Agent Systems. XIV, 249 pages. 2005. (Subseries LNAI).

Vol. 3345: Y. Cai (Ed.), Ambient Intelligence for Scientific Discovery. XII, 311 pages. 2005. (Subseries LNAI).

Vol. 3344: J. Malenfant, B.M. Østvold (Eds.), Object-Oriented Technology. ECOOP 2004 Workshop Reader. VIII, 215 pages. 2005.

Vol. 3343: C. Freksa, M. Knauff, B. Krieg-Brückner, B. Nebel, T. Barkowsky (Eds.), Spatial Cognition IV. Reasoning, Action, and Interaction. XIII, 519 pages. 2005. (Subseries LNAI).

Vol. 3342: E. Şahin, W.M. Spears (Eds.), Swarm Robotics. IX, 175 pages. 2005.

Vol. 3341: R. Fleischer, G. Trippen (Eds.), Algorithms and Computation. XVII, 935 pages. 2004.

Vol. 3340: C.S. Calude, E. Calude, M.J. Dinneen (Eds.), Developments in Language Theory. XI, 431 pages. 2004.

Vol. 3339: G.I. Webb, X. Yu (Eds.), AI 2004: Advances in Artificial Intelligence. XXII, 1272 pages. 2004. (Subseries LNAI).

Vol. 3338: S.Z. Li, J. Lai, T. Tan, G. Feng, Y. Wang (Eds.), Advances in Biometric Person Authentication. XVIII, 699 pages. 2004.

Vol. 3337: J.M. Barreiro, F. Martin-Sanchez, V. Maojo, F. Sanz (Eds.), Biological and Medical Data Analysis. XI, 508 pages. 2004.

Vol. 3336: D. Karagiannis, U. Reimer (Eds.), Practical Aspects of Knowledge Management. X, 523 pages. 2004. (Subseries LNAI).

Vol. 3335: M. Malek, M. Reitenspieß, J. Kaiser (Eds.), Service Availability. X, 213 pages. 2005.

Vol. 3334: Z. Chen, H. Chen, Q. Miao, Y. Fu, E. Fox, E.-p. Lim (Eds.), Digital Libraries: International Collaboration and Cross-Fertilization. XX, 690 pages. 2004.

Vol. 3333: K. Aizawa, Y. Nakamura, S. Satoh (Eds.), Advances in Multimedia Information Processing - PCM 2004, Part III. XXXV, 785 pages. 2004.

Vol. 3332: K. Aizawa, Y. Nakamura, S. Satoh (Eds.), Advances in Multimedia Information Processing - PCM 2004, Part II. XXXVI, 1051 pages. 2004.

Vol. 3331: K. Aizawa, Y. Nakamura, S. Satoh (Eds.), Advances in Multimedia Information Processing - PCM 2004, Part I. XXXVI, 667 pages. 2004.

Vol. 3330: J. Akiyama, E.T. Baskoro, M. Kano (Eds.), Combinatorial Geometry and Graph Theory. VIII, 227 pages. 2004.

Vol. 3329: P.J. Lee (Ed.), Advances in Cryptology - ASIACRYPT 2004. XVI, 546 pages. 2004.

Vol. 3328: K. Lodaya, M. Mahajan (Eds.), FSTTCS 2004: Foundations of Software Technology and Theoretical Computer Science. XVI, 532 pages. 2004.

Vol. 3327: Y. Shi, W. Xu, Z. Chen (Eds.), Data Mining and Knowledge Management. XIII, 263 pages. 2005. (Subseries LNAI).

Vol. 3326: A. Sen, N. Das, S.K. Das, B.P. Sinha (Eds.), Distributed Computing - IWDC 2004. XIX, 546 pages. 2004.

Vol. 3325: C.H. Lim, M. Yung (Eds.), Information Security Applications. XI, 472 pages. 2005.

Vol. 3323: G. Antoniou, H. Boley (Eds.), Rules and Rule Markup Languages for the Semantic Web. X, 215 pages. 2004.

Vol. 3322: R. Klette, J. Žunić (Eds.), Combinatorial Image Analysis. XII, 760 pages. 2004.

Vol. 3321: M.J. Maher (Ed.), Advances in Computer Science - ASIAN 2004. Higher-Level Decision Making. XII, 510 pages. 2004.

Vol. 3320: K.-M. Liew, H. Shen, S. See, W. Cai (Eds.), Parallel and Distributed Computing: Applications and Technologies. XXIV, 891 pages. 2004.

Vol. 3319: D. Amyot, A.W. Williams (Eds.), System Analysis and Modeling. XII, 301 pages. 2005.

Vol. 3318: E. Eskin, C. Workman (Eds.), Regulatory Genomics. VII, 115 pages. 2005. (Subseries LNBI).

Vol. 3317: M. Domaratzki, A. Okhotin, K. Salomaa, S. Yu (Eds.), Implementation and Application of Automata. XII, 336 pages. 2005.

Vol. 3316: N.R. Pal, N.K. Kasabov, R.K. Mudi, S. Pal, S.K. Parui (Eds.), Neural Information Processing. XXX, 1368 pages. 2004.

Vol. 3315: C. Lemaître, C.A. Reyes, J.A. González (Eds.), Advances in Artificial Intelligence – IBERAMIA 2004. XX, 987 pages. 2004. (Subseries LNAI).

Vol. 3314: J. Zhang, J.-H. He, Y. Fu (Eds.), Computational and Information Science. XXIV, 1259 pages. 2004.

Vol. 3313: C. Castelluccia, H. Hartenstein, C. Paar, D. Westhoff (Eds.), Security in Ad-hoc and Sensor Networks. VIII, 231 pages. 2005.

Vol. 3312: A.J. Hu, A.K. Martin (Eds.), Formal Methods in Computer-Aided Design. XI, 445 pages. 2004.